ENCYCLOPEDIA OF

Hand-Weaving

ENCYCLOPEDIA OF

Hand-Weaving

STANISLAW A. ZIELINSKI

FUNK & WAGNALLS

New York

Printed in the United States of America

L.C. Card 75-45519

Library of Congress Cataloging in Publication Data

Zielinski, Stanislaw A
  Encyclopedia of hand-weaving.

  1. Hand weaving. I. Title.
TT848.Z5 1976   746.1′4′03   75-45519
ISBN 0-308-10072-7

FOREWORD

IT IS A PLEASURE to me to write this foreword to the *Encyclopedia of Hand-Weaving*.

The Oxford dictionary defines encyclopedia as "a book giving information on all branches of knowledge or of one subject." The absence of a hand-weaving encyclopedia has long been an obstacle to weavers and I feel this book will be of great benefit to hand-weavers and teachers.

Because hand-weaving terminology is extremely confusing and is a mixture of terms from Great Britain, Europe and America, weavers will welcome this clear, concise and comprehensive book. It will be invaluable as a book of reference—not only for a definition of weaving terms but as a source of general information about weaving.

One of the fascinating features of this book is the many pattern drafts, not only because of the draft but because the country of origin is given and cross reference readily tells when the same pattern appears in different countries under different names.

The numerous illustrations show details of pattern and texture, looms and parts, adding greatly to the reader's interest and enjoyment.

I wish this encyclopedia great success, not only as a tribute to the author, but also for the help and stimulus the book will give to hand-weavers.

CARRIE L. E. OLIPHANT

INTRODUCTION

The terminology of hand-weaving is extremely confusing. This is due to several factors. Different weaving communities in Great Britain remained for centuries sufficiently isolated from each other to develop their own technical language. Then the infiltration of French weavers (in the sixteenth century) often with a superior weaving knowledge introduced a new vocabulary of French words which became later on assimilated or corrupted.

When weaving started in North America, the emigrants, even when good artisans, were not necessarily familiar with the proper weaving terminology. Consequently they adopted some new technical expressions, retaining most of the old ones, but only too often in the wrong meaning.

Then in the beginning of the nineteenth century the hand-weaving practically disappeared, except in the most backward communities, and at its revival nearly a century later, the pioneers were at loss as to the meaning of the simplest weaving terms. It was then that the hand-weaving language was built anew for the third time, and this process is still going on. The parallel development of power weaving resulted in a still different set of terms and this was not without influence on hand-weaving. Thus it came about that we have at the present time not only several terms to designate the same weave or operation, but also cases when one term has several different meanings.

To illustrate: "harness" means in Britain a set of "leaves" or "shafts" (the latter in power weaving) together with the "upper tie-up." In America "harness" is nothing else than one "leaf" or heddle-frame. "Heddle" means always one "leash" (or hook, or needle) in America, but in Great Britain it may be used either in the American meaning, or as an equivalent of "leaf," and it may be spelled: heddle, headle, heald, or even yeld. As a matter of fact, the old English expression "leaf" is hardly ever used now. To designate a row of heddles mounted on one frame the following terms are used: harness, heddle, heddle-frame, harness-frame, heddle-stick, leash-rod, shaft, and leaf. Most of these terms have more than one meaning. On the other hand, some weaving expressions are completely lacking, e.g., there is no American equivalent of the British "harness."

In many cases it is possible to trace back a doubtful word, but not always. As an example we can take the word "Dornick." It came undoubtedly from a weaving centre in Northern Scotland, where a particular kind of turned twill was developed. The fabric was later known by the name "Dornock" or "Dornick," and hence the weave itself got its name. But later on in America the same term has been used for a herringbone twill, and the origin of the word ascribed to Belgium or even Scandinavia. At first it would seem that there is no possible connection between these two weaves, but a closer examination shows that the way of joining blocks in the original weave is exactly the same as the way of joining vertical stripes in the American Dornick. The point in both cases is to avoid long floats. It is obvious then that a colonial weaver familiar with the first weave invented the second one, and called it accordingly "dornick twill," or another similar name which later became just "dornick."

In the case of "harness" it is hard to say who made first the mistake, since even in colonial times the word "leaf" was widely used and there was no reason to change it. What must have happened is that the full expression "four leaf harness" was often shortened to "4'harness," and probably during the revival of hand-weaving this was interpreted as "4 harnesses."

Since most of this terminology has been in use for decades at the least, it is not easy to decide which terms are right, and which are wrong. If an expression is used long enough, it becomes the right one regardless of its original meaning. Consequently what we are going to attempt in this work, is not only to explain the meanings of the different terms, but also to indicate their origin, whenever known, and to select the meaning which seems to be the most appropriate and yet most widely used. It is possible to reconcile these last two conditions in all cases but one, i.e. in the case of "harness," which is most widely used in an obviously wrong sense.

From a purely practical point of view, the main purpose of this encyclopedia is to enable the reader to understand any weaving literature regardless of its age or place of origin, as long as it is written in English. On the other hand, it is quite easy to use this work as source of general information about weaving. Starting with the word "Weaving," and taking advantage of the cross-references, the reader will be able to acquire quite an extensive knowledge of the subject, although the information is given in a condensed form.

When explaining a technical term we must express it in simpler and unequivocal words. For this purpose we have selected the following expressions:

HEDDLE. In the American meaning. The same as British "leash."

SHAFT. A set of heddles mounted on one frame. The same as Am. "harness," "heddle-frame," "harness frame," and Br. "leaf," "heald."

HARNESS. A set of shafts together with their upper tie-up.

In case of synonyms, the description follows the most appropriate term. Other more doubtful, obsolete or rare expressions are explained only as far as their origin is concerned, and in each case a reference to the selected term is made.

The following abbreviations are used in the text: (v) = see . . ., fr. = from, R = rare, Am. = American, AS = Anglo-Saxon, Br. = British, En. = English, Fr. = French, G. = German, Gr. = Greek, Ir. = Irish, Lat. = Latin, Sc. = Scandinavian, Sp. = Spanish, Sw. = Swedish.

ENCYCLOPEDIA OF

Hand-Weaving

ABACA (fr. Filipino).   The same as manila hemp.

ACCIDENTAL (Am.).   When weaving overshot written on opposites (v) small blocks appear in places when none were intended.   This will happen for instance when shed 2, 3 is used in the following draft:

ACCIDENTAL DRAFT, WEAVE.   See Texture Weaves.

ACETATE.   Yarns and fabrics made of Cellulose Acetate (v).

AKLAE.   Norwegian Low-warp (v) tapestry technique.   Wefts interlock between two warp ends.

ALBATROSS (fr. Sp. *alcatruz*).   Light woollen fabric woven in tabby.

ALL-OVER SPOTS (Br.).   A spot weave (v) in which the pattern covers the whole fabric, and consequently gives 3 blocks of pattern with 4 shafts. The pattern is formed by weft floats on one side and warp floats on the other (Bronson). When two shots of tabby are made after each shot of pattern, the warp floats disappear, and the pattern on one side is in tabby only (Swivel effect).

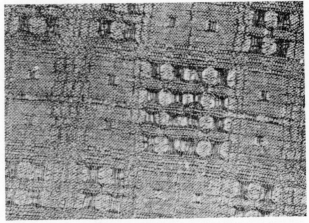

ALL-OVER SPOTS (Barley Corn)

The number of blocks is always one less than the number of shafts in the harness.   E.g.:

1, 2—tabby treadles
3, 4, 5—pattern treadles

5 4 3 2 1

In the above example only one block of pattern can be woven at a time, for instance:

figure: 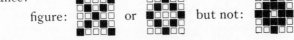 but not:

1

If combination of two or more blocks is necessary, an additional shaft must be used. Its purpose is to space the blocks and thus to avoid too long floats:

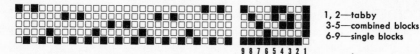

1, 2—tabby
3-5—combined blocks
6-9—single blocks

9 8 7 6 5 4 3 2 1

ALPACA (Sp.).   Yarn and fabric made of wool of Alpaca (*Auchenia Pacos*, South Am.), or any fabric resembling more or less the genuine alpaca.

AMERICAN BEAUTY.   Colonial pattern (v) of the Star-and-Wheel group. Short draft:

```
5  44  7  5 5 5 5 5 5  7  44
  4   4    6 5 5 5 5 6    4   4
  4    4  6            6    4    4
  4  5  4 6              6 4   5   4
```

ANALYSIS OF FABRICS.   Such a description of a sample of weaving, which would enable a weaver to produce a fabric identical with the sample. In analysis the following data must be found:

1. Yarn, or yarns used.   Their composition, colour, twist (direction and degree), count of yarn.

2. Count of cloth.   Number of threads per inch in warp and weft.

3. Weave and pattern if any.

4. Finishing.

1. Probably the most difficult part of analysis is the yarn itself, particularly if the yarn is a mixture of different fibres.   A complete analysis requires a well equipped laboratory; however, here are a few simple tests:

Burning test.   Wool smells like burned feather, and neither burns well, or smoulders.   The burned ends stick together and are covered with thick layer of carbon.

Silk behaves in a similar way.

Linen burns better, and smoulders for a short while.   The ends are straight and clean.

Cotton burns still faster, and smoulders indefinitely.   Ends spread slightly.

Rayon as a rule is fast burning.

Nylon smells like celery, melts near fire.

Fibreglass and metallics do not burn.

Chemical test.   Wool can be dissolved completely when boiled in 5% solution of caustic soda.

Cotton dissolves in 2% sulphuric acid.

Acetate (rayon) fabrics dissolve in acetone or acetic acid.

2

The direction of *the twist* is either right or left hand. The degree of twist in hand-weaving is described in terms: tight, medium tight, loose.

The count of yarn can be established by comparing threads pulled out from the sample with other threads of known number.

2. Number of threads per inch can be easily counted, using special magnifying glass. Correction should be made for shrinkage.

3. Except for the simplest weaves which can be analyzed at a glance, the following procedure is necessary:

One whole repeat in warp and weft must be reproduced on graph-paper (v. Draft). If it is difficult to distinguish between the warp and weft, the sample must be pulled apart thread by thread. When a thread is loosened it is much easier to see how it is interwoven with the opposite set of threads.

When the whole draw-down is made on paper, we examine the vertical lines, giving the same number to all identical lines. The highest number thus obtained is equal to the number of shafts required to weave the sample. Then we repeat the operation for the horizontal lines. Here the highest number gives the number of treadles. Now we write both the threading and the treadling drafts on the same piece of graph paper and in line with the draw-down. By looking up from each line of weft in the draw-down to the threading draft we find out what combination of shafts was necessary to produce this line, and this gives us the tie-up.

Pattern:

Vertical lines have 6 as the highest number which means 6 shafts. Horizontal lines have 5 as the highest number, which means 5 treadles.

The numbers used in analysis now become the numbers of shafts and treadles, and the complete draft will be:

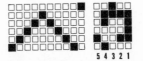

Treadling: 5, 4, 3, 2, 1, 2, 3, 4.

In more elaborate weaves every block of pattern may correspond not to a single thread as in the above example, but to one unit (v) of the weave, and the resulting draft will be a short-draft (v) only.

4. To describe the finishing operations the weaver must have more practice than theoretical knowledge. In extreme cases the finishing may destroy completely the weave, as for instance felting. Even in fulling the shrinkage may be so pronounced that the original thread count remains doubtful. However, since certain standards are usually observed in setting

3

the warp, this original count may be deduced from the count of yarn used. Other processes, such as napping, printing, embossing and so on, are easy to notice and to describe.

ANGORA (fr. *Angora* in Asia Minor). Yarn or fabric made of wool of angora rabbits, or angora goats. Also yarn containing some angora wool, and its imitations.

APRON. A piece of strong fabric nailed to the cloth beam or to the warp beam. Its width should be the same as the length of the reed, and it should be long enough to reach close to the harness. The free end of the apron is hemmed and a steel rod inserted in the hem. Another steel rod is laced to the first one with a cord. This second rod permits the weaver to attach the warp to the apron. It is desirable that the fabric of which the apron is made be as little elastic as possible. Strong linen cloth is the best material.

ARMURE (fr. Lat. *armatura* or Fr. *armure* = weave). 1. Any of the basic weaves. 2. The set-up and threading of the loom for one of these weaves. 3. Cotton, or silk fabric with small pattern. 4. Small spot patterns on corded fabrics. 5. Woollen cloth woven in twill.

ARROW. Colonial pattern (v) of the Wheel-and-Table group. Short draft:

```
10        10 11 10      10  5  5  5  5  5
     11       5  5    11    11 11 11 11 11 11
      4  4             4  4
    10    10         10    10
```

ART LINEN. Rather open tabby fabric used as ground for hand embroidery.

ASTRAKHAN (fr. Russian). 1. Sheep skins with curly fur. 2. Imitation of astrakhan woven like velvet, but the pile made of angora goat wool.

AUBUSSON. Tapestry and rugs made in Aubusson (France) and their imitations.

AXMINSTER. Carpets with rich pile made originally in Axminster, Great Britain.

BACHELOR. Colonial pattern (v) of the Star-and-Table group. Short draft:

```
      9 9 9          9 9 9     9      9
        9 9 9 9 9            9 9   9 9   9 9
    3 3 8 3 3 3 3 8 3 3 8 3 8 8 3 8 8 3 8
```

BACK BEAM. The same as Warp Beam.

BACK HARNESS. The same as Pattern Harness in Two-Harness method.

BACK REST. The same as Slabstock.

BACKING. The same as Ground Weave.

4

BACKING. The same as Maitland cords.

BAIZE (fr. old Fr. *baie*). Imitation of felt made of wool, woven in tabby and napped.

BALANCED DRAFT. Threading draft composed of unsymmetrical repeats, corrected at one end. E.g.:

D   C B   A

The repeat is from C to D and it has been threaded a number of times. The part from A to B has been added to balance the draft.

BALANCED PATTERN. Symmetrical pattern.

BALANCED TIE-UP. Any tie-up is balanced when the same number of shafts is tied to each treadle. In counterbalanced looms, when the tie-up is unbalanced, the sheds do not open on the same level. This can be corrected with a Shed Regulator (v).

BALANCED TWILL. Twill which has the same length of floats in weft and warp, such as 2:2, 3:3 and so on. These twills show the same amount of weft and warp on both sides of the fabric.

BALLOON SILK. A fine rayon or silk fabric very closely woven.

BANK. Bobbin rack of a Warping Mill (v).

BAR. 1. Band of colour in weft. 2. Vertical rib running parallel to the warp in an overshot pattern.

BARK CLOTH. Crinkled woollen fabric. Compare: Crepe.

BARLEY CORN WEAVE. The same as All-Over Spots.

BARRÉ (Fr.). Fabrics with stripes of different colours in weft.

BASIC WEAVE. Any weave which is not a variation of a simpler one, and which has its own variations or derivate weaves. Opinions differ as to which weaves are basic, since every weave can be traced back to tabby or twill, but the following are usually considered as basic: tabby, twill, spot, diaper (turned twills), double, tissue, pile, and cross weaves. Compare: Weaves.

BASKET WEAVE. Derivate of tabby weave in which every thread of warp and weft is replaced by two, three or four parallel threads. Fabrics woven in basket weave are rather loose particularly if more than two parallel threads are used. E.g.:

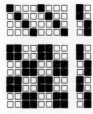

2:2 basket weave

5

BASKET WEAVE (*false*).   Imitation of plain basket weave, which has the appearance of the original weave.   The draft is exactly the same as for Huckaback Lace (v) but two kinds of yarn are used both for warp and weft. In the threading draft ■ is very fine yarn of a neutral colour, and ● heavy and soft yarn of a different colour.   In treadling the fine yarn is used on treadles 2 and 3, and the heavy one on treadles 1 and 4.

Treadling: 3, 1, 3, 1, 3, 2, 4, 2, 4, 2.

4 3 2 1

BASKET WEAVE (stitched).   Variation of plain basket weave, in which the blocks are stitched in the centers.

Treadling: 1, 2, 1, 3, 4, 3.

1 2 3 4

BAST (fr. AS *boest*).   The inner bark of trees.   Hence all vegetable fibres from stalks of plants.

BATISTE (fr. Old Fr. *Baptiste*).   Very light cotton or woollen fabric, made of best quality yarns, and woven in tabby.

BATTEN (fr. Fr. *bâton*).   The frame which holds the reed in place.   It is either hung from a rocking shaft placed across the capes, or propped on two bolts in the lower cross-beams of the loom.   In either case it must be placed so as to move freely between the harness and the breast-piece.   The frame has four parts: the Swords on which it rocks, the lower transversal piece fixed permanently to the swords, the Race Block, and the upper transversal piece, Handtree.   The latter is removable.   The race block has a groove in its upper surface, and the handtree a similar one in its lower surface. The reed fits into these grooves.   When weaving with a hand shuttle the race may have a race-plate, a narrow board which projects forwards, and on which the shuttle runs.   A flying shuttle always requires a race-plate, although this is set at a different angle than one used for hand-shuttle weaving.

   The batten should be adjustable as to its height, axis of rotation, and its weight.   As this last adjustment may prove difficult, several battens are sometimes used with one loom.

   Synonyms: Beater, Lathe, Lay, Ley, Slay.

BAYADERE (fr. Port. *bailadeira* = a Hindu dancer).   A barré fabric in striking colours originally made in India.

BEAD LAMS (En.).   In cross weaving—doups (half-heddles) with beads tied on ends, used always when the heddles are mounted *before* the reed, as

6

for instance in all net weaves (v). The perforated beads are used in view to decrease the friction on the warp (whip), on which they travel several inches during every beat. The bead has a groove on its circumference to hold the doup.

BEAD LENO. A method of producing crossed warp ends, as in leno, gauze, etc., which has beads, or short plastic tubes threaded on pairs of warp ends between the batten and the harness. The tension of each of the warp ends in the bead can be changed so that the bead together with the ends moves to the right or to the left and twists around a third warp end not threaded through the bead.

BEAM. Part of a loom; any of the large rollers on which either the warp or the finished cloth is wound. See Warp Beam, Cloth Beam. Sometimes the Idler (v) is called Knee Beam.

BEAMING

BEAMING FROM WARPING MILL

BEAMING. Winding the warp on the warp beam. Several methods are used:

1. The warp in chain is placed in front of the loom, the batten and harness removed, the warp passed through the raddle or spare reed (v. Spreading), and attached to the warp-beam apron.

If the warp has only one cross (lease) the lease rods remain in the warp during beaming. If there is one cross on each end of the warp the rods are removed for beaming and inserted again in the second cross for threading. When a reed is used instead of a raddle, the cross must be transferred from the front of the reed to the back before the reed can be removed. A helper is needed during beaming to hold the warp.

2. The warp is placed as before with the lease rods close to the reed, then the ends are cut, sleyed and threaded (from the front to the back) before beaming. No raddle is used. The lease rods may be permanently removed after threading, or inserted into the warp in their usual position after beaming.

7

3. The warp is placed behind the loom, with lease rods in the usual place between the slabstock and the harness, then threaded and slayed. It is then tied to the front apron, and beamed on the cloth beam. When the end of warp is reached it is tied to the warp beam, and re-beamed.

4. The warp is placed (chained) in the back of the loom, and then wound through a raddle on the cloth beam. The lease rods are set between the breast-piece and the reed. Then the warp is slayed and threaded, tied to the warp beam and rewound.

5. The warp is made on a warping mill (horizontal model). The mill is placed in front of the loom. The warp passes through the raddle, and is laced (not tied) to the warp beam apron. The lacing permits to get an even tension all across the warp. The brake on the warping mill is set on, and then the warp is beamed only through the raddle without lease rods. When the beaming is finished the lease rods are inserted in the second cross.

6. In sectional warping the warp is not prepared beforehand, but goes straight from the bobbin rack through a tension box and a small raddle on the sectional warp beam. Each section must be beamed separately. Lease rods are optional, although desirable.

Whichever method is used, the beaming should be done so that an even tension of warp is preserved all through. From this point of view the methods 2, 3, 4 are the best, and the most difficult is the sectional warping. As far as the speed of beaming is concerned, the fastest is the 5th method, then the 1st. Methods 5 and 6 do not require any help in beaming.

Synonym: Turning-on.

BEAMING DRUM. A rather obsolete piece of equipment, used in connection with a warping mill in industrial hand-weaving. It is a large wooden cylinder constructed like a barrel, and mounted horizontally. The warp taken from the warping mill is wound on the drum, and then re-wound on the warp beam, which for this purpose must be removed from the loom and set on a special stand opposite the drum. Both the drum and the stand are permanently fixed to the floor.

BEARER. The same as Slabstock.

BEAT. One movement of the batten forward and back.

BEATER. 1. The same as Batten. 2. A heavy wooden fork used in Tapestry Weaving for beating down the weft.

BEATING. Action of pressing the weft (particularly its last pick) toward the cloth. This is done on a horizontal loom with a swinging batten, and on a vertical loom with a sliding batten. In high-warp tapestry weaving a special comb or fork is used.

On the proper manner of beating depends the quality of a fabric, and this operation requires a lot of skill. Several factors influence the spacing of the picks of weft in a fabric. They are: the tension of warp, the angle of the shed, the distance from the cloth to the reed, the weight of the batten, the speed and the strength of beating, and the timing of beating and treadling. Even when all other factors remain constant, the distance from the reed to the cloth changes during weaving, and the force of beating must be changed accordingly to preserve the same spacing of weft.

As a rule the weft is beaten after every pick. If this is done only once, the beating must come at the same time as the changing of the shed; if twice, the first beat comes before and the second after the shed is changed; if three times, one before and two after.

The beating should be done entirely by the weight of the batten, not by the pressure of the hand. Then the force of beating depends only on the speed with which the batten is pulled forwards.

In fly-shuttle weaving, when the loom has a good take-up motion, the beating does not influence the quality of the fabric.

BEAT-UP-POINT. The last pick of weft, the same as Fell.

BEAVER CLOTH. Woollen cloth woven in twill with long nap, or even pile.

BEER (probably a jocular corruption of the word Porter). Nineteen dents of a reed. The number of warp ends passing through 19 dents.

BEETLING (fr. AS *bitan* = to bite). Flattening of the fibres in a finished fabric by beating it with wooden mallets. It differs from fulling inasmuch as it is done in different temperature and humidity, so that no shrinkage results. The same process can be performed with rollers.

BENGAL. Striped muslin originally made in Bengal, India.

BENGALINE. A corded fabric (v) with silk warp, which covers the woollen weft.

BIASED TWILL. Any twill which shows a distinct diagonal.

BIBLIOGRAPHY of Hand-Weaving. Because of a very large number of books about hand-weaving, we give here only the most important ones:

Albers, Anni. *On Weaving*. Wesleyan University Press, Middletown, Conn. 1965.

Atwater, Mary M. *Shuttle-Craft Book of American Hand Weaving* (rev. ed.). Macmillan, New York, 1951.

Beriau, Oscar Alphonse. *Home Weaving*. Institute of Industrial Arts, Gardenvale, Quebec. 1948.

Black, Mary E. *New Key to Weaving*. Macmillan, New York. 1961.

Blumenau, Lili. *The Art and Craft of Hand Weaving*. Crown Publishers, New York. 1955.

Davison, Marguerite P. *A Handweaver's Pattern Book*. Marguerite P. Davison, Swarthmore, Penn. 1951.

Frey, Berta. *Designing and Drafting for Handweavers*. Macmillan, New York. 1975.

Halsey, Mike, and Lore Youngmark. *Foundations of Weaving*. Watson-Guptill, New York. 1975.

Kirby, Mary. *Designing on the Loom*. Select Books, Pacific Grove, California. 1973.

Oelsner, G. H. *Handbook of Weaves*. Dover, New York. 1951.

Overman, Ruth, and Lula Smith. *Contemporary Handweaving*. Iowa State University Press, Ames, Iowa. 1955.

Plath, Iona. *Craft of Handweaving*. Scribner's, New York. 1972.

Regensteiner, Else. *Art of Weaving*. Van Nostrand-Reinhold, New York. 1970.

Thorpe, Azalea Stuart, and Jack Lenor Larsen. *Elements of Weaving*. Doubleday, New York. 1967.

Thorpe, Heather G. *Handweaver's Workbook*. Macmillan, New York. 1966.

Tidball, H. *Weaver's Book*. Macmillan, New York. 1961.

Tod, Osma. *The Joy of Handweaving*. Bonanza Books, New York. 1964.

Tovey, John. *The Technique of Weaving*. Reinhold, New York. 1965.

Worst, Edward F. *Weaving with Foot-Power*. Dover, New York. 1974.

BIGHT (fr. AS *būgan* = to bend).   One group or strand of warp ends tied to the apron.

BINDER.   Shots of weft usually made with fine but strong yarn with the purpose of strengthening the fabric.   In such weaves as overshot, summer-and-winter, crackle, etc., the binder separates the pattern shots and keeps the warp evenly spread.   In all these weaves it is made on tabby sheds.   In warp-pile fabrics the purpose of the binder is to hold in place the loops of yarn which form the pile.   The same applies to the weft-pile fabrics.   For coarse fabrics we use tabby; for finer ones, twills.   In more elaborate pattern weaves binder occurs not only in weft but in warp as well.   Binder is also used in tapestry and carpet weaving.   It is optional in flat tapestry but necessary in knotted rugs.

BINDING PLAN.   Short draft for complicated tie-ups such as used in turned twills, double weaves, etc.   See Short Draft.

BIRD'S EYE.   A pattern in Diamond Twill (v), with all diamonds of about the same size.   Occasionally used to describe diamond patterns in other weaves than twill.

BIRD'S NEST.   Colonial five-block pattern suitable for Summer-and-Winter, lace, turned twills, etc.   Short draft:

```
              12                    12
      4        4      1   4   1      4
    2   2 2    2    1    1 1    1
  2    3 1 3   2    1 1    1  1
  3    3    3  3    1 1    1 1
```

BLANKET TWILL.   The same as 1:2 twill (v).

BLAZING STAR.   Colonial pattern, the same as Walls of Jericho (v).

10

BLEACHING. A chemical or physical process which removes or destroys pigments in a yarn or fabric. Raw or reclaimed yarn must be bleached before being dyed, particularly in light shades.

The most important physical bleaching agent is sunlight. It is still used for bleaching homespun linen. Chemical methods are numerous but they can all be divided into the following groups:

1. Oxidizing agents (e.g., hydrogen peroxide, potassium permanganate).

2. Acids (here belongs burned sulphur, which forms with the moisture in the air, sulphurous acid).

3. Alkalis (ammonia, potassium carbonate).

4. Chlorine and its compounds.

When more than one pigment is present in the yarn, it is sometimes necessary to use several bleaching agents belonging to different groups.

BLOCK (Am.). An element of a pattern, running all across the fabric in the direction of the weft. It may contain one or more components as long as these components are all woven at the same time, i.e., on the same treadle or combination of treadles. For instance, in the pattern at right, the first block has two components (two rectangles), the second the same number, the third only one, and the fourth three components.

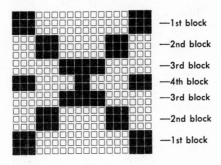

—1st block
—2nd block
—3rd block
—4th block
—3rd block
—2nd block
—1st block

The number of blocks can be also found as described under Analysis.

When the number of blocks in a pattern is known, then it is easy to find out how many shafts are needed to weave this pattern. In the formulas below "N" is the number of blocks, and "L" the number of shafts:

twill, overshot, crackle	$L = N$
all-over-spot, barley corn	$L = N + 1$
summer-and-winter, lace	$L = N + 2$
overshot on opposites	$L = 2 \times N$
dropped tabby, huckaback	$L = 2 \times N + 2$
turned 1:2 twill (dimity)	$L = 3 \times N$
double weave, dornick (turned 1:3 twill)	$L = 4 \times N$
damask (on 1:4 satin)	$L = 5 \times N$

Compare: Short Draft.

BLOCKOUT. The same as Draw-down (v). Sometimes distinction is made between these two terms to the effect that Blockout is made directly from a short draft, and Draw-down from a full draft.

BLOOMING LEAF. Colonial pattern. Short draft:

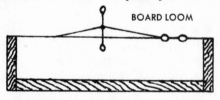

BLOTCH (dialectic corruption of Blot).   A spot in the fabric where the weft misses one or more warp threads.   Synonym: Scobb.

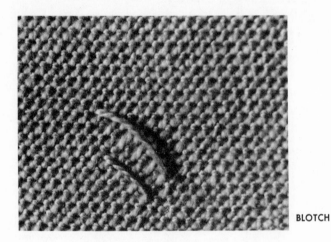

BLOTCH

BOARD LOOM. In principle the same as Frame loom, but instead of a frame a board with raised edges is used. The warp is wound around the loom, and its length is more than twice the length of the loom. It may be equipped with heddle-sticks, or even with a rigid-heddle (v) provided that the front and the back of the loom are high enough.

BOARD LOOM

BOBBIN (fr. Fr. *bobine*).   A wooden or plastic spool about 3 to 6 inches long fitting inside of a shuttle. Also large spool used for warping and holding as much as one pound of yarn.

BOBBIN CARRIER. The same as Bobbin Rack.

BOBBIN FRAME. The same as Bobbin Rack.

12

BOBBIN RACK. A vertical frame made of wood, with horizontal steel rods on which are placed warping bobbins. The rods can be removed. When in place they can be secured with a catch. The racks can hold any number of bobbins from twelve up. When working with a warping mill, as well as in sectional warping, a large quantity of bobbins is required.

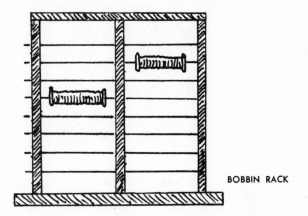

BOBBIN RACK

They are placed on the rack in the same order in which they come in the warp, so that the threads do not cross each other. Very large racks were built in sections which were disposed in a semicircle, so that each section faces the warping mill. Synonyms: Creel, Heck Box, Spool Rack, Bobbin Frame, B. Carrier.

BOBBIN WINDER. A simple machine for winding the yarn on bobbins, spools, quills, or cops. It consists of a large wheel turned by hand, and connected by gears, belt or cord to a much smaller one which consequently turns much faster. The axle of the small wheel has a projecting end which fits tightly inside a spool. The yarn comes from a swift if it is in skeins, or from a tube or cone.

The warping bobbins should be filled with yarn in uniform layers, but the winding of weft is more complicated.

BOBBIN WINDING

In case of a bobbin the winding should start at one end, form a cone pointing inwards (A), then go to the other end to make a similar cone. Then the space between the cones is filled up, but always with a depression in the middle, until the winding is nearly finished. Quills are wound in a

13

similar way, except that at the start two balls are formed instead of two cones (B). Plugs for the flying shuttle are wound to the full size on one end, and then the winding proceeds in conical layers (C) until the other end is reached.

BOILING-OFF. The same as Degumming.

BOLT (fr. G. *bolte* = piece of linen). The full length of finished fabric as taken from the loom. Synonyms: Cut, Piece.

BOLTING CLOTH. Silk fabric, very fine and closely woven in Cross Weave (up to 200 threads per inch).

BONAPARTE'S MARCH. Colonial pattern (v) of the Cross-and-Table group. Short draft:

$$\begin{array}{cccccccc} 6 & 7 & & 7 & & 7 & & 7 \\ & 4 & 4 & 3 & 4 & 4 & 4 & 4 & 3 & 4 & 4 \\ & 4 & & 3 & 3 & & 4 & & 4 & & 3 & 3 & & 4 \\ & 4 & & & & & 4 & 4 & & & & & 4 \\ & & & |8x| & & |6x| & & |8x| \end{array}$$

BORDER. This part of a woven piece which lies along the edges, and which has a different pattern than the centre.

BORDER PATTERN. Any pattern comparatively small may be used for borders. In articles with large central pattern the border may contain either the same pattern in miniature (v Miniature Patterns) or any other as long as it harmonizes with the main design. On the other hand, when the main pattern is small, the border should be designed in as large pattern as possible. In other cases there is no pattern on the woven piece except in borders, or all the pattern is in the central part with plain borders. In such weaves as swivel or lace the border is nearly always plain.

BORE. The length of warp on the loom moved forward at a time. This may be anything from a fraction of an inch to several inches. The expression comes from the holes "bored" in the cloth beams of old looms. A stick inserted in the holes served to turn the beam.

BORE STAFF. A stick which was used for turning either the warp beam or the cloth beam in old looms. These beams were of large diameter and have holes drilled near one end. The staff fits into these holes. The cloth beam has a ratchet wheel which prevents the beam from turning back. The warp beam has no ratchet but the staff is propped against a row of pegs in the frame of the loom, or there is a brake which maintains an even tension of the warp.

BOSOM. The main part of a woven piece as opposed to the selvedges or borders.

BOSS (fr. AS *bozan* = to beat). Linen weft bleached and beaten flat.

BOTTOM BOARD. See Jacquard's Machine.

14

BOUCLÉ (fr. Fr. =curled). 1. Yarn which has two or more strands, of which one is straight, the other forms loops. 2. Fabric woven with bouclé yarn.

BOUND WEAVE. The same as weaving on Opposite Sheds (v).

BOUT (fr. AS *būgan*). The same as Bight.

BOW CORD. A cord which connects a couper (v) with corresponding shaft (R).

BOW-KNOT. Colonial pattern or component of a pattern. See Maple Leaf.

BOW-KNOT. A knot sometimes used to tie the warp in, i.e., to attach the warp to the apron.

BOX LOOM. One of the "no-harness" looms. It works on the same principle as a Frame Loom. Its main part is an open box with the two long sides much lower than the front and back. The warp is wound around the box. Due to its height the loom is suitable for weaving with a rigid heddle.

BOX BATTEN. A batten equipped for fly-shuttle weaving.

BOX-IN-THE-BUSH. Colonial pattern, the same as Dutchman's Fancy.

BRAID (fr. AS *bragdan*). A plaited work which is not considered as woven (no distinction between warp and weft), but which is often used for finishing fringed edges of a woven piece. The braids are either knotted or plaited flat in which case they resemble weaving.

BRAKE. An optional part of a loom. It replaces the ratchet wheel. The disadvantage of a ratchet wheel is that it does not permit to control the warp tension in a continuous way, the tension being changed by steps corresponding to the dents in both the back and front wheel. Usually the brake is placed on the warp beam.

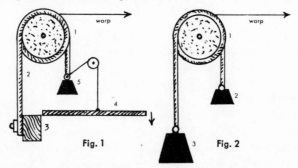

Fig. 1   Fig. 2

There are two kinds of brakes: one gives positive braking action, and has to be released before the warp can be moved forwards. The other releases the warp whenever the tension becomes too great. In the first

15

(Fig. 1) a cord (2) is attached to the frame (3) of the loom, then passed around the warp beam (1). Its free end is pulled down lightly by a weight or a spring (5). The brake is released with a treadle (4) which lifts the weight.

The second kind of brake (Fig. 2) has a very heavy weight (3) attached to the back end of a cord wound around the warp beam (1), and a smaller one to the front end (2). It works in a permanent way as long as the heavy weight does not touch the warp beam. Then it can be reset by lifting the small weight.

BREAKING. A process which follows the retting, and in which the flax stalks are broken so that the fibres are not damaged, and can be separated from the lignous parts of stalks in the next operation.

BREAST BEAM. The same as Cloth Beam.

BREAST PIECE. Part of the loom frame. The beam or board over which passes the cloth before it is wound on the cloth beam. In some looms, particularly the old ones, there is no breast piece: its place takes the cloth beam.

BREAST ROLLER. The same as Cloth Beam.

BRIDLE (fr. AS *bridel*). A piece of cord tied to every Lash of a Draw-Loom (v).

BRILLIANTINE (fr. Fr. *brillantine*). A fabric similar to Alpaca, very closely woven in tabby or twill. Cotton warp, and angora goat wool in weft.

BRITCH WOOL. Coarse wool from the hind legs of sheep.

BROADCLOTH. Woollen yardage of good quality. Originally woven wider than other fabrics.

BROCADE (fr. Sp. *brocado*). 1. A brocaded fabric (see Brocading). 2. Any fabric with metallic threads in weft (R).

BROCADING. A free weave of the Inlay type. Real brocading differs from other inlay weaves inasmuch as the pattern weft is cut to the proper length before it is laid in the shed. Every shed is filled in its entire length with pattern weft. The pattern floats are rather short. Short floats combined with very hard beating give a very firm fabric. When the ground or binder is woven in tabby, the brocading thread passes under one and over two warp ends. There is only one pattern shed, consequently the pattern texture is similar to corded fabrics. Usually a separate shaft with long-eye heddles is hung in front of the standard harness:

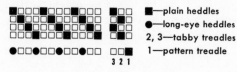

■—plain heddles
●—long-eye heddles
2, 3—tabby treadles
1—pattern treadle

3 2 1

To avoid vertical stripes in the texture, at least two pattern sheds must be used. E.g.:

Sheds 1 and 2 are used alternately. The floats in this case will be longer (3 instead of 2).

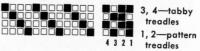

3, 4—tabby treadles
1, 2—pattern treadles

The term Brocading is loosely applied to nearly all Inlay weaves.

BROCATELLE (Fr.). A tissue weave (v) in which the ground warp is very tightly stretched, and the pattern warp rather loose. Thus the pattern is raised above the ground.

BROCHÉ (fr. Fr. *brocher* = to brocade). One of the Tissue weaves (v) in which the ground is tabby. There are usually three pattern picks to one pick of binder. Every pick of pattern in three consecutive pattern sheds is of a different colour. Thus the general effect is of only one pick of weft of changing colour, between each two picks of binder. The three colours do not remain the same, but are changed according to the part of the design woven. Although the colours thus form horizontal stripes, these stripes show only at the back of the fabric, when the face of the Broché resembles Brocade.

BROKEN TWILL. A weave which has the same qualities as a biased twill but where the diagonals do not show, because they are "broken."

The twill can be broken by changing the tie-up as in the following examples or by changing the treadling: 1243 instead of 1234 in a standard tie-up.

Twill woven on three shafts (1:2) cannot be broken. Twills of the type 1:N are called Satins when N is 4 or more, and when the breaking is

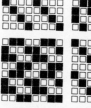
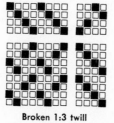

Broken 2:2 twill   Broken 1:3 twill   Broken herringbone

performed so that no trace of the original diagonal remains. Thus: 1:4 twill may be:

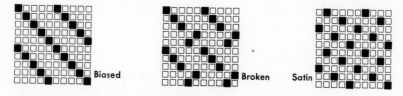

Biased   Broken   Satin

Sometimes the Dornick twill (v) is called broken twill.

BRONSON WEAVE (Am.). Properly speaking, this name should be applied to all Spot Weaves with a tie-up, as in Fig. 1. As far as it is known this tie-up and consequently a whole class of spot weaves has been mentioned for the first time in the English weaving literature by Bronson, although he did not claim it as his invention. Tie-up, in Fig. 2, has been used before then in England for what was then called Spot Weaves, and what we know now in hand-weaving as Swivel. To avoid confusion we distinguish now between: Spot, All-Over-Spot (or Barley Corn), Spot Lace, which all can be called Bronson, Bronson Lace, etc., and Spot Swivel, or simply Swivel.

In the first case the pattern is formed by floats. In the second case the floats are cut off, and coloured weft must be used to make the pattern visible. See Spot Weaves.

BROWN YARN. The same as unbleached yarn. See Bleaching.

BRUSSELS TAPESTRY (fr. *Bruxelles* in Belgium). Weft or warp pile fabrics with uncut loops. The better quality has weft pile. Some have the pattern printed on warp, and are woven as terry velvet.

BUNTINE, or **BUNTING** (fr. G. *bunt*). Thin cotton or woollen fabrics used for flags, signals and so on.

BURLAP (fr. Lat. *burra* = coarse hair). A coarse fabric woven in tabby from jute or hemp fibres.

BURLING (fr. Fr. *bouril*). Action of removing knots from a finished fabric. Synonym: Deknotting.

BUTTERNUT. Colonial pattern (v) of the Cross-and-Table group. Short draft:

CAAM (prob. fr. AS *camb*). 1. The same as reed (R). 2. The same as Back—or Pattern-Harness in Two-Harness method (v).

CAAMING. The same as Sleying (R).

CALENDERING (fr. Low Lat. *calendera* = cylinder). Pressing a fabric with hot cylinders, instead of flat irons.

CALICO (fr. *Calicut* in India). 1. Any plain cotton fabric. 2. (Am.) Printed cotton fabric woven in tabby.

CALICO WEAVE. The same as Tabby weave (R).

18

CAMBLET or **CAMLET** (fr. Arabic *khaml* = pile).   Any fabric resembling one made of camel's hair.

CAMBRIC (fr. Fr. *cambrai*).   Fine linen fabric well bleached, or its imitation made of cotton.

CANDLEWICK.   1. Thick cotton yarn used for weft.   2. Rough design on fine, unbleached, cotton tabby ground.

CANE.   Warp prepared for beaming.   The name comes from a warping process in which the warp is wound around a stick (cane) before beaming (R).

CANE ROLLER.   The same as Warp Beam (R).

CANE STICK.   Some old looms have a groove made in the warp beam. To attach the warp to the beam a stick is passed through the first loop in the portee cross, and then after the warp is spread, the stick and the warp on it are pressed into the groove.   This method is satisfactory on long

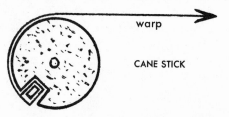

warp

CANE STICK

warps only, since about a yard is wasted at the end of every warp.   On the other hand, it is the simplest and fastest way of attaching the warp to the warp beam.

CANNELÉ (Fr.).   In hand-weaving, a method of distorting the weft which follows a wavy line on the surface of the tabby ground.   For instance:

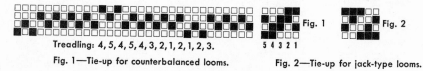

Treadling: 4, 5, 4, 5, 4, 3, 2, 1, 2, 1, 2, 3.

Fig. 1

Fig. 2

5 4 3 2 1

Fig. 1—Tie-up for counterbalanced looms.   Fig. 2—Tie-up for jack-type looms.

The weft used on treadle 3 is much heavier than the ground.

CANVAS (fr. Lat. *cannabis* = hemp).   Heavy linen or cotton fabric woven in tabby.

CAPE (fr. Lat. *capa*).   1. Part of a loom frame, one of the two horizontal beams, which support the Top-Castle, and the hanging batten.   2. The upper part of a raddle (v).   It is removed before spreading the warp.

CARBONIZING.   Cleaning of wool with strong acids.   Wool is acid-resistant, but all other organic matter clinging to the fibres is dissolved (carbonized) by the acid.

19

CARD. 1. A perforated plate which opens one shed in a Dobby, or in a Jacquard Machine (v). 2. An implement used in Carding (v). 3. A thin square plate with holes in the corners used in Card Weaving.

CARD WEAVING. A special weaving technique used for making very narrow fabrics (up to 2 inches wide). The warp may be stretched between any two supports several feet apart. The shed is opened by turning a set of Cards—thin square plates made of cardboard, plastic or metal. Each card has four holes: one in each corner. Every warp end passes through

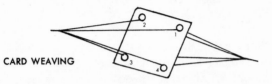

CARD WEAVING

one of these holes. By turning the set of cards different sheds are opened (four sheds in all), and at the same time the warp ends threaded through the same card are twisted around each other. The resulting weave is consequently a Cross-Weave (v) in which the warp covers completely the weft. Card weaving is a slow process, but it presents very interesting possibilities. Synonym: Tablet weaving.

CARDED WOOL. Wool with comparatively short fibres (less than five inches) which has undergone the process of carding.

CARDING (fr. Lat. *carere*). A process in which the wool is prepared for spinning. In principle carding is executed with two cards, or flat pieces of wood with a great number of short wires set in (similar to wire-brushes). The wool is rolled between them and forms shorter or longer slivers (rolag). In machine carding the wool passes through several sets of cards which have cylindrical form, and the sliver is produced in a continuous way.

CARDINGS. Wool after carding, but before spinning. Cardings are used exceptionally as weft for making very heavy blankets. Synonym: Rolag.

CARPET WEAVING (fr. Lat. *carpere* = to pluck). Carpets or pile-rugs, when hand woven belong to the weft-pile fabrics. Rows of thick weft are separated with several shots of thin, strong binder, usually woven in tabby. The pile weft makes a knot around one or two warp ends, then a loop, then a knot again, and so on. There are several knots used in carpet weaving (compare Ghiordes, Sehna, Single Warp knot). The length of loops left between knots is regulated with a gauge (flat stick or rod) around which the loops are wound. After one whole row of knots is made, the loops may be cut, or left uncut. The cutting is performed in the same way as in other pile weaves (v), then the gauge is withdrawn. The pattern is obtained exclusively by changing the colours in weft. The quality of a carpet depends mostly on the material used, the number of knots per inch square, and on the pattern; the weaving technique itself is of secondary importance.

CARRIAGE. In a Draw-Loom, the frame which supports the Pulley Box. It corresponds to the Top-Castle in an ordinary loom.

CARTRIDGE SILK. Coarse, natural silk fabric of inferior quality, woven in tabby. Originally used for powder containers in artillery shells.

CASEMENT FABRIC. Any light fabric suitable for curtains.

CASHMERE (fr. *Kashmir* in India). 1. Wool of a mountain goat from Tibet and Northern India. 2. Fabric made of this wool. 3. Brocaded shawls made in India.

CASSIMERE (fr. Turk. *Quazmir*). Soft, light woollen fabric, woven in twill.

CAT TRACKS. Colonial pattern (v), the same as Snail Trail.

CATALOGNE. French term designating rag rugs and runners usually made by the yard. Striped, plaided or hit-and-miss.

CATALPA FLOWER. Colonial pattern (v) of the Star-and-Table group. Short draft:

```
12 5 5 12
       12              5 5 5 5 5 5 5 5 5                12
           12 5 5 12 5 5 5 5 5 5 5 5 5 12 5 5 12
    5 5 5        5 5 5                          5 5 5
```

CATGUT. A Cross-Weave (v) similar to Gauze, but with warp ends making a full turn around each other between two shots of weft, instead of half a turn, as in Gauze.

CELLULOSE ACETATE. Rayon fabrics and rayon fibre obtained by the action of acetic acid on cotton fibres.

CHAIN (fr. Lat. *catena*). The same as warp (R). Properly: warp taken from the warping reel, and made into a chain to keep it from getting tangled.

CHAIN

When making the chain the weaver starts from the porrey-end of the warp, forms a loop and passes another loop of the warp through it, then a third through the second and so on. The chain is easily unravelled by pulling the portee-end of the warp.

CHALLIE, CHALLIS, or **CHALLY** (fr. Fr. *chale* = shawl). Light, woollen fabric woven in tabby.

CHAMBRAY (fr. Fr. *cambrai*). Plain fabric with one colour in the warp, and a different colour in the weft.

21

CHARIOT WHEEL. Colonial pattern (v) of the Wheel-and-Star group. Short draft:

CHECKS. Simple pattern usually obtained by crossing stripes of dark and light colours in warp and weft, as in Fig. 1. However, to get the proper "chessboard" effect, a pattern weave is needed, such as overshot, crackle, spot or turned twill (Fig. 2).

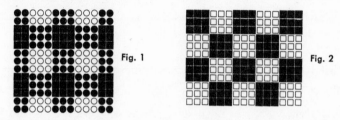

Fig. 1 Fig. 2

CHEESECLOTH. Light, very open cotton fabric woven in tabby, originally used for wrapping cheese.

CHENILLE (caterpillar in Fr.). 1. Yarn with short fringe perpendicular to the core of the yarn, all on one side, or on two opposite sides of the core. Chenille yarn can be woven on a hand-loom. The warp is set as follows: 6 to 8 ends very close, then skip about one inch, and repeat as many times as necessary. Weave as tabby, using for weft comparatively thick and soft yarn. After weaving, cut the floats half way between the strands of warp. The stripes thus obtained can be used as weft in weaving chenille fabrics.

2. Chenille fabrics have pile on one or both sides. This pile is formed by the fringe of the chenille yarn. In weaving, the fringe must be combed before beating, to avoid its being enclosed in the shed. It is combed all up, if pile is on one side only, or both up and down for pile on both sides.

Hand-woven chenille fabrics are called Twice-Woven (v).

CHEVIOT (fr. *Cheviot Hills* in Scotland). Breed of sheep, yarn spun from their wool, and fabric woven from cheviot yarn.

CHEVRON THREADING (fr. Fr. *chevron* = rafter). Threading for herringbone twill.

CHIFFON (fr. Fr. *chiffon* = rag). Thin, light, and soft silk fabric.

CHINA DOUBLE. Colonial pattern (v) of the Sunflower group. Short draft:

22

CHINCHILLA CLOTH. Heavy woollen fabric napped on one side. Woven in double twill.

CHINÉ (fr. Fr. *chiné* = multicolour). Any pile fabric with design printed on warp before weaving. See Warp Printing.

CHINTZ (fr. Sanskrit *chitra* = spotted). Printed cotton fabric woven in tabby.

CIRCULAR WEAVE. One of double-cloth weaves. Two layers of cloth are connected by the selvedges, thus forming a tube. Circular weave is suitable for cushion covers, bags, etc. It may be woven in any standard weave with or without pattern but the number of shafts required is always twice the number for one layer only. The draft for circular tabby weave is:

Treadling: 1, 2, 3, 4.

4 3 2 1

When the two layers are connected on one side only, the weave is called semi-circular, or double-width, and the treadling is 1 3 2 4. The side on which the layers join depends on the direction of throwing the shuttle, and this direction should never be changed. It should be, for instance, from the right for treadles 1 and 2, from the left for 3 and 4. Synonym: Hose.

CISELÉ (fr. Fr. *ciselé* = finely cut). Pile fabric with pattern formed by blocks of cut and uncut pile.

CLASPED HEDDLES. String heddles made each of two interlocking doups, or half-heddles. The warp ends pass between these doups. When moving the warp forward, the tension on the heddles must be somehow released. Consequently clasped heddles are not mounted on a frame, but between two shafts, of which the lower one can be slightly raised. The advantage of clasped heddles is that they hold firmly the warp ends and consequently there is less friction between the warp and the harness. This is of some importance when weaving very fine fabrics.

CLASPED WEFTS. See Locked Wefts.

CLEMATIS. An overshot pattern. Short draft:
$$\begin{array}{cccc} & 6 & 3 & 6 \\ & 7 & & 3 \\ 4 & & 4 & 3\,3 \\ 6 & & 6 & \end{array}$$

This pattern is written partly on opposites. When developing the short draft into full draft it must be remembered that the opposed blocks do not overlap.

CLOCK WORK. Colonial Summer-and-Winter pattern. Short draft:

$$\begin{array}{ccccc} 1 & 3\,1\,3 & & 3\,1\,3 & 1 \\ 1 & 3\,3 & & 3\,3 & 1 \\ 2 & 2 & 6\,1\,1\,1\,1\,6 & 2 & 2 \\ 1\,2 & 2 & 3\,3\,1\,1\,1\,1\,3\,3 & 2 & 2 \end{array}$$

CLOTH. (fr. AS *clath*). Any woven fabric. The word is used also to designate woollen fabrics only.

CLOTH BEAM. The rotating beam in front of a loom, on which finished cloth is wound. It is made of wood, and can be either round, hexagonal or octagonal. In the latter case it is usually made of triangular sections glued together. It revolves on two steel shafts embedded in the ends of the beam, and supported in two bearings set in the loom frame. If the frame is of hardwood, the bearings are not necessary: holes bored in the frame are quite sufficient. On one end the cloth beam has a ratchet wheel (v); a handle with a pawl (or dog) is used for turning the beam. Old looms have a ratchet wheel, but no handle. Holes are bored in the beam, and pegs set permanently in the holes, or removed when not in use. In fly-shuttle looms the beam is often equipped with Take-Up Motion (v). Synonyms: Breast Beam, Breast Roller, Fore Beam, Front Beam, Web Beam.

CLOUDLESS BEAUTY. Colonial pattern (v) of the Three-Block-Patch group. Short draft:
```
9 9 9 9  9                    9
        9 9 9 9 9 9 9 9 9 9 9 9
3 3 3 3  3  3 3 3 3 3 3 3   3
```

CLUSTER OF VINES. Colonial pattern (v) of the Sunflower group. Short draft:
```
4 5 4 | 5| 4 5 4  4         4  4| 5| 4'5 5           |  |
      5 |5     4    4      5 |5     4   4   5 5 4     |  |  4
          4    4 5 4 5| 4 5 4  4               4| 5| 4
5 5        5 5  4  5 5   5 5  4  5 |5             11 |11
    |2x|         |2x|          |2x|          |6x|
```

COLONIAL. A term loosely applied to early American weaving, and weaving patterns. The period covering colonial weaving extends roughly from the beginning of the seventeenth century to the beginning of the nineteenth century, i.e., to the introduction of power looms. It is characterized by an extensive use of overshot technique, particularly the four-block overshot, and by a total absence of tissue weaves, brocades, warp-pile weaves, pile carpets, cross-weaves, lappets and knotted tapestry. Besides overshot, and standard weaves, there were used: spot weave (later called Bronson), double spot-weave (Summer-and-Winter), double weaves and turned twills, but not to any great extent. Compared with contemporary English weaving, the Colonial weaving is rather limited on the technical side, but it has developed an extraordinary richness of design. Colonial patterns are nearly all four-block, or their more elaborate derivatives.

Looms in use during the colonial period of weaving had from 4 to 16 shafts. There is no indication of draw-looms being ever used in America.

COLONIAL PATTERNS. All colonial patterns can be divided in the following way (classification of M. M. Atwater. See Bibliography):

1. *Diamond and Cross*: (a) Cross and Table
   (b) Diamond and Table

2. *Star and Rose*:   (a) Star and Table
   (b) Rose and Table
   (c) Star, Rose and Table
   (d) Group of Stars and Table

3. *Wheel*:   (a) Star and Wheel
   (b) Wheel and Table
   (c) Wheel and Rose
   (d) Group of Stars and Wheels, and Table
   (e) Wheel, Star, and Rose

4. *Radiating Patterns*: (a) Sunrise and Table
   (b) Blooming Leaf
   (c) Bow-Knot

5. *Patch Patterns*:   (a) Two-Block
   (b) Three-Block
   (c) Four-Block

6. *Miscellaneous*:   (a) Sunflower
   (b) Unclassified

In all: nineteen groups in six classes. The name of every class indicates the elements of which the pattern is composed. These elements are described separately under: Cross, Table, Rose, etc. Drafts given under proper names of colonial patterns are all short drafts. For their interpretation see: Short Drafts, and Development of Drafts.

The names of colonial patterns included in this book are all classical patterns. Names of patterns not included are of later origin, usually doubtful and of local importance only.

COLOUR. The names of colours are often misleading and they vary with nearly every producer of dyes and paints. Several attempts to standardize them have been made. Originally Ostwald placed all colours in the rainbow's order on a circle and divided this circle into 100 parts. Later for practical reasons this circle was divided into eight groups, each group having three shades—24 pure colours in all. These 24 colours are called Range NA. By adding a certain amount of black to every colour we have Range NE, and still more black gives Range NI. Adding more or less white to each colour we have Ranges EA and IA. Still more ranges are obtained by adding black and white simultaneously. Any particular shade is then defined by the number of range and the number of colour. Thus, for instance, NI-12 will be very dark bluish-purple.

A similar but more practical theory was developed by Munzell. Besides classifying colours, it gives certain rules which can guide an unexperienced designer. See *Munzell's Theory of Colour*.

COMB. 1. The same as Reed (v). 2. In tapestry weaving (High-Warp Tapestry) a wooden fork which is used for beating down the weft. It consists of a heavy piece of wood about a foot long, with a handle on one end, and a head with serrations cut in the wood on another. The number of serrations or grooves per inch corresponds to the sett of warp.

COMBED WOOL. Better quality of wool with fibres from 5 to 12 inches long. This wool passes through an additional carding operation, called combing.

COMBER BOARD (word of uncertain origin; it either comes from *Cambrai* in France, and was brought to British Isles by French weavers, or is an obsolete form of "cumber," fr. Lat. *cumulus* = heap). A board with tiny holes serving as guides for heddles. The holes are not placed in one row, but in several, and the board is usually composed of a number of sections, called Slips, held together in a frame.

Comber board is used in all types of Draw-Looms. Synonym: Hole Board.

←slip

COMBER REPEAT. Repeat of a pattern which does not change its direction, as opposed to Point Repeat, where the direction changes. Usually this kind of repeating any pattern, part of a threading draft, is referred to as "plain repeat" or just "repeat." Compare: Point Repeat, Turnover R., Drop Turnover Repeat.

Comber repeat

COMBER SLIP. One section of a comber board.

COMBING. A process similar to carding, and used only with better quality long fibre wool. It straightens the fibres instead of tangling them.

26

COMPOUND HARNESS. More than one harness mounted on the same loom, so that every warp end is threaded through one heddle in every harness. Compare: Two-Harness Method.

COMPOUND MONTURE. A Draw-Loom which has the ground harness replaced by a Split Harness (v).

COMPOUND TIE-UP. Tie-Up made in such a way that a part of it is a Direct Tie-Up, and another part plain tie-up.

COMPOUND TREADLING. Treadling which requires the use of both feet to open a shed. Two, three or even four treadles are depressed at the same time. This method is used whenever the number of treadles is smaller than the number of sheds required. For instance, double face twill, combinations of blocks of pattern in Summer-and-Winter, etc. Compound treadling is rather slow, and should be avoided if possible.

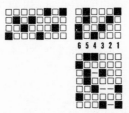

COMPOUND WEAVES. There are several definitions of Compound Weaves: 1. Any weave which has more than one warp. 2. Any weave composed of two different simpler weaves. 3. A weave composed of two different pattern weaves.

In the last case the weaving can be done with Two-Harness method. The back harness is threaded for one weave, the front harness for another. When the front harness remains in neutral position (neither raised nor sunk), the loom works as if it had the back harness only, and the first weave is executed. When the front harness is used alone, the second weave appears. More than two weaves require still more harnesses, and since the distance between two consecutive harnesses is at least 12 inches, the loom becomes difficult to operate, and a Draw-Loom is to be preferred. Compare: Tissue Weaves, Two-Harness Method.

CONE. One of several ways in which yarn is wound and sold. It has the advantage over tubes or spools in that the yarn can be taken off the cone without revolving it, which simplifies such operations as warping, bobbin winding, etc. The cone should be placed so that the yarn will unwind in the vertical direction. When this is impossible for any reason, a special stand properly inclined must be used. The cones are then placed on pegs set in the stand.

27

COP (fr. AS *cop* = summit). A cone of yarn wound on a quill or tube. Sometimes the tube itself.

COPPIN. The same as Cop (R).

CORD (fr. Lat. *chorda*). One horizontal line of a weaving pattern. The term comes from the draw-loom, where the number of cords (lashes) in the Simple is equal to the number of the sheds in a certain pattern. The number of cords applies to the pattern only, as the ground is woven on a separate harness.

The word Block is used in the same meaning as Cord.

CORD. Any corded fabric (v), particularly Corduroy.

CORD WEAVE. Any weave which produces corded fabrics.

CORDED FABRICS. Fabrics with raised ridges parallel to the warp or weft. There are several ways of making them:

1. The yarns in warp are alternately coarse and fine, or between two thick ends, two or more thin ones are placed. The weft covers the warp.

2. The picks of weft are alternately thick and thin—the warp covers the weft.

3. Fine tabby alternates with only one shed of twill made in heavier weft:

Treadling: 5, 2, 5, 1,
or: 4, 2, 4, 1, and so on.

4. When a weft-pile fabric is woven with pile always in the same shed, it will present ridges parallel to the warp after the floats are cut:

Treadling: 1, 2, 3 or 3, 2, 3, 1.
3—pile weft; 2, 1—binder; r—ridge.

5. Thick and widely-spaced weft, with closely set, fine warp, or *vice versa*.

Fancy corded fabrics have floats in the covering fine yarn, whether it is weft or warp, and the floats form patterns, in the same way as in other weaves.

CORDING. The same as Tie-Up.

CORDUROY (fr. Fr. *corde du roi* = King's thread). A weft-pile cotton fabric. Ridges parallel to the warp. In hand-weaving Corduroy can be produced on many drafts. E.g.:

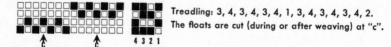

Treadling: 3, 4, 3, 4, 3, 4, 1, 3, 4, 3, 4, 3, 4, 2.
The floats are cut (during or after weaving) at "c".

This draft will produce ridges typical for corduroy. But the ridges can be avoided by staggering the floats:

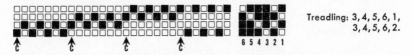

Treadling: 3, 4, 5, 6, 1,
3, 4, 5, 6, 2.

The yarn for the pile is usually heavier and softer than the yarn for warp. The cutting can be done on the loom, or after the piece is woven, and taken off the loom.

Light rugs can be woven in this way, if extremely heavy yarn is used both for weft and warp. Synonym: Thicksett.

CORE. The central or binding part of fancy yarns such as Bouclé, Chenille, and so on.

COTTON (fr. Arabic *qutun*). Vegetable fibres from the fluff covering the seeds of several tropical bushes, all belonging to the Mallow family, order *Gossypium*. Cotton yarn is obtained through the following operations: ginning (breaking the fibres from the seeds), sifting, mixing, and beating or willowing. Then follow the same operations as for wool.

Cotton yarn is one of the easiest to work with. It is strong, elastic, resistant to friction, and it can be spun very thin. On the other hand, it has a dull look unless mercerized (v), and has poor absorbing and insulating qualities.

COUNT OF CLOTH. The same as Thread Count (v).

COUNT OF YARN. System of numbers designating the thickness of yarn. Since the thickness itself is too difficult to measure in fractions of the inch, the weight of a certain length of yarn is adopted as the unit of measure. These units, however, vary with different yarns. Thus:

Cotton, Rayon, sometimes *Wool*: Number 1 has 840 yards to the pound. Any other numbers indicates how many times *thinner* is the corresponding yarn. E.g.: No. 5—4,200 yards, No. ½—420 yards to the pound. When the yarn has two or more plies, two numbers are used: one indicates the number of plies, the other the thickness of every ply. E.g.: 3/2 means three plies of No. 2 or 560 yards per pound. But the order in which these numbers are written is not always the same.

Linen: Number 1 has 300 yards to the pound. Other numbers can be figured out in the same way as for cotton. E.g.: No. 10—3,000 yards per pound, No. 3/15—1,500 yds./lb.

Hemp, Ramie, Jute: as Linen, but only low numbers of yarn are made.

Silk: 1. As cotton, with the difference that the first number indicates the count, and the second the number of plies.

29

2. In "Deniers," No. 1 has 4,500,000 yards per pound. Higher numbers indicate how many times the yarn is heavier than No. 1. Thus No. 100 will have 45,000 yds./lb.

3. In "Drams," the number indicates the weight in drachms of 1,000 yards of yarn. No. 1 has 135,000 yds./lb., No. 10—13,500, and so on.

Wool: Several different systems are used:

1. The same as for cotton.
2. Similar as for cotton, but No. 1 has 560 yards per pound.
3. Similar to the above, but No. 1 has 320 yds/lb.
4. The count is in number of yards in one dram.
5. The count is in number of yards in one ounce.
6. The count number indicates the weight in drams of a length of 80 yards.
7. The count number indicates the weight in grains of a length of 20 yards. To figure out the number of yards per pound, divide 140,000 by the count number.

The length of yarn is measured in yards. Larger, but rather obsolete, units are:

For cotton: one spindle = 18 hanks (840 yards each) = 126 shifts = 252 knots = 15,120 yards.

For linen: one spindle = 2 hesps = 24 heers = 48 cuts (300 yards each) = 14,400 yards.

Wool was measured either in hanks of 560 yards, or in snaps of 320 yards.

Synonym: Grist of Yarn. See: Metric Count of Yarn.

COUNTERBALANCED LOOM. A foot-powered loom in which all shafts are interdependent, i.e., movement of one of them affects all others, even when no tie-up has been made.

Advantages of these looms are: they are simple in construction, and consequently cheap; they are light and easy to operate; they have a very simple tie-up; the shedding motion is two-directional, which is important with sticky yarn. On the other hand, they are suitable only for weaves requiring balanced tie-ups.

All counterbalanced looms operate on sinking shed. The

COUNTERBALANCED LOOM

lamms (one for each shaft) are placed between the treadles and the harness. By depressing one treadle, the weaver pulls down the shafts tied to this treadle and at the same time raises all remaining shafts.

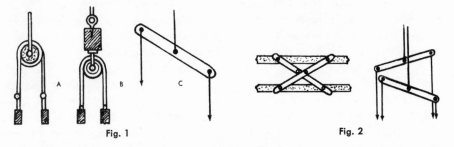

Fig. 1   Fig. 2

The construction of the harness depends on the number of shafts and the way they are connected. Fig. 1 shows three different methods of connecting pairs of shafts: A—roller, B—pulley, C—horse. Any of them can be used alone or in combination with others. The roller is probably the most satisfactory inasmuch as it keeps the two shafts parallel and horizontal as long as the connecting cord does not slip on the roller. The horse has the advantage of being very simple and practically noiseless, but it tends to pull apart the shafts in neutral position. To obviate this, two crossed horses are sometimes used (Fig. 2), but then the arrangement is much too complicated when compared with a roller. The pulley is as good as a roller, but only when there is no danger of shafts getting out of horizontal, which happens whenever a narrow warp is set in a wide loom, or when there is even a slight difference in tension between the two edges of the warp.

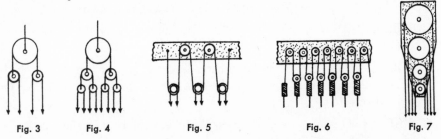

Fig. 3   Fig. 4   Fig. 5   Fig. 6   Fig. 7

The usual 4-shaft harness is shown on Fig. 3, and an 8-shaft harness on Fig. 4. By placing pulley wheels on ends of rollers, a better arrangement is obtained, and at least theoretically it can work with any number of shafts (Fig. 5) because the force pulling up the shafts is more equally distributed. Most counterbalanced harnesses do not work satisfactorily with an odd number of shafts unless pulley-wheels are set in the upper shafts of heddle-frames, and one continuous cord connects all the shafts

31

(Fig. 6, page 31). Such a harness will work well with a small number of shafts, but with a greater number the friction becomes too great even when using ball-bearings.

A particular model of counterbalanced harness is one in which the shafts are tied in pairs, but the pairs are independent of each other. Its use is rather limited, and care must be taken when making the tie-up, not to tie two shafts of the same pair to one treadle (Fig. 7, page 31).

An ordinary counterbalanced harness does not work well with unbalanced tie-ups, because the different sheds open at different heights, which means that in extreme cases they do not open at all. Wide reeds help to a certain extent to overcome this difficulty. Shed regulators are still better. They raise or lower the whole harness, so that the shed opens always in the same place regardless of the tie-up. Thus corrected harness can be even used as a ground harness in Two-Harness method (v), provided that the ties are of different length: short for the sunk shafts, and longer for the shafts remaining in neutral position. These long ties correspond to the missing ties in a jack-loom tie-up. E.g.:

Jack loom   Counterbalanced loom

COUNTER MARCHE. The same as Lamm (R).

COUNTER-MARCHE LOOM. Spelled also "Contra-marche" and "Kontra-marche." The same as Double-Tie-Up Loom (See Independent Action Looms).

COUNTERPOISED HARNESS. The same as Cross' Draw Loom.

COUPER (fr. Fr. *couper* = to cut). The upper lever in a jack-loom. Synonym: Tumbler.

COURSE. The shortest repeat in threading. E.g., in plain threading the course has a number of warp ends equal to the number of shafts. The same as repeat (R).

COVER. In Tissue weaving, particularly in Broché (v) the number of colours in the same horizontal stripe. In Swivel all colours used to make one shed of tabby. One, two, three covers means: one, two, three colours.

COVERLET (fr. Fr. *couvre-lit* = bed cover). At the present "coverlet" means in North America a colonial bed cover, woven usually in wool on cotton warp in overshot, summer-and-winter, or double weave, later also on Jacquard looms.

COVERLID. The same as Coverlet.

COVERT (fr. Fr. *couvert* = covered). Woollen fabric woven in twill. Warp made of two colours twisted together, of which one dark and one light.

CRACKLE WEAVE. The name comes from the fissures in the texture of the fabric woven in crackle (which is diminutive of *crack*). The weave is a derivate of Diamond Twill, but the direction of the diagonal in

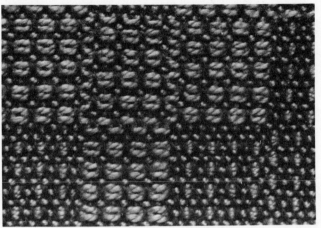

CRACKLE WEAVE

threading changes so often that nearly all floats are of 3 ends. Crackle gives 4 blocks of pattern with four shafts. Each block is written on a different "unit" of threading (Fig. 1).

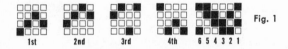

1st   2nd   3rd   4th   6 5 4 3 2 1   Fig. 1

Each unit can be repeated any number of times, therefore the blocks of pattern can be of any size. But when joining two blocks, an "incidental" heddle must be inserted to preserve the continuity of the draft as in Fig. 2.

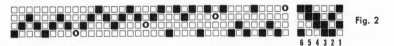

6 5 4 3 2 1   Fig. 2

There are three classical ways of weaving crackle:

1st. One pattern treadle is repeated as many times as necessary to weave one block of pattern. One shot of binder follows each shot of pattern. E.g., treadling for the draft in Fig. 2: 6162616251525152414 2414231323132. Here the blocks of pattern overlap each other by about one-half of their length.

2nd. Two treadles are used alternately: 61526152415241524132 413261326132. The blocks do not overlap, and they have exactly the

33

same structure as summer-and-winter. We have here also half-tones as in overshot.

3rd. The threading draft is followed in the same way as in overshot:
3132616231326152516261525162615241425152414251524132314241323142

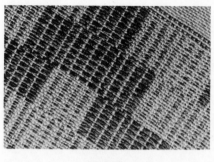

CRACKLE

4132. Here also the blocks do not overlap.

Crackle can be woven as a bound weave (on opposite sheds). The best treadling is 6543 all through the woven piece. The blocks are formed by changing the order in which the colours are used. For instance: 1st block: 6b, 5b, 4w, 3w; 2nd block: 6w, 5b, 4b, 3w; 3rd block: 6w, 5w, 4b, 3b; 4th block: 6b, 5w, 4w, 3b. Here "w" is white, and "b" black.

The advantage of crackle is that it gives very uniform and firm structure of the fabric.

CRADLE LOOM. Small weaving loom of a very simple construction used for educational purposes and in occupational therapy. Its main part is a frame made of four round sticks set between eight flat ones (four horizontal and four vertical). One of the round sticks is eccentric, and by turning it the weaver can regulate the warp tension. The warp is wound around the loom, and slides on the round sticks. The loom has no proper harness, but a rigid heddle (v), i.e., a reed and a heddle-frame combined into one. This heddle serves to open the shed, and to beat the weft as well. The only weaves suitable for cradle-loom are tabby and free weaves.

CRAPE (fr. Lat. *crispus* = curled). The same as Crepe (v).

CRAPES. A cross-weave (v) with a pattern of more than two blocks.

CRASH (fr. Lat. *crassus* = coarse). Any fabric woven from rough yarn, particularly linen or cotton.

CREEL (Scot. fr. Gaelic *criol* = chest). The same as Bobbin Rack.

CREPE (fr. Fr. *crêpe*). Any fabric which remains permanently wrinkled, or which resembles one. This effect can be obtained in weaving or after weaving by treating the fabric with chemicals or heat. In weaving there are several methods of producing crepe: 1st, by using crepe weaves (v); 2nd, by using yarn strongly twisted in the same direction for both warp and weft; 3rd, by using two opposite twists of yarn in warp, or in weft, or in both.

34

CREPE WEAVE. Any weave which produces crepe effect in a fabric. The principle of all such weaves is that one part of the fabric is woven in firm texture (short floats) and another in loose texture (long floats). These two parts must alternate very closely in both directions, or at least in one. In the latter case we have striped crepe. E.g.:

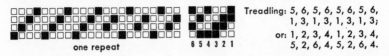

Treadling: 5, 6, 5, 6, 5, 6, 5, 6,
1, 3, 1, 3, 1, 3, 1, 3;
or: 1, 2, 3, 4, 1, 2, 3, 4,
5, 2, 6, 4, 5, 2, 6, 4.

one repeat   6 5 4 3 2 1

To get vertical stripes we use only one-half of the treadling: 56, or 1234. A larger number of shafts will give better results:

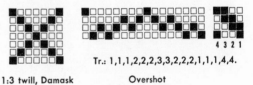

one repeat   4 3 2 1   repeat   8 7 6 5 4 3 2 1

Vertical stripes; Tr.: 1, 2, 3, 4.   All-over crepe; Tr.: 1, 3, 2, 4, 5, 7, 6, 8.

CRETONNE (fr. Fr. *Creton*, name of the manufacturer). Upholstery fabric, cotton or linen, printed.

CROSS. In the warp: the same as Lease.

CROSS. Element of weaving patterns. Threading is the same as for Diamond, but the treadling reversed.

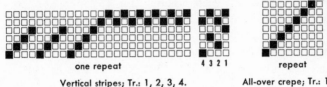

Tr.: 1,1,1,2,2,2,3,3,2,2,2,1,1,1,4,4.

2:2 twill, Crackle   Barley corn   1:3 twill, Damask   Overshot

Cross in different weaving techniques.

CROSS BRIDLE. In a draw-loom, a short cord stretched between the two guide ropes (v). Whenever several colours in weft are used simultaneously, the corresponding lashes are not tied directly to the Guides, but to the bridles. In this way the lashes are less crowded and their selection is easier.

CROSS COMPASS. Colonial pattern (v) of the Star-and-Wheel group. Short draft:

CROSS' DRAW LOOM (fr. the inventor's name). A draw-loom equipped with a shedding machine similar to Jacquard's, but with perforated boards and knotted cords instead of cards and needles.

35

CROSS DYEING. Dyeing of fabrics woven of different yarns, of which one takes the dye and the other does not. For instance, when linen and cotton are used in the same fabric, most of ordinary dyes will dye the cotton but not the linen.

CROSS OF TENNESSEE. Colonial pattern (v) of the Cross-and-Table group. Short draft:

```
5 5 5 5 5 5 5 5   4   4     4   4
              14    4   5   4    14
           12    4   4 4   4    12
    5 5 5 5 5 5 5    4   4   4   4
```

CROSS STICKS. The same as Lease-Rods (v).

CROSS WEAVE (or Crossed Warps). Any weave in which two or more warp ends are twisted around each other during the process of weaving, either by pick-up method (Free Cross Weave), or by a special arrangement of heddles.

The simplest cross-weave is Gauze (v). When one shot of gauze is followed by an odd number of tabby shots, the weave is called Leno.

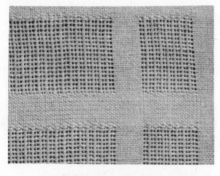

CROSS WEAVE (Riddles)

When stripes of gauze alternate with tabby in the direction of warp, we have Pickets. When there are blocks of gauze with tabby all around, it is called Riddles. Cross weave used as an ornament on tabby ground particularly if made in a different yarn is called Veining. All above weaves have warp threads making half a turn around each other. If they make a whole turn between two shots of weft, the weave is Catgut.

When the gauze blocks alternate with tabby blocks, the weave is known as Purles. If they form a pattern we have Victories. When one thread of warp is twisted with *two* adjacent ends, the weave is Turkey Gauze.

All these weaves can be executed with the same equipment which is required for plain gauze. However, if more than three threads of warp are to go around each other, a set of heddles placed *before* the reed is necessary. This set is mounted on the batten and swings with it. To avoid excessive friction between heddles and the warp, special heddles called Bead-Lams are used. Instead of mails or eyes they have perforated beads tied to the doups. The weaves made on this mounting have a common name of Net Weaves (v). They require, beside the bead-lams, at least two warp beams.

The latter method has nothing to do with so called "Bead Leno" (v), in which the beads are not tied to the doups at all, and are placed behind the batten.

CROSS WEAVE (Leno)

If some of the ends of warp cross so many others that they are woven rather horizontally than vertically, and to a certain extent replace the pattern weft, the weave is called Lappet, or Embroidery Weave (not to be confused with embroidery weaves executed with tapestry technique). Lappet weave (v) requires a batten of special construction.

Synonym: Leno.

CROSSED DIAMOND. A simple pattern suitable for diamond twill, crackle, overshot, etc. E.g.:

one repeat

A B 4 3 2 1

Treadling (plus binder):
2, 3, 4, 1, 2, 3, 4, 1, 1, 4, 3,
3, 4, 1, 1, 4, 3, 2, 1, 4, 3, 2.

CROSSED WARPS. The same as Cross Weave.

CROSSING. The same as Interlocking (v).

CUP AND SAUCER. Colonial pattern (v) of the Wheel-Star-and-Rose group. Short draft:

```
 4   4   6    3 3 3 3    6   4   4   10 3 3 3 10
   4   4   10 3 3 3 10    4   4   6     3 3 3 3    6
 4   4   10            10   4   4   8               8
 4   4   8              8   4   4   10             10
```

CUT. 300 yards of linen yarn.

CUT (of cloth). The same as Bolt.

CUT. In weaving Diapers, Damasks, etc., "to cut" means to design the drafts so that no floats cross the border between two blocks.

CYLINDER. A part of Jacquard's machine (v).

37

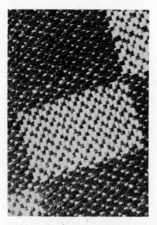

DAMASK (8 shaft)

DAMASK. Fine silk, or linen fabric woven in damask weave.

DAMASK WEAVE (fr. *Damascus* in Syria). Damask weave is based on the same principle as all Turned Twills (v) but the ground weave is satin, usually 1:4 since higher ratios require too many shafts. The blocks of pattern are obtained by reversing the ratio between weft and warp. As the simplest satin requires 5 shafts, a four-block damask calls for 20 shafts. For this reason Damasks are often woven with the Two-Harness Method (v).

Threading and tie-up for two-block damask based on 1:4 satin:

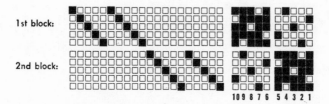

1st block:

2nd block:

10 9 8 7 6 5 4 3 2 1

Treadling for the 1st block: 6, 7, 8, 9, 10; for the 2nd block: 1, 2, 3, 4, 5. Both the tie-up and the treadling must be so arranged that not only both blocks are woven in true satin, but that there are no floats which would cross the line between two blocks.

Damask weave is particularly suitable for silk, linen, and any glossy yarn, because the pattern is visible only due to the reflected light and not to the colour of the yarn.

When instead of satin, a broken 1:3 twill is used, the resulting weave is called sometimes "rough damask," or "eight-shaft-damask." So-called "semi-damask" may be any simpler pattern weave (overshot, crackle, summer-and-winter) woven so that the same yarn is used for warp, pattern and binder. See: *Diaper*.

DAMASSÉ. Linen fabric woven in such a way as to resemble damask (v).

DAMASSIN. Damask with silver or gold in the weft.

DANISH LOOM. The name given sometimes to half-folding foot-power looms, with the back part of the loom frame being hinged to the front.

DEGUMMING. Removing of the gum from the raw silk, by boiling it in very strong solution of soap. Silk can be spun and even woven with the gum, but the fabrics cannot be used unless degummed. Synonym: Boiling-off.

DEKNOTTING. Removing the knots from a finished fabric. The knots are untied, and if the ends are long enough they are darned into the fabric; if not they are cut off, and a short piece of yarn darned parallel to the broken yarn.

DENIER (fr. Fr. *denier* = old unit of weight). Unit of count of silk, based on the following principle: when 450 yards of silk weigh one denier (.05 gm.) we call this silk No. 1. All higher numbers indicate how many times the yarn is *heavier* than No. 1. Compare Count of Yarn.

DENIM (fr. Fr. *"de Nimes"* = of the city of Nimes). Coarse cotton fabric woven in twill.

DENT (fr. Fr. *dent* = tooth). The space between two adjacent blades of a reed, or of a raddle. "Empty Dent," dent in which there is no warp; "Strong Dent," dent with too many ends; "Weak Dent," dent with too few warp ends. Synonym: Split.

DENTAGE. The same as Sett (v) of reed. Number of dents per inch (R).

DENTFUL. All warp ends passing through the same dent. Synonym: Splitful.

DERIVATE WEAVE. Any weave developed from a simpler one, without changing the principle of the structure of the weave. Typical example: basket from tabby.

DEVELOPMENT. The same as Draw-Down (R).

DEVELOPMENT OF DRAFTS. (See Draft, Short Draft.) Arranging a draft in such a way as to make it ready for threading. Most drafts in weaving literature are condensed, or at any rate not complete. Several operations are necessary to develop a draft:

    1. Find out the number of repeats of the main pattern necessary to fill

39

nearly the whole woven piece, so that the whole pattern will be balanced (v) and that enough warp ends will remain for borders and selvedges.

2. Find appropriate draft for borders.
3. Repeat operation No. 1 for borders.
4. Match the borders with the main pattern (see Matching).
5. Figure out proper selvedges and match them with the border.

DIAGONAL. An oblique ridge which appears in all biased twills. In pattern weaving we have diagonals in colour or in texture running across the fabric from one corner to another, whenever the fabric is "woven-as-drawn-in."

DIAGONAL THREADING. The same as plain threading, i.e.: 1, 2, 3, 4, or 4, 3, 2, 1, and so on.

DIAMOND. An element of a pattern. It is a square or a rhomb with one of its diagonals parallel to the warp, and the other to the weft. E.g.:

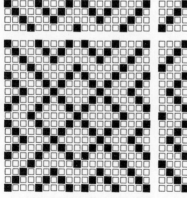

Diamond in twill

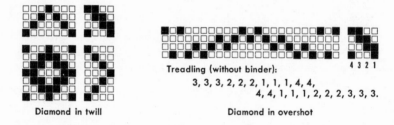

Treadling (without binder):
3, 3, 3, 2, 2, 2, 1, 1, 1, 4, 4,
4, 4, 1, 1, 1, 2, 2, 2, 3, 3, 3.

4 3 2 1

Diamond in overshot

DIAMOND TWILL. The simplest of the Pattern Twills (v) usually woven on 4 to 6 shafts. It produces the smallest patterns possible in hand-weaving. They are composed entirely of diamonds and crosses, although vertical bars and therefore hexagons are also possible.

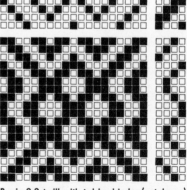

A—in 1:3 twill without binder   B—in 2:2 twill with tabby binder (not shown)

40

DIAMOND TWILL (4-shaft) DIAMOND TWILL (6-shaft)

The following twills can be used here: 1:2, 1:3, 2:2, 1:4, 2:3, 1:1:1:2, 1:5, 2:4, 3:3, 1:1:1:3, 1:1:2:2. The patterns can be woven with or without binder. Traditional treadlings are either Woven-as-drawn-in, or Rose-Fashion; but any fancy treadling is possible. See also: Pattern Twill, Lined Work, Bird's Eye, Goose Eye, Rosepath.

DIAMOND WOOL. Rather coarse and long wool from the hollow of the back, and from above the hind legs of sheep.

DIAPER (fr. Fr. *diapre* = figured cloth). Any fabric decorated all over with small patterns (R).

DIAPER WEAVE (Br.). This term means the same as Turned Twill, but it is more often applied to 4 shaft twills, biased or broken. E.g.:

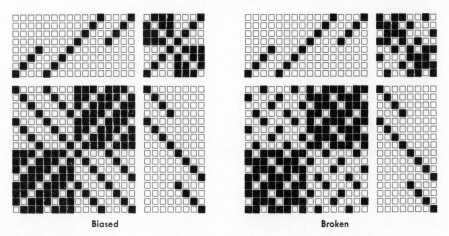

Biased Broken

The pattern can have any number of blocks, but 4 shafts are required for each block. Therefore multi-block patterns are woven in Two-Harness Method (v).

41

DIMITY CORD (fr. Gr. *dimitos* = having two threads). Fine, corded cotton fabric. The corded effect is obtained by alternating narrow strips of 1:2 and 2:1 twill in warp.

DIMITY WEAVE. The simplest of Turned Twills, based on 1:2 twill. A two-block dimity can be woven on 6 shafts of a single harness, or on three ground and two pattern shafts in case of Two-Harness Method.

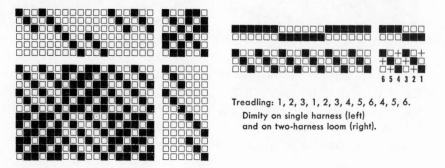

Treadling: 1, 2, 3, 1, 2, 3, 4, 5, 6, 4, 5, 6.
Dimity on single harness (left)
and on two-harness loom (right).

DIRECT TIE-UP. A tie-up in which only one shaft is tied to each treadle.

DISTAFF (fr. AS. *distoef*). In spinning a short stick which holds the unspun fibres.

DIVISION. In turned twills woven on a plain harness: set of shafts necessary for each block of pattern. The number of shafts in one division is equal to the number of warp ends in one repeat of the twill (3 for 1:2 twill; 5 for 1:4 twill, etc.), and the number of divisions equal to the number of blocks in the pattern.

DOBBY (prob. Scot. for *Robert*, inventor of the machine). A shedding machine similar to Jacquard's, but simpler and used on looms with comparatively small number of shafts.

DOFFER, or **DOFFING KNIFE** (fr. *"to do off"*). Part of a carding machine which collects the fibres from cylindrical cards.

DOG. Colloquial name of the Pawl of a Ratchet wheel (v).

DOG TRACKS. Colonial pattern of the Star-and-Rose group. Short draft:

DOGWOOD BLOSSOM. Colonial pattern of the Star-and-Rose group. Short draft:

```
8 3 8     4  4 4  4      9  4              4
    8 3 8    4   4   8 3 8 4   6 5 5 5 5 6   4
        7 7   4    4  7 7   4   5 5 5 5 5    4
    7 7      4    7   4         4            4
```

42

DOMINO 6's. Overshot pattern. Short draft:

```
3 6 5     5 6
   7 4   4 7
         3
7 7     3 3
```

DOORS AND WINDOWS. Colonial pattern of the Four-Block-Patch group. Short draft:

```
4 4 4 4 4 4 4 4
                12
  4 4 4 4 4 4 4
              12 12
```

DORNICK TWILL. The name comes from Dornick Weave (v), because in both these weaves the diagonals going in two opposite directions do not meet, i.e., do not form a point. Thus the long floats in corners or turning points are avoided, which may improve the quality of the fabric. The principle of "cutting" the floats (see "cut") is the same as in all turned twills. Dornick Twill is sometimes called Broken Herringbone.

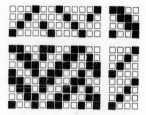

DORNICK WEAVE (fr. *Dornoch* in N. Scotland). Spelled also Dornic, or Dornock. A 1:3 Turned Twill (v) usually biased. Dornick with more

DORNICK
WEAVE

than three blocks in the pattern is usually woven on a double harness (see Two-Harness Method). E.g.:

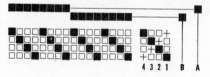

Treadling:
1st bl.: 1+A, 2+A, 3+A, 4+A.
2nd bl.: 1+B, 2+B, 3+B, 4+B.

43

DOUBLE CLOTH WEAVE. Any weave which gives two distinct layers of cloth at the same time. They may be completely separated from each other, or connected at the selvedge on one side (semi-circular, or double-width weave), or on both sides (hose, or circular weave). They can be also stitched together (Stitched double cloth, Quilt weave), or they can penetrate each other forming a pattern (Double weave). Completely separated layers are never woven in practice.

The advantage of Double Width weave is that it makes possible weaving of a wide cloth on a narrow loom. On the other hand, it requires twice as many shafts as in plain weaving, the warp is subjected to twice as much friction, and one side or layer of the cloth is always a little more stretched than the other.

The draft for the simplest double cloth weave, when both layers are woven in tabby, is:

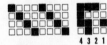

Treadling: 1, 2, 3, 4 gives semi-circular, and 1, 3, 2, 4 circular weave. If two independent layers are wanted, one shuttle should be used for sheds 1 and 2, and another for 3 and 4

Both layers can be stitched together in a number of ways. Compare Stitched Double Weave. An example of stitching is shown here:

Treadling: 1, 3, 2, 4. This kind of stitching is not very satisfactory as the stitches come too close, but it is the only possible with 4 shafts

In the above examples every layer was woven in tabby, but it is quite easy to have both layers woven in twill. Double 1:2 twill can be woven on 6 shafts as in the following draft:

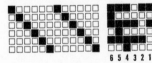

Treadling:
For semi-circular cloth: 2, 4, 5, 3, 1, 6, 4, 2, 3, 5, 6.
For circular: 1, 4, 2, 5, 3, 6.

The layers can be woven in two different weaves, e.g., tabby and twill, two different twills, any pattern weave on one side and tabby on the other (if stitched together the tabby serves as lining), etc. E.g., very open basket weave, lined with fine tabby:

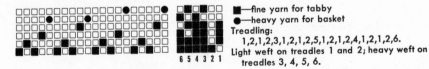

■—fine yarn for tabby
●—heavy yarn for basket
Treadling:
  1,2,1,2,3,1,2,1,2,5,1,2,1,2,4,1,2,1,2,6.
Light weft on treadles 1 and 2; heavy weft on treadles 3, 4, 5, 6.

DOUBLE-ENDED CLOTH. Any fabric in which the warp-ends are threaded in pairs (i.e., two heddles on the same shaft).

DOUBLE-FACE WEAVE. Any weave which produces a fabric with one side of a different colour or texture than the other side. Double-face cloth can be woven even on two shafts:

■—white warp ends ●—black warp ends
Very heavy weft on treadle 1, very fine on 2

The cloth will be mostly white on one side and mostly black on the other.

Any twill except the balanced ones (2:2, 3:3, etc.), and particularly twills of the 1:N type, whether biased, broken, or satins will show more weft on one side and more warp on the other. Consequently the two sides may be made in two different colours, or with one kind of yarn showing on one side only.

Stitched double cloth will give the same effect. E.g.:

■—white warp
●—black warp
Treadles 1 and 3—black weft
Treadles 2 and 4—white weft

In all above cases the colours will be not quite pure, because of the stitching ties. The ties may be concealed, however, provided that the warp will be covered by the weft. Then two colours of weft or two different yarns are used:

Black weft on treadles: 1, 3, 5, 7.
White weft on treadles: 2, 4, 6, 8.
Treadling: 1, 2, 3, 4, 5, 6, 7, 8.

DOUBLE GENOA. The same as 2:2 twill (v. Genoa).

DOUBLE HARNESS. Two separate harnesses mounted on one loom. One harness weaves the ground, and the other the pattern. Compare: Two-Harness Method.

DOUBLE-POINT TWILL. Variation of Herringbone Twill (v). E.g.:

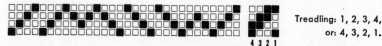

Treadling: 1, 2, 3, 4,
or: 4, 3, 2, 1.

DOUBLE ROSE. Colonial Pattern of the Sunflower Group. Short draft:

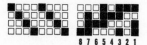

DOUBLE SHEDDING MOTION. The same as Double Tie-Up.

DOUBLE SPOT WEAVE. 1. Any pattern weave which requires two shafts for the ground, e.g., Summer-and-Winter, Paper Spots. 2. Any spot weave woven in double cloth.

45

DOUBLE TIE-UP. A tie-up in Jack-type looms with two sets of lamms: one for the sinking shed, and one for the rising shed. Such a tie-up gives a perfect control of the shed, but requires twice as many ties as a single tie-up. Compare: Independent Action Looms.

DOUBLE TWILL. 1. Double cloth woven in twill (both layers). 2. (Am.) The same as Turned Twill.

DOUBLE WEAVE. 1. The same as Double Cloth Weave. 2. A pattern weave which produces two layers of cloth penetrating each other. The two layers are woven on the same principle as in the Double Cloth Weave (v), but for every block of pattern a separate set of shafts is used. Thus when both blocks are woven in tabby, four shafts are required per each block. To make the pattern visible, each layer must be woven in a different colour. The large number of shafts and treadles involved limits the number of blocks in the pattern to two or three in most cases. From three blocks up it is advisable to use the Two-Harness Method.

The draft for a two-block pattern in tabby is:

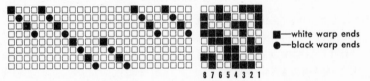

■—white warp ends
●—black warp ends

8 7 6 5 4 3 2 1

Treadling for the 1st block: 8, 7, 6, 5; white weft on 8 and 6, and black on 5 and 7. For the 2nd block: 4, 3, 2, 1; white weft on 4 and 2, and black on 3 and 1.

DOUBLE
WEAVE

Patterns in double weaves are usually woven in tabby, but any twill and even satin can be used, provided that the loom has sufficient number of shafts. For the simplest twill (1:2) and simplest pattern 12 shafts are necessary, and for the satin at least 20.

46

With two-harness method a smaller number of shafts are required, but the economy here is not as large as in case of damasks and turned twills. This is because we must have two pattern shafts per block, one for each colour. E.g.:

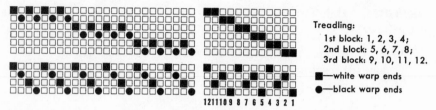

Treadling:
1st block: 1, 2, 3, 4;
2nd block: 5, 6, 7, 8;
3rd block: 9, 10, 11, 12.

■—white warp ends
●—black warp ends

12 11 10 9 8 7 6 5 4 3 2 1

The blocks of pattern can be combined, i.e., two blocks can be woven at the same time. In the above example, treadles 1 and 5, 2 and 6, 3 and 7, 4 and 8 can be pressed at the same time to combine blocks one and two, or the tie-up can be changed accordingly.

DOUBLE WIDTH CLOTH. A fabric woven in a semi-circular weave. Compare Double Cloth Weave.

DOUBLING. Twisting together of two or more yarns. This can be done on a spinning wheel, particularly when a strong twist is required, or on a Doubling Stand for a loose twist.

DOUBLING STAND. A simple wooden appliance for twisting several

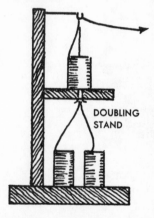

DOUBLING STAND

yarns together. It consists of a board, or base, an upright piece of wood, and a shelf attached to the upright about half-way up. One or more tubes of yarn stand on the base, and one more on the shelf which is perforated in the centre. The yarn from the tubes on the base passes through the hole in the shelf and through the upper tube. When the yarn is pulled up over a hook in the stand, the yarn from the upper tube encircles all the other yarns coming from below. The twist thus obtained is always very loose, and depends only on the diameter of the upper tube.

DOUP, or **DOUPE** (fr. Icelandic *daup*). The long loop on each end of a string heddle. A short heddle used in cross-weaves (Leno), and made of a single loop. Each half of a clasped heddle.

DOWEL ROD. A steel rod, or a flat stick to which the warp is attached. The dowel rod is either laced to the Apron, or tied directly to the warp beam or cloth beam.

47

DOWNFALL OF PARIS. Colonial pattern (v) of the Blooming Leaf group. Short draft:

12   7 7 7 7   4   14   4 7 4   14   4   7 7 7 7
    4 3 3 3 8   14   4   4   14   8 3 3 3 4
  4   4   14   4 2 2   4   14   4
  4   4   14   4   4   14   4   4

DRACHM. Unit of count of silk. It is the weight in drachms of 1,000 yards.

DRAFT. A graphic representation of: (a) threading, (b) tie-up, (c) treadling, and (d) resulting fabric (draw-down). A draft may contain all four, or just one of them. It can be full (expanded, developed), or short.

DRAFTS

A full draft shows all the warp ends of at least one repeat in threading, all ties in the tie-up, and all picks of weft in one repeat of treadling. If the draft is short, it may be either numerical, or graphical (Profile). The way of condensing a draft is a matter of convention and varies in different times, countries, and even with different authors.

A full threading draft shows as many horizontal lines (or spaces) as there are shafts in the harness. Either the lines or the spaces between the lines correspond to the shafts. A mark on the line or between two lines means that in this place one warp-end passes through one heddle. When the draft is typed, the lines are omitted: all marks in one row correspond to one shaft. Marks placed *on* lines are usually short strokes. Marks between the lines may be either full squares, crosses, diagonal strokes, vertical strokes, or numbers. Numbers indicate either the number of the shaft, in which case they are superfluous, or number of warp ends going into one heddle-eye. Numbers on short drafts have still another meaning.

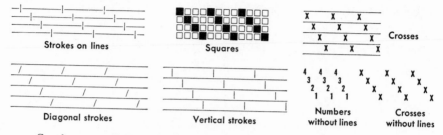

Strokes on lines	Squares	Crosses

Diagonal strokes	Vertical strokes	Numbers without lines	Crosses without lines

Strokes are of English origin, and are rather obsolete now, whether on lines or between them. Black squares are Scandinavian, and are very popular. So are the crosses, particularly convenient when typing a draft. Numbers were used in Scotland; their only advantage is that they can be easily memorized during the threading. Whenever they are used the draft may be written in one line: 432143214321 etc., but then it is no more a graphic representation of the threading.

Usually the draft does not contain any directions for sleying. If the texture of a fabric requires a special arrangement of warp-ends in the reed, the directions are given separately, and only exceptionally on the draft itself (compare Sleying).

In the Tie-Up draft the horizontal lines correspond to the lamms, and the vertical ones to the treadles. Wherever a tie is made, it is shown

on the draft as a circle (Fig. 1, Scottish), or black square (Fig. 2, Scandinavian), or a cross on the line (Fig. 3, English). Sometimes it is necessary to make distinction between the sinking shed (v) and the rising one (v). Since both sheds appear on the same tie-up, for instance in Double-Tie-Ups (v), two marks are used: one for short lamms, and another for the long ones. In most cases these two marks are not necessary, because each treadle is tied to all shafts, and consequently lack of a tie to the long lamm means a tie to the short one. But in the Two-Harness method (v) some lamms are not connected at all with certain treadles, and then two marks as well as empty spaces must be used in the tie-up.

The direction of the draft in Anglo-Saxon countries is from the right to the left now, but it was not always. On the continent of Europe the

49

opposite direction of writing is prevailing. The shafts are counted from the bottom up (from the top down in Europe), and the treadles from the right (but there are many exceptions).

The treadling may be shown on a draft similar to the threading draft, but placed vertically under the tie-up draft. Crosses, horizontal strokes, circles, or numbers are used. Numbers may be written in one line but then the treadles should be numbered on the tie-up draft.

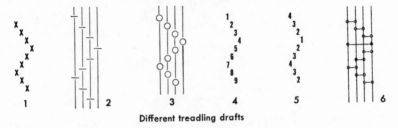

Different treadling drafts

When more than one treadle is depressed at the same time, two or more marks are placed in the same row, or a horizontal stroke is made between the two vertical lines corresponding to the treadles (Fig. 6). The latter method is often used in drafts for the Two-Harness Method.

A complete weaving draft contains all the above elements; the tie-up to the right or to the left of the threading, and the treadling below the tie-up. The shafts on the threading draft are in line with the corresponding lamms on the tie-up, and the treadles of the tie-up are in line with the treadles of the treadling draft. Such an arrangement has an additional advantage, that in the free space below the threading draft we can fill in the picture of the woven fabric, or so-called Draw-Down, or Block-Out, or Development.

DRAM. The same as Drachm.

DRAUGHT. An alternative spelling of the word Draft. Both spellings are correct but "draught" is rather obsolete.

DRAW-BOY. A helper who pulls the lashes of a Simple in the Draw-Loom. Later replaced with Shedding Machines (v). The draw-boy had usually a draw-loom-fork to pull the lashes.

DRAW-BOY MACHINE. The same as Parrot (v).

DRAW-CORDS. Cords which pull different pattern sheds, or individual pattern heddles in a Draw-Loom operated by the weaver alone, or by machinery (i.e., a draw-loom without a draw-boy).

DRAW-DOWN (Am. term of recent origin). Pattern or texture of the fabric drawn from a draft on graph paper. To make a draw-down we must have a complete weaving draft properly arranged, i.e., the shafts

50

must be in line with the tie-up and the treadling marks exactly under the tie-up draft. At least one and a half of a repeat is drawn both in threading and in treadling. Then the pattern is filled in on the assumption that the warp is white and the weft black (in power weaving very often the contrary). When making a draw-down from a full draft, we draw not only

DRAW-DOWNS:

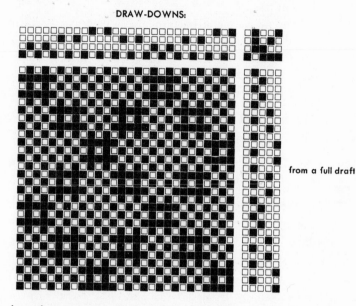

from a full draft

the pattern but the structure of the fabric as well. If only the pattern is required, the draw-down can be made from a profile (short draft).

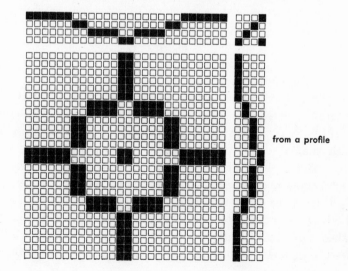

from a profile

51

If the purpose of the draw-down is to examine, or represent the structure of the fabric, special graph paper is often used. This has a number of divisions per inch proportional to the actual count of the warp and of the weft. For instance, if a cloth has 60 ends and 40 picks per inch, the paper will have 10 divisions per inch in one direction, and 15 divisions in the other.

When the fabric has a pattern in colour only, it will not show on a draw-down made in white and black. Then the colours must be marked both in warp and weft, which will show the pattern, but not the structure of the fabric. If both structure and pattern are required, two draw-downs must be made. Synonyms: Block-Out, Pattern Draft, Weave Plan.

DRAWING-IN. 1. The same as Threading (R). 2. Drawing-in of the edges. See Selvedge.

DRAW-KNOT. A knot similar to the Bow-Knot, and used for tying-in (tying the warp to the cloth beam).

DRAW-LOOM. A loom in which each heddle, or at least each pattern-heddle (heddle in the back or pattern harness), is operated separately. A draw-loom may have only one harness, as on the drawing, and then each warp end passes through one heddle. Or it may work on the principle of the Two-Harness Method (v). Then the front or ground harness has plain shafts (usually from 4 to 8), and the back harness independent heddles. These heddles (pattern heddles) control often more than one warp end.

The first, classical type, cannot be operated without a helper, or a shedding machine, therefore it is unsuitable for an amateur. The second may be operated entirely by one person, from the front.

A classical draw-loom has in common with an ordinary loom only the batten, the cloth beam, and the warp beam. Treadles, if any, operate only the ground harness, or the shedding machine. The heddles are hung separately in several rows. They are kept in the proper position by a board with rows of holes in it (Comber Board), and they are weighted with small lead sinkers (Lingoes). To open a shed some of the heddles are pulled up by Pulley-cords. When several heddles are tied together, each heddle is connected with the Pulley-cord by a Necking-cord. The cords go up to the Pulley Box, over the pulleys, and then horizontally to the back of the loom frame, or to the wall. These horizontal cords are called the Tail. Half-way on the tail-cords are tied vertical cords descending down to the floor. They form a Simple. To these in turn are tied short cords (Tacks) gathered in bunches named Lashes. By pulling a lash the helper lowers the corresponding cords in the Tail, and consequently opens a shed. The number of Lashes in each set-up is equal to the number of sheds required in one repeat of the pattern.

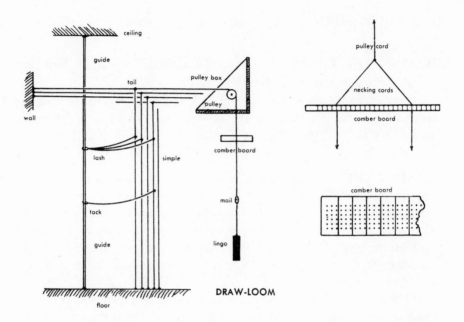

DRAW-LOOM

If the pattern woven has more than one repeat, more than one heddle is attached to each tail cord. In most cases the number of cords in the tail and in the Simple is much smaller than the number of heddles.

The weaver cannot conveniently operate the Simple, and a helper (draw-boy) is needed to pull lashes in proper order. When pattern has a limited number of blocks, a Draw-Boy machine (v) can replace the boy. For a larger number of blocks a Jacquard machine is more appropriate.

A draw-loom is the only *perfect* loom for a hand-weaver, since it gives a complete freedom of design and of texture, but it is much too complicated, requires too much space, and too much time for the set up. Its use may be justified only in production of very high quality fabrics in large quantities.

On the other hand, draw-looms with two harnesses—one for weaving of the ground, and the other for the pattern—are much smaller, easier to operate, and they may be built so that they have no tie-up except for the ground harness. They work slower, however, and are not suitable for double weaves. Compare Two-Harness Method.

Finally, the principle of a draw-loom may be applied to any loom, by mounting in the front of the loom an additional harness with individual heddles operated by hand. See Pattern Harness.

DRAW-LOOM FORK. A lever which helps opening sheds in a Draw-Loom.

DRESSING THE LOOM. Preparing the loom for weaving. Different operations are performed in the following order:

1. Warping. 2. Spreading the warp. 3. Beaming. 4. Distributing the heddles on shafts. 5. Hanging the shafts (upper tie-up). 6. Tying up (lower tie-up). 7. Threading. 8. Sleying. 9. Tying-in. 10. Gating, or adjusting.

DRESSING THE WARP. Making the warp more resistant to wear by treating it with different chemicals. The dressing is done either before beaming on the warping reel, or in chain—or gradually during weaving. The yarn may be dressed before warping. The purpose of dressing is twofold: to give the yarn more tensile strength, and to diminish the friction. The first requires such components as glue or starch, the second: fats, waxes or oils.

The compound or solution used for dressing is called Size (v). The warp or yarn should be immersed in a warm solution, then wrung and dried. Synonym: Sizing.

DRILL, or **DRILLING** (fr. Dutch *drillen*). Strong cotton twill.

DRIVER. The same as Picker.

DROP BOX. A part of the equipment of a flying shuttle loom, used when more than one shuttle are required.

DROP TURNOVER REPEAT. A repeat of threading or of a pattern in which the diagonal not only changes direction but is lowered by its whole length:

DROPPED NETS. Any Net-Weave (v) in which the pattern is formed by dropping or not crossing certain ends and picks.

DROPPED TABBY. A weave in which blocks of pattern (usually very small) are not woven at all—the warp remains on one side and the weft on the other side of the fabric. E.g.:

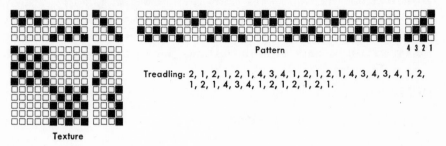

Pattern   4 3 2 1

Treadling: 2, 1, 2, 1, 2, 1, 4, 3, 4, 1, 2, 1, 2, 1, 4, 3, 4, 3, 4, 1, 2, 1, 2, 1, 4, 3, 4, 1, 2, 1, 2, 1, 2, 1.

Texture

The same weave for a higher number of shafts is usually called Paper Spots (v).

DROPPED WEAVE. Any weave in which the pattern is formed by the warp and weft being kept apart in places where they should interlace. Then they both form floats, vertical on one side and horizontal on the other side of the fabric. These floats have no tabby between them.

Dropped weaves require a large number of shafts if woven on a single-harness loom. E.g., 2:2 twill asks for 4 shafts per block of pattern plus 4 shafts for the ground. Thus three-block patterns cannot be woven on less than 16 shafts. Therefore in hand-weaving the most common dropped weave is Dropped Tabby (v).

In double harness weaving the ground harness has only 4 shafts with plain heddles, and the pattern harness is placed *in front* of the ground harness. The pattern heddles have long eyes. This kind of a harness may be added to any 4-shaft loom.

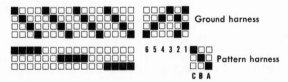

Ground harness

6 5 4 3 2 1

Pattern harness

C B A

The treadling for dropped tabby is: 1, 2 for plain tabby; 1+A, 2+A for the 1st block of pattern; 1+B, 2+B for the 2nd block; and 1+C, 2+C for the 3rd block.

The treadling for dropped twill is: 6, 5, 4, 3 for plain twill; 6+C, 5+C, 4+C, 3+C for the 1st block; 6+B, 5+B, 4+B, 3+B for the 2nd; and 6+A, 5+A, 4+A, 3+A for the 3rd. The tie-up given is for a rising shed loom.

The number of blocks may be as high as the number of pattern heddles (compare Pattern Harness).

55

DUCK (fr. Dutch *doek* = linen cloth). Strong and heavy linen fabric woven in tabby.

DUKAGANG (Sw. *dukågang* = cloth-path). Swedish tapestry technique probably of Oriental origin, but developed in Sweden. The pattern weft goes over three and under one warp end, always in the same shed, so that long vertical bars appear in the texture. Binder is necessary after every shot of pattern.

DUMB SEED (Compare Seeding). Overshot pattern in warp (R).

DUNGAREE (fr. Hindu). Heavy blue cotton fabric used for navy uniforms.

DUTCHMAN'S FANCY. Colonial pattern (v) of the Star-Rose-and-Table group. Short draft:

DYEING. A chemical process which leaves a certain amount of pigment in the yarn. When the process is a purely physical one, i.e., the pigment is simply deposited on the fibres, the resulting colouring is not a fast one.

Dyeing has usually three stages: 1. Preparing the fibres so that the pigment will penetrate them. This is accomplished by treating the yarn with a mordant. 2. Impregnating the fibres with pigments. 3. Fixing the pigment (this stage is often omitted).

Dyes are either natural (vegetable, animal, or mineral) or artificial (synthetic).

Most common natural commercial dyes are: Catechu, from an acacia tree—brown; Fustic, from morus tree—yellow and orange; Indigo, from indigo plant—blue; Haematein, from logwood tree—black, violet, blue; Cochineal, from the insect coccus cacti—red, purple. Besides these there are hundreds of common plants suitable for dyeing.

Most of the artificial dyes belong to the coal-tar group. There are: Anilin dyes, Phenol dyes, Azo dyes, Quinolene dyes, and Anthracene dyes. In all, several thousands of dyeing compounds.

The natural dyes have no advantage on the artificial ones, as any natural dye can be duplicated synthetically. The common prejudice against artificial dyes is due to the fact that "home dyes" or "salt dyes" are usually of very poor quality, and are neither fast nor light-proof. On the other hand, the peculiar charm of old, vegetable dyed fabrics is due to the unevenness of dyeing and not to the dye itself.

EDGE. See Selvedge.

EGYPTIAN COTTON. Cotton plant native of Egypt, with fibres darker than those of plain cotton. Yarn made of this plant, and its imitations.

EMBOSSED FABRICS. Fabrics with a pattern in relief on one or both sides obtained by passing the fabric between hot metal cylinders with the pattern cut out on the metal.

EMBROIDERY WEAVE (Am.). Several Free Weaves are sometimes called Embroidery weaves, particularly when a small pattern is executed with tapestry technique on shuttle-woven background. Thus "French embroidery" corresponds to Brocade; "Swedish" to Dukagang; "Russian" to inlaid twill; "Inlay" means usually patterns picked-up in tabby sheds.

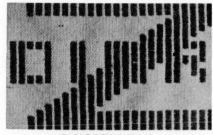

EMBROIDERY WEAVE

EMBROIDERY WEAVE. The same as Lappet (v).

END. One yarn (thread) in the warp.

ENGLISH FLOWERS. Colonial pattern (v) of the Star-Rose-and-Table group. Short draft:

```
3|4  6 3 3 6   6 3 3 6  4       4 4        4  |3|4       4 4       4  6 3 3 6   6 3 3 6
 3 | 4       4 4       4  4       4  4       4 |3|3  4       4 4       4  4       4 4       4
   | 4       4 4       4  6 3 3 6   6 3 3 6  4 |3|4  6 3 3 6   6 3 3 6  4       4 4       4
15x| 4  3 3 3   5  3 3 3  4  3 3 3   5  3 3 3  4 |14x| 4  3 3 3   5  3 3 3  4  3 3 3   5  3 3 3  4
```

ENTERING. The same as Sleying.

ENTERING HOOK. A very flat steel hook used for sleying. Synonym: Reed Hook.

EVENER. The same as Raddle.

EVERYBODY'S BEAUTY. Colonial pattern of the Diamond-and-Table group. Short draft:

```
              7 |3 |7   7  7        7  7  7  7  7    7  7
              3 | 3 6  7 7   7  6 6   6 6 6    7  7 7   6
               |14x|
```

EYE. The central loop in a string or wire heddle, through which a warp end is threaded. It should be large enough to let the threading hook through, but not much larger. Long Eyes used in the Two-Harness Method are much longer: from 2½ to 4 inches. Compare: Heddle, Mail.

EXPANDED DRAFT. A full or detailed draft of threading, developed from a short draft.

EXTRA DIAMOND WOOL. The best part of a fleece. It comes from the shoulders and flanks.

FABRIC (fr. Lat. *faber* = worker). In weaving: finished web, cloth.

FANCY CORD. See Corded Fabrics.

FANCY TWILL. See Twill.

FANCY WEAVE. Any simple weave made more intricate by introduction of small changes in the draft, so that essential qualities of the weave are preserved.

FEDERAL KNOT. Colonial pattern (v) of the Star-and-Table group. Short draft:

```
10 5 10                    10 5 10   5  |3 |3   5
      10 5 11 |3 |11 5 10        4     6 |3 |6
         5 5  |3 |3  5 5         4     4      4   4
   5 5        |10x|          5 5     4 4 |7x|  4 4
```

FELL (fr. Gaelic *fill* = to fold). The last pick of weft beaten down (R). Synonym: Beat-up-point.

FELT (AS *felt*). A fabric which is usually made without weaving by pressing together any animal fibres in presence of moisture and heat. But the fibres may be spun and woven first, and then the process of felting may be stopped at any stage.

FELTING. The process of making felt. This term is often used improperly to designate Fulling.

FIBRE (fr. Lat. *fibra*). A comparatively long and thin piece of vegetable or animal tissue. Yarn is composed of fibres twisted together. When the fibres are very long, as in case of silk, they are called filaments.

FIBREGLASS. Artificial yarn spun from very fine filaments of glass.

FIFTY-FIFTY. When applied to fabrics, it means the same number of ends and picks per inch.

FIG LEAF. Colonial pattern (v) of the Bow-Knot group. Short draft:

```
6| 5| 6 4   6      12    6  4 9|5 8   8|5 9 4   6      12     6  4
  |  |  4    8     10    4        4 4 |        4    10         8  4
  |  |  2  4    10      10  4  2       3  |  2  4    10      10  4  2
  5 |5    4    10       8   4 |9 9     |9 9   4    8      10    4
  |6x|                       |← 3x →|
```

FIGURE HARNESS. The same as Pattern Harness.

FILAMENT (fr. Lat. *filum* = thread). A very long fibre such as in silk or in synthetic yarns.

FILLER. See Rug Filler.

FILLING. The same as weft (R).

FINGER WEAVE. The same as Pick-Up.

FINISHING. Every fabric after being woven must undergo all or some of the following finishing processes:

1. Mending and Deknotting. All mistakes, dropped yarns and so on are mended with a darning needle. Knots are untied and the ends darned in.

2. Washing. This may be done in hot or tepid water, with or without soap.

3. Boiling. This may be done together with washing or separately.

4. Fulling (v).

5. Felting. Used seldom, and only when the texture of weaving is not supposed to show at all.

6. Napping (v).

7. Pressing.

All fabrics require Nos. 1 and 7. Most: 1, 2 and 7. Besides these, wool may go through the operation 4, 5 and 6; linen, 3. All of them are optional.

FINNWEAVE. A free double weave, with both layers woven in tabby. Although the pattern is independent from the way the loom is set up, it helps a lot if we use a 4-shaft loom threaded and tied-up for double weaving:

8 7 6 5 4 3 2 1

The weft is carried first on one of the treadles: 1234, but only part way through the shed. Then the shuttle is removed from the shed, and this is changed to the one of the opposite group: 5678. This operation is repeated according to the requirements of the pattern, until the shuttle will get across the whole width of the fabric. One repeat of treadling will look as follows: white on 1 and 7 (alternately according to the pattern); black on 3 and 5; white on 2 and 8; black on 4 and 6.

Very simple patterns are not woven in Finnweave, because they can be woven much faster on a multiharness loom.

FISH-IN-THE-POND. Colonial pattern (v) for Summer-and-Winter weave. Short draft:

$$\begin{matrix} & & & & 5 & & & 5 \\ & 1 & & 1 & 5 & & 5 \\ & 1 & 1 & 1 & 1 & 5 & 1 & 5 \\ 1 & & 1 & & 1 & & 5 & 1 & 5 \end{matrix}$$

FLAG OF UNION. Colonial pattern (v) of the Star-and-Table group. Short draft:

4 3 3 3 3 3 3 3 3 3 3 3 3 3 3 3 3 |4 5 4 |4 5
                                    5 5 | 5 5
                                       9 9
3 3 3 3 3 3 3 3 3 3 3 3 3 3 3 3   8 5 8
                                   |←—2x—→|

FLANNEL (fr. Fr. *flannelle*). Light, napped woollen fabric woven in tabby or twill.

59

FLANNELETTE. Imitation of flannel; cotton flannel.

FLAT STEEL HEDDLE. A heddle similar to a wire heddle but made of one piece of flat steel.

FLAT TAPESTRY. Any tapestry (v) without pile. Sometimes this term is used in more restricted sense: tapestry woven in tabby only. E.g.: low, and high warp, Navaho, kilims, etc.

FLAX (fr. AS *fleax*). Vegetable fibres from the plant *Linum Usitatissimum*. Spun flax is called Linen. The yarn is obtained from the plant through the following operations: Deseeding (or Rippling)—separating stems from seed; Retting—separating individual fibres by a process of fermentation; Breaking—removing parts of stalks which cling to the fibres; Scutching and Heckling—further stages of cleaning the fibres.

The yarn is not elastic, and not resistant to friction, but it has a remarkable tensile strength, and resistance to chemical action.

FLEECE (fr. AS *fleos*). The wool from one sheep. Different parts of the fleece produce different wool (See Sorting).

FLEMISH WEAVE. High-warp tapestry weave.

FLOAT. This part of a warp or weft yarn which crosses several other yarns without forming a tie. The length of a float is measured by the number of crossed (skipped) yarns. Floats are seldom longer than 16. Synonym: Skip.

FLOATING HARNESS. A harness built in such a way that the lamms are not hinged, but keep horizontal position when moving up and down

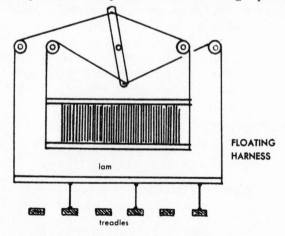

FLOATING HARNESS

lam

treadles

(Fig.). This means that all treadles have the same leverage (the same pressure is required regardless of the position of the treadle), and consequently that more treadles and better spaced can be mounted under the harness.   On the other hand, Floating harness must have additional levers or pulleys, or both, which increases the friction.   It is used mostly in Double-Tie-Up looms, or in multishaft jack-type models.

FLOCKS (fr. Lat. *floccus* = lock of wool).   Short wool fibres.

FLOOR LOOM.   The same as Foot-Power Loom.

FLOSS (fr. Lat. *fluxus* = loose).   Weft yarn made of long fibres, not twisted together.

FLOSSA (Sw. = pile).   Any knotted pile rug.   In Scandinavia as elsewhere rugs are woven on the same principle as Oriental rugs.   Knots such as Ghiordes, Sehna, and Single-Warp knot are used in Flossa, and there is nothing to distinguish it from ordinary knotted rugs.   It is definitely not a weaving technique, and there is no excuse to use this term in English language.

FLOWER POT.   Colonial pattern, the same as Lisbon Star (v).

FLUSHING (En.).   Any weaving technique in which the pattern is formed by floats either in warp or weft.   This term is somewhat wider than Overshot, and comprises such weaves as Crackle, Spot Weaves (but not Swivel).

FLYING SHUTTLE.   The same as Fly Shuttle.

FLY SHUTTLE.   A simple machinery which propels the shuttle across the shed, so that the weaver's hand does not touch the shuttle.   The principle of fly-shuttle is used not only in industrial weaving on power looms, but to a certain extent in hand-weaving as well.   Its advantages are: 1st, greater speed, because only one hand controls the shuttle, when the other operates the batten; 2nd, greater width of the woven fabric, when compared with hand-shuttle weaving.

The main part of the fly-shuttle equipment is mounted on the batten. The batten itself must have a race-board as long as the batten, and inclined towards the reed.   On both ends of this board there are two Shuttle-boxes in which the shuttle rests after every pick of weft.   In the centre of each box there is a metal rod (Picker) which slides in the horizontal direction.   A cord is attached to the outer end of each picker.   This string can be pulled with a handle (Picking Stick) which hangs from the rocker above the reed.

During the work the weaver has one hand on the batten, when the other holds the picking stick.   When the shed is opened he pulls the picking stick to the right, which makes the left hand picker throw the shuttle across the shed and into the right hand shuttle box.   Then comes

61

the beat, the shed is changed and the picking stick pulled to the left, which makes the shuttle travel in the opposite direction.

Usually the looms equipped with a fly-shuttle have also a Take-Up Motion (v) as well as a Let-Off mechanism (v), so that the weaver does not waste time to move the warp forwards. The finished cloth and the warp move a fraction of an inch after every beat, so that the shed and the tension of the warp remain the same as long as the weaving progresses.

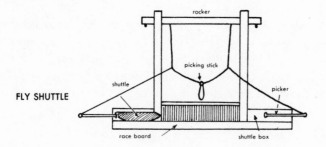

When two or more shuttles are used, the shuttle boxes have a more complicated construction, which allows the shuttles to be thrown alternately, or in any order whatsoever. A shuttle box of this kind is called a Drop Box.

A fully equipped fly-shuttle loom resembles a power loom, and can produce as many as fifty yards of cloth a day. Modern fly-shuttle looms are made all in metal, and are fully automatic, so that the weaver operates only two treadles, and does not even touch the batten.

The fly-shuttle is best adapted for yardage, such as tweeds, plain upholstery and similar fabrics. It is less suitable for pattern weaving, and entirely unsuitable for irregular fabrics, or for stripes of different colours in weft. Patterns are woven so that the pattern yarn as well as the binder are set in the warp, and only one shuttle is used.

A majority of hand-weavers considers the fly-shuttle weaving as unethical, unless advertised as such. This of course does not apply to fabrics which could not be produced on a hand loom, such as fabrics wider than fifty inches. The term proposed to designate fly-shuttle woven fabrics is "hand-loomed."

FOLD. Yarn doubled without twisting. Two parallel yarns wound on the same bobbin.

FOLDING LOOM. Any foot-power loom with a frame so constructed that it can be folded when not in use. Smaller looms of this kind are portable. There are also looms which fold only partly, i.e., only the warp beam is mounted on a hinged support.

FOOTMAN. In a spinning wheel, the stick or rod which connects the treadle with the crank.

FOOT-POWER LOOM. Any loom with shedding motion operated by treadles. This type of loom is, and always has been, the most widely used one. The oldest foot-power looms were probably used in China or India. A light frame of bamboo sticks is set in the ground, which serves also as a seat for the weaver. The treadles or stirrups are placed in a dugout under the loom. The oldest European looms were built like a cage (Fig. 1) which contained inside all the working parts of the loom, and the weaver as well. They were often built into the house and could not be moved. Later on the looms became of lighter construction and movable. The cage was reduced to the most essential beams with the weaver outside.

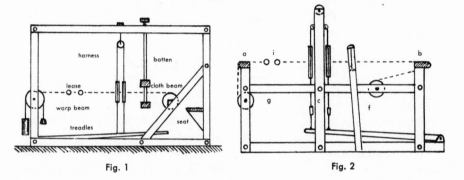

Fig. 1   Fig. 2

A foot-power loom as used at the present (Fig. 2) has the following parts: a frame made of eight horizontal and four vertical pieces. Two of the horizontal ones are: the Slabstock (a), and the Breast-piece (b). On the sides there are two more uprights (c), which supports the harness either directly, as in the roller type of counterbalanced loom, or indirectly through the top-castle (v). In looms with a hanging batten, two more horizontal supports (capes) are necessary. These are fixed to the uprights. In older looms the capes extend all the way to the back of the loom. The batten (f) is either hung, or propped on two bolts set in the lower horizontal side pieces of the frame. The harness hangs from the top-castle or from a roller. It is tied farther down to the lamms, which hang horizontally at right angle to the treadles. These are usually hinged in the front— in older or very heavy looms: at the back. The warp-beam and the cloth-beam are fixed between the upper horizontal side pieces of the loom frame. The warp beam has a brake which can be released from the front; the cloth beam has a ratchet wheel with two catches (or "dogs") of which one is stationary and the other fixed on a handle which turns the

63

beam. Between the harness and the slabstock we have the lease-rods, either free or tied to the loom frame (Fig. 3).

Looms used for special weaving techniques may have additional parts, as for instance one or more warp beams (Pile Weaves, Double, and Tissue Weaves), a second harness (Two-Harness Method), two or three

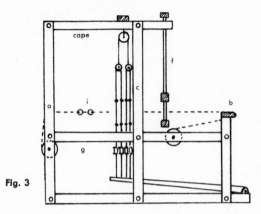

Fig. 3

sets of lamms or levers (Independent Action Looms), flying shuttle equipment, take-up or let-off motion, Shed Regulators, Pattern Harness, Bead Lamms (for Net Weaving), Lappet frames and wheels and so on.

Modern looms of this type do not differ essentially from the described above. They are sometimes simplified, particularly their shedding motion. Sometimes they have only as many treadles as shafts, and consequently only a direct tie-up. Single tie-up harness of the jack type is often used. The general tendency is to make the looms lighter and more compact—even folding looms. They have often a sectional warp beam, or a special shaft for a prefabricated warp. As a rule the modern looms are much more limited and less efficient than the standard ones.

Half-automatic hand looms constitute a separate group. They are all-metal, highly precise, and highly efficient. They work on the same principle as a power loom, have the same limitations, and are suitable for industrial hand-weaving only. They are used whenever the speed of a power loom is too great for a given yarn, or where the labour is cheap enough to compete with power.

FORE BEAM. The same as Cloth Beam.

FORE LEAF. In Spot Weaves (Bronson, Swivel, Barley Corn, etc.) the first shaft which carries half of the warp.

FORTY-NINE SNOWBALLS. Colonial pattern (v) of the Rose-and-Table group. Compare Snowball. Short draft:

FOULARD (Fr.). Light, printed silk fabric, or its imitation in cotton.

FOUR-LEAVED CLOVER. Colonial pattern (v) of the Star-and-Diamond group. Short draft for plain overshot:

Short draft for overshot on opposites:

```
6  67      77       76
 6      12 12    12 12   6
 6  6        6         6  6
 7   12  4  13   13  4  12   7
```

FOUR O'CLOCK. Colonial pattern (v) of the Two-Block-Patch group. Can be used for Overshot on Opposites, Summer-and-Winter, Damask, or Double Weave. Short draft:

```
4 8  8 4 2 2 2 2 6 14 6 2 2 2 2
 6 14 6 2 2 2 2 4 8  8 4 2 2 2 2
```

FRAME. The same as Harness-frame, Heddle-frame, Shaft.

FRAME LOOM. A square wooden frame with notches cut in the two short sides, or with rows of nails driven in the lower and upper cross-pieces. The warp is either wound around the frame, one end into every notch,

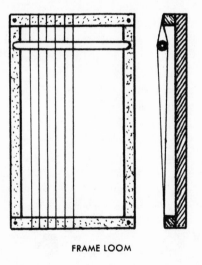

FRAME LOOM

or it is stretched between nails. The weft may be introduced between the warp ends with a large needle, and the beating is done with a comb. Sometimes short half-heddles tied to a stick are used to open one shed, when a flat stick placed permanently between the even and odd warp ends

65

opens the other. Small frame-looms are used for educational purposes, or for making samples. Variations of this kind of looms are known under different names: Board Loom, Cradle Loom, Box Loom, etc.

Large looms working on the same principle, but set vertically, and equipped with a simple shedding mechanism are used for tapestry weaving, particularly for high-warp tapestry. When such a loom has also a warp beam and a cloth beam, a batten, and two treadles it is called a Vertical Loom.

FREE LACE WEAVES. Any Lace Weave made by pick-up method. It may be executed on any simple loom in a variety of ways, with fingers, a needle, or a pick-up stick. This method is hardly justified if it produces the lace effect which could be obtained much faster and easier with a proper threading draft (Gauze, Leno, Bronson). On the other hand, there are Lace Weaves which could not be made in any other way (e.g., Spanish Lace).

FREE WEAVING. Any weaving in which at least some of the weft picks do not cross the entire shed, and in which the warp ends must be picked by hand to place the weft in proper position. When the weave is made by the pick-up method but all weft picks cross the whole width of warp from one selvedge to another, the weaving should not be called "free," as it can be executed on a loom with a sufficient number of shafts by ordinary methods. For instance, twill may be woven by pick-up on two shafts, which does not make it a free weave.

Free Weaving proper comprises the following techniques: Tapestry (knotted, flat, low and high warp), Embroidery Weaves or Inlay (except Lappet Weave), Brocade (but not Broché or Brocatelle), and Free Lace. All free weaving techniques have one point in common: they can be executed on a two-shaft loom, or even on a "no-harness" loom. However, when available, additional shafts are used to make the pick-up easier. This is particularly important in Embroidery Weaves, and Brocades where twill sheds are used throughout. Fig. 1 shows an example of threading and tie-up for Brocade; Fig. 2, for Dukagang; and Fig. 3, for Twill Embroidery. Treadles 1 and 2 in each case are used only for the binder (Brocade) or ground (Embroidery).

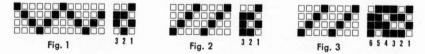

Fig. 1   3 2 1   Fig. 2   3 2 1   Fig. 3   6 5 4 3 2 1

Free weaving on a frame-loom survived to the present days from immemorial times, and is still the highest and purest form of hand-weaving. Unfortunately it is also a very slow technique.

66

FRENCH DRAW LOOM. A draw-loom equipped with a Jacquard's machine (R).

FRENCH EMBROIDERY WEAVE. Any Brocade which does not cover completely the ground.

FRENCH WEAVING TERMS. *Armure* = weave; *attache* = tie; *attachage* = tie-up; *baguette d'encrois* = lease-rod; *banquine* = breast beam; *basse lisse* = low warp; *bati* = loom frame; *battant* = batten; *bobinage* = winding of warp bobbins; *bobine* = bobbin; *bobineuse* = bobbin winder; *bordure* = border; *bref* = draw down; *bride* = float; *cannelier* = bobbin rack; *cannetage* = weft bobbin winding; *cannette* = bobbin; *cannetteuse* = bobbin winder; *cantre* = bobbin rack; *cardage* = carding; *chaine* = warp; *contremarche* = lamm; *corde* = cord; *cordes-des-remises* = upper tie-up; *coton* = cotton; *cotele* = corded; *croise* = twill; *damas* = damask; *defaire* = to unweave; *devidoir* = swift; *duite* = pick of weft; *echeveau* = skein; *embuvage* = shrinkage; *enrouloire* = breast beam; *ensouple derouleuse* = warp beam; *ensoupleau* = cloth beam; *envergeur(e)* = lease; *etoffe* = cloth; *etoupe* = linen tow; *feutre* = felt; *fil* = yarn; *fil de liage* = binder; *filage* = spinning; *finissage* = finishing; *flotte* = float; *fond* = ground; *foulure* = fulling; *frange* = fringe; *frappe* = overshot; *frein* = brake; *goffre* = waffle weave, honeycomb; *harnais* = harness; *laine* = wool; *lame* = shaft; *lisse* = heddle; *lin* = flax; *lisiere* = selvedge; *losange* = diamond; *maille* = heddle; *maillon* = heddle-eye; *marche* = treadle; *marchure* = treadling; *marmousset* = jack, couper, lever; *marquoire* = sampler; *metier* = loom; *m. contrebalance* = counterbalanced loom; *m. mecanique* = power loom; *m. pliant* = folding loom; *modele* = sample, sampler; *natte* = basket weave; *navette* = shuttle; *navette volante* = flying shuttle; *nid-d'abeilles* = honeycomb weave; *noeud* = knot; *numero du fil* = count of yarn; *ourdir* = to warp; *ourdissage* = warping; *ourdissoire* = warping reel; *pas* = shed; *passage en ros* = sleying; *patron* = pattern, draft; *passage en lammes* = threading; *pedale* = treadle; *picquage en peigne* = sleying; *plie* = ply; *pliage* = spreading; *poil* = pile, nap; *poitriniere* = breast beam; *peus* = dent; *raccord* = treadling draft; *rapport* = threading draft; *rateau* = raddle; *remettage* = threading; *remise* = harness; *rentrage* = threading; *renverse* = reversed; *repetition* = repeat; *reps* = rep weave; *retrait* = take-up, shrinkage; *ros* = reed; *rouleau* = roller; *satin* = satin; *serge* = twill; *soie* = silk; *sommier* = race board; *tablier* = apron; *tapis* = rug; *tapisserie* = tapestry or upholstery; *taffetas* = tabby; *teinturage* = dyeing; *tendoir* = templet; *tenture* = hangings; *tissage* = weaving; *tisseur* = weaver; *tisse-a-la-main* = hand-woven; *tissu* = cloth, fabric; *toile* = tabby; *trame* = weft; *velour* = velvet; *velour cotele* = corduroy. (Accents omitted.)

FRIAR'S CLOTH. A fabric woven in 4:4 basket weave.

FRICTION BRAKE. Type of brake used on the warp beam which releases the warp, and permits a very fine adjustment of the warp tension. It has a steel wire wound around one end of the warp beam. One end of the wire is fixed to the loom frame (a), when the other is pulled down by a spring (b) in the same direction in which the beam turns when unwinding the warp. The greater the pull on the brake, the stronger is the braking

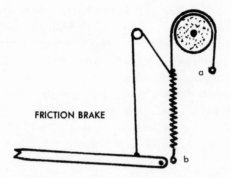

FRICTION BRAKE

action. A treadle is needed to release this type of brake. The treadle is tied to a cord which stretches the spring and thus releases the brake. There is also another type of brake which releases the warp whenever the tension becomes too great. It consists simply of a steel band fixed to the loom frame, and another one encircling the end of the warp beam. Both bands are concentric and the outer one can be tightened with a screw around the inner band. This brake works well if precisely built, but it requires very light beating, or it will let the warp slip.

FRINGE. A border made of free ends of warp or weft left on a finished article. Usually we have fringe in warp, particularly on pieces of tapestry, etc. To get fringe on all sides, we make the warp wider by the double length of fringe, and later on pull out the extra warp ends. If we do not cut the edges we shall have fringe made of loops instead of single ends.

FRISE (fr. Fr. *friser* = to curl). Upholstery fabric with warp pile. The pattern is produced by leaving some of the pile uncut on the background of cut pile.

FRONT BEAM. The same as Cloth Beam (v).

FULLING (fr. AS *fullere*). One of the stages of processing the cloth. Originally the fabric was beaten with wooden mallets in the presence of heat and moisture. Now it is pressed between hot cylinders, and considerable shrinking and thickening of the cloth results.

68

GANG (fr. G.). The same as Portee (v).

GATHERER (En.). Two short rods, or a loop of wire behind the heddles in a Heck-Block (v). The gatherer collects together the warp ends of one portee after they pass through the heddles. Synonym: Guide.

GATING (Scot. fr. AS *geat*). Adjusting of the different parts of the loom after the warp has been threaded and tied-in. Gating depends on the construction of the loom, but in most cases it is done in the following order:

1. The heddles (particularly cord heddles) are properly spaced and set vertically.

2. Shafts are hung horizontally and at proper height, i.e., a little lower than the tightly stretched warp. This is done to have the lower portion of the shed (on which the shuttle slides) stretched more than the upper part.

3. The reed is set exactly at the centre of the warp (by sliding it in the batten) so that both edges have the same tension.

4. The position of the batten is adjusted so that there is no friction between the warp and the shafts of the reed, or the batten itself. This is done by moving the batten up and down on the swords, or by moving the swords in the rocker. Then the reed should strike the cloth when the batten is vertical. This may require further adjustment of the batten.

5. The tie-up is re-made or at any rate corrected. The ties should be of such a length as to produce a perfectly flat lower part of the shed.

6. As the last operation, a "heading" is woven and mistakes in threading or sleying corrected.

GAUGE (in warp-pile fabrics). A flat piece of brass or steel inserted into the pile during weaving. Its width is equal to the length of the pile, and the rod must be longer than the width of the fabric. If the pile is to be cut, the gauge must have a groove in the upper edge, so that a knife travelling in this groove will not slide off the gauge and into the warp. The rods or gauges may be of any size, or nearly so. The ones used for

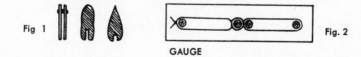

Fig 1   Fig. 2

GAUGE

velvet weaving are extremely fine, when so-called "flossa rods" for rugs may have a width of several inches. The very large sizes are made of wood (Fig. 1). Synonyms: Velvet Rod, Flossa Rod.

69

GAUGE. A block of wood with four pegs, screws, or nails driven into it, used for making cord heddles. The heddle is tied around the pegs as shown

GAUGE
(heddle-block)

in the sketch. Either granny or reef knots are used (Fig. 2, page 69). Synonyms: Heddle-block, Heddle-gauge, Jig.

GAUZE (fr. *Gaza* in Palestine, where it originated). Any light and open fabric woven in tabby, or cross-weave.

GAUZE WEAVE (See Cross Weave). A cross-weave in which the warp-ends are twisted around each other in pairs, making half a turn between two shots of weft, and then another half a turn in the opposite direction.

Special harness is required for weaving gauze. It consists of two shafts with ordinary heddles set in the back, and two additional ones in

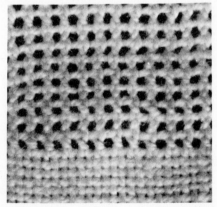

GAUZE WEAVE

the front. The first from the front is called Standard, and has ordinary heddles, too. The number of heddles on the Standard is equal to one-half of the number of warp ends. The second shaft has special heddles called Doups. They are only half-heddles made of cord, i.e., loops of cord

70

hanging from the upper shaft of the second frame. The doups are permanently threaded through the corresponding heddles in the Standard (Fig. 1).

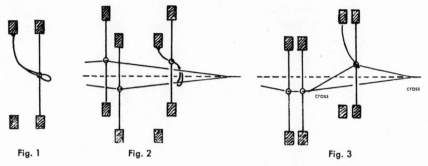

Fig. 1   Fig. 2   Fig. 3

When the Doup frame is lowered, and the Standard raised, the two front shafts do not affect the work of the back ones, so that plain tabby can be woven (Fig. 2). In the following draft treadles 1 and 3 give tabby (Fig. 4). When both the Standard and the Doup shafts are lowered, or

Fig. 4

when both are raised, a warp end threaded through the Doup will go together with the Standard, and behave exactly as if it were threaded through Standard only. This happens when treadles 2 or 4 (Fig. 4) are used. The crossing takes place when after a tabby shot the Gauze treadle (No. 4) is depressed (Fig. 3). The doup has been loose on treadle 1 and 3, and did not prevent the normal working of the loom. On treadle No. 4 the doup is pulled through the eye of the Standard heddle, thus forcing the

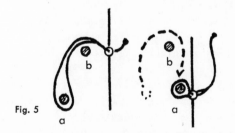

Fig. 5

warp-end "a" (Fig. 5) to go around the end "b". The threading of a Gauze harness is different from any other inasmuch as one-half of the warp ends are threaded through *two* heddles (2nd and 4th) while the other half go through one heddle only, and because no warp ends are threaded through the Standard. The order of threading is of utmost importance,

71

because the doup must go around the free end in each pair or no crossing will take place.

Besides the above classical harness there are simpler arrangements of frames for Gauze weaving. The Standard may be dispensed with, since its role is limited to clearing the shed of tangled doups, and to preventing the doups from moving forward with the advancing warp. The shed may be cleared by an additional treadle (No. 5 in Fig. 6), and the

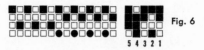

Fig. 6

5 4 3 2 1

doups may be pushed back by hand every time the warp is moved forward. Thus more complicated cross-weaves may be woven on a 4-shaft harness, as for instance Riddles or Pickets. In Fig. 6 tabby will be woven on treadles 2 and 4; gauze on 3 and 4; tabby and gauze on 1, 3 and 4.

GEER (Weaving Geer) Obsolete fr. *Gear*. Weaving implements.

GENOA (fr. *Genoa* in Italy). Single Genoa = the same as 1:2 twill; double Genoa = 1:3 twill. Contrary to popular belief, Twill did not originate in Genoa, but was extensively manufactured there, and fabrics woven in 1:2 or 1:3 were known under this name or its corruption, "jean."

GENTLEMAN'S FANCY. Colonial pattern (v) of the Diamond-and-Table group. Short draft:

```
12  12| 12|  12                  |4 4          |4 4
                        13 13    |      13 13  |      13 13
    10  |4  |10    12  5  4 |4  4  5  4 |4  4  5  12
                12              6|  6       6|  6        12
        |10x|                   |←—2x—→|
```

GEORGETTE (Fr.). Light silk fabric woven in tabby. The yarn is tightly twisted, which gives the fabric an appearance of crepe.

GERMAN WEAVING TERMS. *Appretur* = finish; *atlas* = satin; *aufbaumen* = beaming; *baumwolle* = cotton; *bindung* = weave; *bindfaden, bindschuss* = binder; *blatt* = reed; *blattstechen* = sleying; *bleichen* = bleach; *breithalter* = templet; *bremse* = brake; *brocat* = brocade; *doppeltuch* = double fabric; *draht* = twist; *dreherbindung* = gauze weave; *effectkoper* = fancy twill; *einarbeiten* = take-up; *einlaufen* = take-up; *einzug* = threading; *einzugrapport* = repeat; *einfache bindung* = basic weave; *einziehnadel* = threading hook; *fach* = shed; *faden* = thread; *fadenkreuz* = cross; *farbe* = colour; *faser* = fibre; *filzen* = felting; *flachs* = flax; *flor* = pile; *gang* = portee; *garn* = yarn; *gaze* = gauze; *gebrochen koper* = broken twill; *gelese* = lease; *genuakord* = corduroy; *geschirrolle* = roller; *gestell* = (loom) frame; *gewebe* = cloth; *grund* = ground; *handscherbaum* = warping mill; *haspel* = reel; *helfe* = heddle; *kattunbindung* = tabby; *kamm* = reed; *kammeinzug* = sleying; *kette* = warp; *kettenbreite* = width of warp; *kettendichte* = sett of warp; *kettenscheren* = warping;

72

ketteln = chaining (the warp); *koperbindung* = twill; *krepp* = crepe; *lade* = batten; *leinen* = linen; *leinwand* = tabby; *leiste* = edge, selvedge; *litze* = heddle; *muster* = pattern; *pedal* = treadle; *rand* = border; *reissflachs* = tow; *riet* = reed; *rietzahn* = blade of reed; *rippe* = rib; *rips* = rep; *samt* = velvet; *samtnadel* = velvet rod; *schaft* = shaft; *schlitz* = dent; *schrumpfen* = shrinkage; *schuss* = weft; *schutze* = shuttle; *seide* = silk; *spinnen* = spinning; *spinrad* = spinning wheel; *spule* = bobbin; *spulen gatter* = bobbin rack; *spuler* = winder; *steppen* = stitching; *stickerei* = embroidery; *stuhlgestell* = loom frame; *teppich* = rug; *treten* = treadling; *tritt* = treadle; *tuch* = cloth; *vlies* = fleece; *walken* = fulling; *weben* = to weave, weaving; *weber* = weaver; *weberknotten* = weaver's knot; *webstuhl* = loom; *wolle* = wool; *wurfelbindung* = basket weave; *zigzackkoper* = herringbone twill.

GHIORDES KNOT (fr. *Ghiordes* in Asia Minor). A carpet knot used very often in Oriental rugs, brought to Europe and quite common now in modern weaving.

GIMP (fr. Fr. *guimpe*). 1. Heavy thread or wire used for edges of very open lace, usually free lace. 2. Flat tinsel wound around a soft core.

GINGHAM (fr. Fr. *guingan*, or *guingamp* in Brittany). A checked or striped cotton dress fabric.

GINNING (fr. *Gin* = short for "engin"). Process of separating cotton fibres from the seeds.

GOBELIN. High-warp (v) tapestry originally made at Gobelins in Paris, a weaving factory established in the fifteenth century.

GOOSE EYE. Small pattern in Diamond Twill (v).

GOVERNOR'S GARDEN. Colonial pattern of the Diamond-and-Table group. Short draft:

GRANITE STATE. Colonial pattern of the Star-and-Table group. Short draft:

GRIFT (orig. unkn.). Part of a Jacquard's Machine (v).

GRIST (fr. AS *grindan*). Thickness of yarn; count of yarn.

GROSGRAIN (Fr. = large grain). Corded fabric with ribs parallel to the weft.

GROUND. In pattern weaving, the weave which forms the background for the pattern. It is uniform and woven in one of the standard weaves, from tabby to satin. It is usually sunk when the pattern is raised. There is ground in such weaves as Tissue, Embroidery, Overshot, Spot, Lace, but none in Damask, and all Turned Twills. Double Weaves may have the ground or not.

In all Pile Weaves there is always ground, but in most cases it remains invisible.

In certain Double Weaves, and in all Warp-Pile Weaves, the ground is woven on a separate warp; in all other weaves, on the same warp as the pattern. In Spot and Lace the same weft forms the ground, and the pattern as well.

GROUND HARNESS. In Two-Harness Method (v) the front harness with long-eye heddles is nearly always used for weaving the ground and is called therefore the Ground Harness, when the back harness may be either a set of shafts or a draw-loom harness.

GROUND LEAF (En.). In Spot Weaves: the second shaft from the front. It weaves tabby ground together with the first frame called Fore Leaf. It is absent in All-Over-Spots and Barley Corn.

GROUND WARP. Whenever more than one warp beam is used in one loom, one of the warps is called Ground Warp. It has usually a comparatively high tension, and is made of fine, strong yarn. Other warps form then a raised pattern, or pile.

GROUND WEAVE. Any weave used for Ground (v).

GUIDE. 1. Part of a Draw-Loom (v).
2. The same as Gatherer in a Heck-Block of a Warping Mill.
3. Heavy light coloured thread wound around a warping reel before the warping starts. It serves as a guide for the warper.

GUILD (fr. AS *gild* = payment). Professional organization for mutual protection of the members. Until the Industrial Revolution weavers' guilds were very strong societies not unlike our trade unions.

After the revival of handicrafts the name was adopted by societies of hobby weavers, and even by commercial companies.

The present Weavers' Guilds help their members with buying and selling, organize lectures, competitions and exhibitions; sometimes publish small periodicals. Several guilds have tests of skill for members and issue certificates. There is a parallel here to the old titles of: Apprentice, Journeyman, Junior Master and Senior Master. The requirements, however, are comparatively low.

GUNNY (fr. Bengali *goni*). The same as Burlap.

74

HACKLE (fr. G. *hechel*). 1. The same as Heckle. 2. Any fine fibres before spinning (R).

HACKLING. The same as Heckling.

HAIR CLOTH. Fabric which has horse hair used in weft.

HALF-BLEACHED YARN. Any yarn not completely bleached; linen most often. The bleaching process is stopped before the yarn becomes quite white.

HALF FLOSSA. Any pile weave in which only the pattern is woven with the pile, when the ground is flat.

HALF-HEDDLE. The same as Doup.

HALF-TONES. In overshot Weave—areas in which the pattern weft forms tabby. They occur on each side of a float.

HALKRUS (Sw.). The same as Honeycomb (Colonial).

HAND-LOOM. Any loom operated by hand, or by hand and foot power. Consequently all looms except power looms and half-automatic foot-looms belong here. The same term is sometimes used to designate a table-loom as opposed to a foot power-loom.

HAND-LOOMED. A term proposed to distinguish fabrics woven with a flying shuttle, from "hand-woven" fabrics.

HAND-SHUTTLE. Any shuttle which is thrown by hand during weaving as distinguished from flying shuttle.

HANDSTICK. A stick on which the warp is wound after it is taken off the warping reel, instead of being made into a chain. This method of transferring the warp to the loom is rather obsolete and suitable for short warps only. Synonym: Cane.

HANDTREE. Upper horizontal part of a batten, which keeps the reed in place. It has a groove in its lower surface, and rests on the reed either by its own weight or secured with bolts. Its upper part is sometimes made into a handle. Synonym: Cape (R).

HAND-WOVEN. Woven with a hand-shuttle.

HANGER. In a Draw-Loom—the cord which connects the Mails with the Lingoes.

HANK (fr. Icelandic *honk* = skein). 1. The same as Skein. 2. 840 yards of wool or cotton yarn. In different parts of England the size of a Hank varies.

HARMONY. Colonial pattern, the same as Walls of Jericho.

HARNESS (fr. Fr. *harnais*). Originally the word designated all shafts (then called "leaves") with the upper tie-up, i.e., with rollers, pulleys,

75

or horses and all connecting cords. It is still used in this meaning in Great Britain.

In the United States the word "harness" acquired quite a different meaning, and means a single frame, leaf, or shaft. This change took place probably toward the end of the last century, because in the first half of the nineteenth century the word "leaf" was still in use. Later "leaf" was abandoned in both hemispheres, and replaced by: heddle, or heald in Britain and harness in U.S.A. Strangely enough, both these terms are at least ambiguous if not positively wrong. At the same time "harness" is still used in its old meaning (*Encyclopedia Americana*). Everything seems to indicate that the proper meaning of "heddle" is preserved in U.S.A., while the proper meaning of "harness" survived in Britain.

The harness is the most important part of every loom. On its construction depend all the limitations and advantages of a loom. On the number of shafts depend the weaves and patterns which can be woven, when the way the shafts are hung decides on the general performance: versatility, speed, adjustability, etc. Looms are often named according to the type of harness they use. For instance: counterbalanced, jack type, single tie-up, double tie-up, independent action, sinking shed, rising shed, double harness, triple harness.

HATCHEL. The same as Heckle, and of the same origin.

HEAD. A loop at the end of a Lash in a Draw-Loom.

HEADER. The same as Heading.

HEADING. A piece of fabric woven at the beginning of a new warp to check the threading and sleying, as well as the uniformity of warp tension.

HEADLE. The same as Heddle (R).

HEALD. The same as Heddle (R), or the same as a shaft (En.).

HEATHER. Yarn spun from mixed fibres of different colours.

HECK. The main part of a Heck-block. An arrangement of two small frames with heddles for making a single cross in the warp.

HECK-BLOCK. Part of a Warping Mill (v). It guides the yarn coming from a bobbin rack, and distributes it on the drum or reel.

HECK BOX. The same as Bobbin Rack.

HECKLE (fr. G. *hechel*). An appliance for combing the flax. Synonyms: Hackle, Hatchel.

HECKLING. One of the operations in which flax fibres are freed from fragments of stalks.

76

HEDDLE (fr. AS *hefeld*, or Scand. *heidle*). The word has two meanings. In Britain it designates a shaft (Am. harness). In U.S.A., a wire or cord which controls a single warp end.

A heddle may be made of cord, wire or flat steel. The simplest heddle is a loop attached to a heddle-stick or shaft. The warp end passes through the loop. In this form the heddles are used in simple frame looms, inkle looms and in cross weaving (doups). Similar heddles but with a perforated bead at the end are required for Net Weaving.

HEDDLES

So-called "clasped heddles" are made of two interlocking loops. The warp end passes through both of them, and is held tight as long as the heddles are stretched between the shafts of the frame.

A typical heddle has three openings: at the top and bottom for the steel rails (in modern frames) or for the maitland cords, and in the centre for the warp end. The cord heddles have two large loops, called doups, and a small one in the centre—heddle-eye. They are usually made singly on a heddle-block (v), but they were also made in groups. This latter method keeps the heddles evenly spaced, but makes threading very difficult.

Wire heddles are similar to cord heddles, except that the wire is twisted and soldered between loops, and that the loops are smaller. Flat heddles are punched in sheet steel; they are usually made of stainless steel.

77

The allover length of ordinary heddles should be from 9½ to 12½ inches. The eye, about ½ inch long. Special heddles have different dimensions. For instance, heddles in Two-Harness Method have much longer eyes in the Ground Harness than in the Pattern Harness.

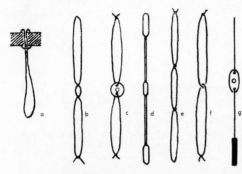

There are special wire heddles (so-called Patent Heddles) for Cross Weaving (v). Another special heddle is one for correcting mistakes —Repair Heddle.

a doup, or half-heddle; b, cord heddle; c, cord heddle with a mail; d steel heddle; e, long eye heddle; f, clasped heddle g, draw-loom heddle.

Steel heddles are made always of the same thickness, regardless of the yarn used for warp. In cord heddles the thickness of the cord should be more or less adapted to the kind of work performed—the heavier and more open the work, the stronger the heddles. Synonyms: Headle, Heald, Yeld, Leash, Lash, Hook, Needle, Heeld.

HEDDLE BEARER.   The same as Top-Castle.

HEDDLE-BLOCK.   The same as Gauge (v).

HEDDLE CORDS.   In a Draw-Loom, the same as Tail-cords.

HEDDLE-FRAME.   The same as Shaft (v).

HEDDLE-FRAME (in Eng. only).   A wooden frame used for making cord-heddles in groups. It corresponds to the heddle-block or gauge for individual heddles. All heddles in one group are tied together, and are made in a continuous way. The frame has two horizontal bars for the two ends of the heddles, and a third one for the eyes. Of the two upright pieces one is removable to let the whole group of heddles slide off the frame when the tying is finished. The heddles tied in groups are suitable mostly for plain weaving, since they cannot be spaced as required by the pattern. But they are preferable for very fine weaving with setts of warp about 100 per inch and higher, because they can be made of very fine and smooth yarn, and they will keep straight and at a proper distance one from another, which reduces the friction between warp and heddles to a large extent.

HEDDLE-GAUGE.   See Gauge.

HEDDLE-REED.   A modern variety of Rigid Heddle (v). It is made of flat steel heddles soldered to a steel frame. It is used both as a heddle-frame and a reed in connection with narrow "no harness" looms.

HEDDLE-STICK. The same as shaft (v). The term is often applied to the stick with half-heddles (doups) used on tapestry looms, or even in foot-power looms for very elaborate patterns (See Two-Harness Method).

HEELD. The same as Heddle (R).

HEER (fr. old Icelandic *herfa* = skein). 600 yards of yarn.

HEMP (fr. AS *henep*). Vegetable fibres from the plant *Cannabis Sativa*. Fibres from other plants are often called Hemp as well. E.g.: Manila Hemp from *Musa Textilis*; Sisal Hemp from *Agava*, and so on. The fibres are similar to flax, but they are coarser. Hemp is used for heavy fabrics but more often for cordage. The count of yarn is the same as for linen.

HERRINGBONE TWILL. A twill weave in which the diagonal changes direction at regular intervals. E.g.:

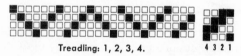

Treadling: 1, 2, 3, 4.   4 3 2 1

To avoid long floats on treadles 2 and 4 a variation of this weave called Dornick Twill is often used.

HESP (Scot.). 3,600 yards of linen yarn.

HERRINGBONE TWILL

HEXAGON. A component of weaving patterns. It can be executed in any weave which gives 4 blocks of pattern, and has tabby binder. E.g.:

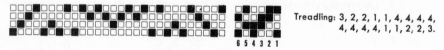

6 5 4 3 2 1

Treadling: 3, 2, 2, 1, 1, 4, 4, 4, 4, 4, 4, 4, 4, 1, 1, 2, 2, 3.

The binder on treadles 5 and 6 has been omitted, but it must follow each pattern shot.

HIGH WARP. In tapestry weaving any weave which does not require a reed. Originally this kind of weaving was always done on vertical looms of fairly large size (hence "high" warp). The beating is done with a heavy wooden fork or comb. This comb is only one or two inches wide; it is used on small sections of warp at a time. The weft consequently hardly ever lies in a straight line across the warp, as in the Low-Warp technique (with a reed and batten). What is more the pattern is never woven up to the same height all across the loom. As far as it is possible, every component of the pattern is finished independently. The only technical limitation in building the pattern is not to let the finished part overhang the unfinished one, or the filling-in of the background may become difficult if not impossible.

The High-Warp technique is not suitable for simple geometrical patterns, or at least it does not present any advantage over the Low-Warp technique in weaving such designs. But it is particularly well adapted for curved lines, because the texture of the fabric actually follows the pattern.

HIGH WARP

The weave used is of secondary importance, as long as it does not require a binder. Plain tabby is most often used. The question of interlocking seldom arises, because vertical lines are rather exceptional in this kind of tapestry.

HIGHER TWILLS. Twills woven on more than 4 shafts.

HISTORY OF WEAVING. Very little is known about the development of weaving technique, except in quite recent times.

It seems that weaving is older than agriculture. It reaches at any rate the Stone Age (Swiss Lake Dwellers), i.e., at least several thousand years before our era. In historical times weavers are mentioned 2,000 years B.C. in Babylon. In the 15th century B.C. Egypt produces striped fabrics, embroidery and netting. In the Far East weaving was probably not less advanced at the time.

All we know about Western Europe is that weaving was at a high level in Gallia before the Roman conquest. For instance, twill was produced on a large scale, although we do not know by what means. On the other hand, weaving was unknown in the British Isles during the same period.

It is probable that weaving equipment hardly developed at all during thousands of years. All Egyptian, Greek and early Roman looms were vertical, or horizontal frame looms, probably without any mechanism opening the sheds, and without shuttles (as we understand this term).

Even the finest and most complicated fabrics were executed by pick-up. The same method was used by native populations all over the world even in modern times. The only native loom with any shedding motion is Hindu (see Foot-Power Loom), but it is impossible to say when, or from where it came to India. We can only conjecture that it must have been known in China much earlier, because the weaving of any quantity of fine silk would be impossible with pick-up method only (it would take ten years to make one square yard). Another conjecture is that this loom came to Europe together with Indian cotton, or with Chinese silk toward the end of the Roman Empire.

From the few data available we can gather that before the tenth century most of Europe already knew simple foot-power looms, and the Western Europe was familiar with the Draw-Loom. In the eleventh century very complicated fabrics, such as damasks, etc., have been woven. Weaving technique developed steadily until it reached its peak in the eighteenth century. By this time practically all weaves which we use now, and which we are likely to use in the future, were already invented.

From then on the development of weaving entered a different phase. The factor of speed neglected so far became of the first importance. Consequently all new inventions were either time-saving, or labour-saving devices. In the beginning of the eighteenth century the flying shuttle appears. Later on the draw-boy (helper) was replaced by increasingly complicated shedding machines, which culminated in Jacquard's mechanism (1804), and finally even the weaver got eliminated by power. The quality of weaving deteriorated rapidly and the main chapter of hand-weaving was closed.

The next period, from the appearance of the power loom to the revival of handicrafts, was characterized by peasant weaving, which survived in the countries where labour was cheap enough to compete with power. This kind of weaving, even if valuable from the artistic point of view, was necessarily on a low technical level, and could not safeguard the refinement of the eighteenth century hand-weaving. This period covered about one hundred years.

When hand-weaving was re-discovered in the beginning of the twentieth century, there was no link left with the old traditions. Consequently the new craft took what it could from the still existing peasant weaving, and developed from there on. Curiously enough in this mechanized age, it did not go for intricate techniques and complicated looms. It tried and still tries to find new ways of self-expression rather in the direction of texture and colour.

HOLE BOARD. The same as Comber Board.

HOMESPUN. Originally, a fabric hand woven from yarn spun by hand. At the present the term indicates only the rough texture of any material woven on hand- or even power-loom.

HONEYCOMB. The same as Waffle Weave (v).

HONEYCOMB (Colonial). This weave has nothing to do with Waffle. During colonial times it was called "Honey Comb," and it has no other name in English. The fabric woven in this way has a very uneven surface with rather long floats on one side. Between blocks of pattern we use very heavy weft which then does not remain straight but follows a more or less wavy line. Nearly all over-shot drafts can be used for weaving Colonial Honeycomb.

The treadling: 6, 5, 4, 3, 4, 3, 4, 3, 6, 5, 2, 1, 2, 1, 2, 1, 6, 5, 4, 1, 4, 1, 4, 1, 6, 5, 2, 3, 2, 3, 2, 3, 6, 5, etc. Very heavy weft on treadles 5 and 6, the same as warp on treadles 1, 2, 3 and 4.

Woven in the traditional way, the weave is not particularly interesting or practical. But it has possibilities for effects in texture weaving. Synonyms: Halkrus, Spetsvav.

HONEYSUCKLE. A small overshot pattern greatly abused by all beginners.

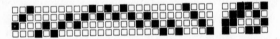

HOOK. 1. The same as Heddle. 2. Part of a Jacquard Machine.

HOOKABAG. Obsolete spelling of Huckaback.

HOP SACKING. Coarse tabby fabric. Hence the term designates sometimes the tabby weave, and sometimes the basket weave.

HORIZONTAL LOOM. Any loom in which the warp is stretched horizontally. Nearly all looms are of this type.

HORIZONTAL WARPING MILL. See Warping Mill.

HORSE. A horizontal wooden lever hung on a cord. It supports two shafts, or two smaller horses. Horses are used in the same way as pulleys, or rollers. Their main advantage is that they produce less friction, and are comparatively noiseless, but they have a tendency to separate the shafts when in neutral position. To overcome this difficulty, crossed horses are sometimes used, each set at a different angle so that only one of them may be in a horizontal position at a time.

HOUND'S TOOTH. A small pattern woven in two colours. The pattern is due entirely to the colour combination, and not to the weave, which in this case is tabby. The draw-down shows the colours only regardless of whether they are in warp or weft.

Identical pattern can be woven in 2:2 basket. Then four black ends will alternate with four white ones in the warp and four black picks with four white ones in the weft. Synonym: Stars.

HUCK. The same as Huckaback.

HUCKABACK (fr. G. *hukkebak*). Originally wares carried on the back by travelling merchants. Then towelling sold by them. Finally the weave used for making towels, etc.

There are many ways of drafting the Huckaback weave. But there are only three basic hucks shown below. They are called 6 x 6, 10 x 10, and 14 x 14. The numbers refer to the number of picks and warp-ends

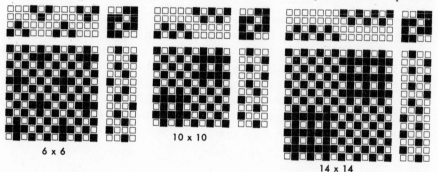

6 x 6   10 x 10   14 x 14

in each repeat of the fabric. The fabric is fairly strong particularly 6 x 6 huck; 14 x 14 is the weakest.

Huckaback weave is used for towels because of its strength and absorbing qualities. But it can be applied to nearly any kind of weaving.

Besides the "true" huckaback there is a number of variations woven with the same threading but different tie-up and treadling. For instance: Huckaback Lace, Double Waffle, Turned Huck, Turned M's-and-O's.

HUCKABACK LACE. A weave which gives imitation lace effect. The threading draft is the same as for huckaback, and so is the treadling. The only difference is in the tie-up: treadle 4 is tied to frames 1 and 2 instead of 1, 2 and 3; and treadle 1 is tied to frames 3 and 4 instead of 2, 3 and 4. There are three kinds of huckaback-lace exactly as there are three kinds of huckaback: 6 x 6, 10 x 10 and 14 x 14. Huckaback lace is very easy to weave, because it has a balanced tie-up, and works well with any yarn. It gives only one block of pattern with 4 shafts and requires 2 more shafts for each additional block.

IDLER. A wooden roller placed between the Breast Piece, and the Cloth Beam in a foot-power loom to prevent the cloth from touching the weaver's knees. Synonym: Knee-Beam.

IMPREGNATING. Fabric which is to be waterproof, or windproof, must be impregnated after weaving. Different chemicals are used according to the qualities required. When only the fibres are saturated with a substance insoluble in water, we have fabrics called "water repellent," "water shedding" or "shower proof." When not only fibres but also the spaces between them are filled with impregnating material, the fabric is "waterproof" and "windproof." Chemicals used are: rubber, waxes, resin, grease (e.g., lanolin for wool), plastics and certain salts (lead- or aluminum-acetate).

INCIDENTAL HEDDLE. In threading drafts of certain pattern weaves, a heddle which joins two blocks of pattern. Compare: Crackle, Modern Overshot, Swedish Lace.

INDEPENDENT ACTION LOOMS. Looms in which any number of shafts may be raised by one treadle, without affecting the height of the shed. The independent action looms may have either single or double tie-up. Looms of this kind with a single tie-up have the shafts weighted, so that they return to the lower position by the action of their weight alone. The weights should be adjustable, as each fabric requires a different tension of the warp, but in most cases they are not. Single tie-up looms have long lamms (Fig. 1) extending the whole width of the

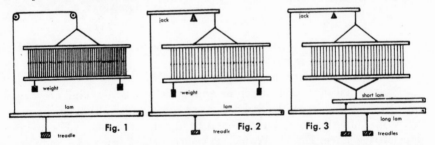

Fig. 1   Fig. 2   Fig. 3

loom. To the end of each lamm a cord is attached. This cord goes around two pulleys and it pulls the shaft up when the treadle is depressed. This method is the simplest, but it requires more pressure on the treadles than any other arrangement. Consequently it should be used only in narrow looms. A better but more complicated shedding motion is used in so-called "Jack Type" looms (Fig. 2). Here the cord is not tied directly to the shaft, but to a horizontal lever mounted on the Top Castle. This lever, called "Jack," is supported not in its centre, but nearer to the end which supports the shaft. Thus the length of the lamm is compensated and the pressure necessary to open the shed remains normal. The shafts must be weighted as in the preceding type.

The advantage of single tie-up looms is that they are simple, easy to set up and adjust. They work reasonably well with any tie-up, and what is more, with any number of shafts. Two or more treadles can be used at the same time, which is very important in such pattern weaves as Summer-and-Winter, Double Weaves, etc. On the other hand, they are less suitable for wide fabrics, as the weight of shafts increases with the width, and is quite considerable with a large number of shafts. Also the speed of weaving is never as high as with a counterbalanced loom.

Both types described above belong to the "rising shed" class (compare "Shedding Motion"). Any Counterbalanced loom with a Shed Regulator can be turned at a moment's notice into an Independent Action Loom, much superior to any single tie-up Jack-Type.

The Double-Tie-Up Loom has two sets of lamms, and one set of upper levers, coupers, or jacks (Fig. 3). The shafts are not weighted. Each treadle is connected through the long lamms to the coupers, and consequently to the rising shafts; and at the same time through the short lamms to the sinking shafts. Thus the shed opens in two directions, exactly as in a counterbalanced loom, but it opens always at the same height. The tie-up has two kinds of ties (short and long) and their number is much higher than in other types of looms. For instance, a loom with 8 shafts and 10 treadles has 80 ties regardless of the weave or pattern woven. Another disadvantage of a double-tie-up loom is that only one treadle can be used at a time.

The double-tie-up loom is the best all-purpose loom designed so far, but its price is comparatively high, and the setting up and adjusting rather complicated.

INDIAN WAR. Colonial pattern (v) of the Diamond-and-Table group.
Short draft:

INDIAN WEAVING. This term is loosely applied to any native weaving in North, Central or South America. In U.S.A. it usually means Navaho weaving—the only genuine Indian weaving which survived to our times, and which probably descends from Cliff Dwellers or Pueblo Indians. Weaving of other Indian tribes (e.g., Chimayo) was imported from Europe by Spanish settlers.

INDIANA ROSE. Colonial pattern (v) of the Wheel-and-Rose group.
Short draft:

85

INKLE (fr. Old Fr. *ligneul* = thread). 1. Thick weft. 2. Tape or belt.

INKLE LOOM. A simple loom for making belts, or sashes of limited width and length. The fabric is warp-face, i.e., the weft is completely covered by warp, except at the edges. Only tabby weave is possible unless the weaver uses pick-up method.

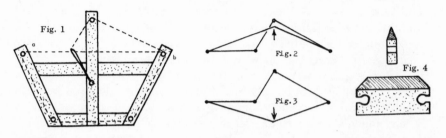

The warp is wound around pegs set in the frame (Fig. 1). One of the pegs should be eccentric. We adjust the tension of the warp by turning this peg in its socket. The heddles are tied to the central peg; they are made as single loops. The warping and threading are done at the same time. The first warp end goes through a heddle and around the upper peg; the second, in a straight line from A to B (Fig. 1), then all odd ends follow the first, and all even ends the second. The sheds are opened by lowering or lifting the horizontal portion of the warp by hand (Figs. 2 and 3). The shuttle is flat with one sharp edge, which beats the weft (Fig. 4).

INKLE LOOM

The pattern is formed entirely by colour combinations in warp. Stripes parallel to the warp are made by setting the warp in groups of different colours, each group of two or more ends. When all even ends are of one colour and all odd ones of another, we have stripes parallel to the weft. Small patterns can be woven by combining the two methods. More complicated, two-block patterns can be made in Rep Weave (v). Two wefts of very different count are used then.

The drafts for Inkle loom are written on two lines. The upper line

86

for ends threaded through heddles, and the lower line for ends which are not threaded.   The letters indicate colours.   E.g.:

R R R B B R R B B B B B B R B B B B R R B B R R R R
R R R R R R R R B B R R R R B B R R R R R R R R

The threading for pick-up patterns is slightly different: RR RR RR RR RR RR RR RR
B B B B B B
and so on.

INLAY.   Any free weave (v) in which the pattern weft is "laid in" with fingers, and not thrown in as usual.   There are several kinds of Inlay, but only the first is the Inlay proper.

1. Small patterns, initials, etc., with the pattern weft rather widely spaced on a plain background.   The pattern weft usually goes there and back across the pattern.

2. The same as Embroidery Weave.

3. The same as Brocade.

In all the above cases we have pattern woven on a plain ground of tabby or twill.

INLAY

INTERLOCKING.   In tapestry weaving there is always a problem as to how to weave the vertical lines which divide two colours.   A slit between blocks of colour is often left in Oriental tapestries, but this technique calls for a very high skill.   The wefts of two different colours may be linked

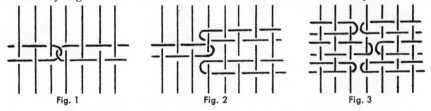

Fig. 1   Fig. 2   Fig. 3

between two warp ends (Fig. 1), or *on one* warp end (Fig. 2), or alternately *on two* warp ends (Fig. 3).   The first method is the best but slow and hardly possible in high-warp tapestry (v).   The second gives a ridge between the two colours, and the third blurrs the line.   This is why vertical lines are often avoided in tapestry weaving.   Synonym: Crossing.

INTERVAL.   In Satin Weave—the same as Move.

IRISH CHAIN.   Colonial pattern (v) of the Star-Wheel-and-Table group.
Short Draft:

8 | 7 | 8 | | 8 | 7 | 8 | | | | 5 5 | | | |
| | | 4 | 3 | 4 | | | 4 | 5 5 | 4 5 4 | | 5 5 | 4 |
| | | | 3 | 3 | | | | 4 | 4 3 4 4 | 4 | 4 3 4 4 |
3 | 3 | | | | 3 | 3 | | | 5 | 5 | | 5 | 5 |
5x | | 4x | | | 5x | | ←——2x——→ |

ISLE OF PATMOS.   Colonial pattern (v), the same as Star-of-the-Sea.

87

JACK (fr. old Fr. *jacque*).   1. The same as Couper (Am.).   2. The same as Horse (En.).   In any case, a lever supporting the shafts.

JACK-IN-THE-BOX.   One of the simplest shedding machines (v), which can operate a large number of shafts with two treadles only.

JACK-TYPE LOOM (Am.).   A loom with shafts hung on coupers (levers), usually with a single tie-up and rising shed.   See Independent Action Looms.

JACQUARD LOOM.   Any loom equipped with a Jacquard's Machine.

JACQUARD MACHINE.   A shedding machine used for industrial pattern weaving, and in a simpler form for all industrial weaving.

The development of the machine started with an invention of B. Bouchon (1725) in which perforated cards were used for the first time. This was improved by M. Falcon (1728) and J. de Vaucanson (1745). Finally the invention was perfected in 1804 by Joseph Marie Jacquard.

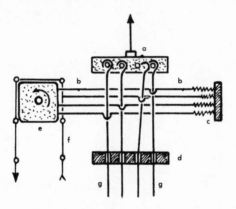

The machine is placed above the loom, on the top-castle, or in case of a draw-loom in place of the pulley box.   The heddles or shafts hang on steel wire hooks (g) which pass through a bottom board (d), then through loops in the Needles (b), and they reach a row of pegs in the Grift (a). When the hooks remain in the vertical position, the upper curved ends of the hooks fit around the pegs, and consequently are lifted, when the Grift is lifted.   But the Needles move horizontally, and when pushed against the springs (c) they pull the corresponding hooks out of the vertical—these hooks will not be lifted by the Grift.   The action of pushing the needles is performed by the cards (f) on the cylinder (e). The cards have holes opposite the needles.   A needle which fits into a hole is not pressed by the card, and therefore the hook will remain vertical and be pulled up by the grift.   In other words, a hole means rising shed, and the lack of hole, sinking shed. With proper arrangement of holes, any combination of heddles may be lifted. Of course each shed requires a separate card. The cards form a chain, and are moved forward by the cylinder one after another. The cylinder in turn is operated by a treadle. Thus the whole work of changing sheds is fully automatic.

When a Jacquard Machine is used in Two-Harness Method (v), it operates the pattern only, when the ground is woven with treadles. This means, of course, a great economy of cards.

The cards are made of cardboard, or of metal if they are made for long use. A special templet serves to perforate the cards with the required precision.

Jacquard Machines for draw-looms have hundreds of hooks and needles. Those used for plain weaving are much simpler.

JEAN (corruption of *"Genoa"*). Cotton fabric usually woven as 1:2 twill.

JENNING'S SHEDDING MOTION. The same as Jack-in-the-Box.

JIG. The same as Gauge (v).

JISP (orig. unknown). Streak in the fabric due to uneven beating of the weft. Synonym: Shire.

JOB'S TROUBLE. Colonial pattern (v) of the Sunflower group. Short draft:

JOHN WALKER. Colonial pattern (v) of the Cross-and-Table group. Short draft:

JUSTERS (fr. *'just*=adjust). Small wooden frame which keeps the shafts or coupers in a horizontal position during threading and sleying. The ends of justers are tied with long cords to the loom frame, thus keeping the harness tight and all frames separated. In case of counterbalanced looms with rollers, the justers are hardly ever used,

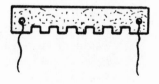

because the harness has a tendency to remain in neutral position by itself. Synonym: Mounters.

JUTE (fr. Hindu *"jūt"*). Fibre of the plant *Corchorus*, native of India. It gives a coarse yarn similar to hemp, and is used for making bags and similar fabrics. American Jute, fibre from the plant Velvetleaf (*Cissampelos*).

89

KAPOK (fr. Hindu). Short soft fibres from the tree Eriodendron, which grows in India.

KEMP WOOL (fr. AS *campe* = rough). Stiff, dead wool occurring mostly in cross-breeds. It is usually of inferior quality, discoloured, and it resists dyeing.

KEMPTY. The same as Kemp wool.

KERSEY (fr. *Kersey* in Suffolk, England). Heavy woollen or wool-and-cotton fabric, lightly felted and napped, woven as twill.

KILIM (doubtful origin, Persian or Greek, spelled also: Khilim or Killim; pron.: keeleem). Flat tapestry in low or high warp technique common in Eastern Poland, White Russia and Ukraine. It is distinguished from other similar tapestries by lack of interlocking of the weft between warp ends. Vertical lines are either avoided, or executed in a fine wave. Old Kilims have geometrical patterns not unlike Navaho weaving, later naturalistic motives of distinctly Oriental origin, and still later they show influence of Western weaving. Kilims are always made of thick wool on heavy linen warp.

KING'S DELIGHT. A colonial pattern (v) of the Cross-and-Table group. Short draft:

```
      13  13  13
           4  4
        6   6   5 5 5 5 5 5 5 5 5
        4     4 4 5 5 5 5 5 5 5 5 4
```

KING'S FLOWER. Colonial pattern (v) of the Star-and-Table group. Short draft:

```
      10 7 7 7 7 10  4 4 4   8 7 8   4 4 4
              10         10     10       10
                        9 4 4 9       9 4 4 9
        7 7 7 7 7               7 7
```

KIVER or **KIVVER** (obs. *kiver* = cover). The same as Coverlet.

KNEE-BEAM. The same as Idler (v).

KNOT (fr. AS *cnotta*). 60 yards of woollen or cotton yarn.

KNOTS. The following knots are used in weaving:

> *Bow Knot*, for tying-in the warp.
> *Draw Knot*, tie-ups with single cords, tying-in.
> *Granny Knot*, cord heddles.
> *Reef Knot*, broken weft, and sometimes warp.
> *Snitch Knot*, tie-ups with two cords.
> *Weaver's Knot*, broken warp ends, tying-on the warp.
> A different class of knots is used in Rug weaving (v).

KNOTTED PILE. Pile attached to the ground with simple knots, such as in Oriental rugs. Woven pile (Velvet, Corduroy) is fixed to the ground by interweaving with the ground warp or with binder. Cheap rugs have very often a pile which is woven but not knotted.

90

LACE (fr. Lat. *laqueus*=loop). Any fabric which imitates lace, and woven as one of the Cross-Weaves.

LACE AND COMPASS. Colonial pattern (v) of the Star-and-Wheel group. Short draft:

$$
\begin{matrix}
3\,2\,2\,2 & 4 & 8\,5\,8 & 4 & 2\,2\,2 \\
 & 5\quad 6\,5\,6 & & 6\,5\,6\quad 5 & \\
2\,2\,2\,4\,4\quad 7\,7 & & & 7\,7\quad 4\,4\,2\,2\,2 \\
4 & & 9\,9 & & 4
\end{matrix}
$$

LACE WEAVE. Real Lace is not woven, therefore any "lace weave" is an imitation of lace. The weaves which may give lace effect are: Cross Weaves, Net Weaves, Huckaback Lace, Swedish Lace, Bronson Lace, or Spot Lace (v).

LACEY WEAVE (Am.). The same as Honeycomb (Colonial).

LADIES' DELIGHT. Colonial pattern, the same as Sunflower.

LAG (Celtic). The same as Card in a Jacquard's Machine (R).

LAID-IN. Pattern woven in Inlay (v).

LAITH. Rare spelling of Lathe (the same as Batten or Beater).

LAM (fr. Fr. *lame*=shaft). The same as Shaft (R).

LAM or **LAMM** (fr. Icelandic *lemja*=beat). A short lever placed under each shaft. It has usually eyelets in its lower surface, and a hook on the upper one. The hook is attached to the corresponding shaft, and the eyelets to the treadles, through the ties of the lower tie-up. The lamm itself is hinged at one end to the loom frame. The purpose of the lamms is to make the vertical movement of shafts independent of the position of treadles. Should the treadles be tied directly to the shafts, the latter would be pulled sidewise, and it would be hard to keep them level.

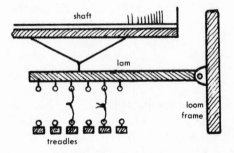

Lamms are not always hinged, sometimes they are simply suspended from the shafts (see Floating Harness).

In double-tie-up looms (Swedish Looms) we have two sets of lamms: short and long ones. These are called respectively: Marches and Counter-marches. Synonyms: Countermarche, Lamb, Lever.

91

LAMB. The same as Lamm, and probably a corruption of this word (R).

LAMÉ (fr. Fr. *lame* = blade). 1. A fabric which has silk warp and flat metal threads in weft. 2. Any fabric with flat metal yarn.

LAMPAS (Fr.). Originally a Chinese silk fabric. A weave similar to Brocatelle (v).

LAPPET (fr. AS *loeppa* = fold). The genuine embroidery weave. It differs from other so-called Embroidery Weaves inasmuch as the yarn for the embroidered pattern is taken from a separate warp, and not from the weft. From the theoretical point of view Lappet Weave belongs to the Cross-Weaves, and what is more any cross-weave may be executed by Lappet process.

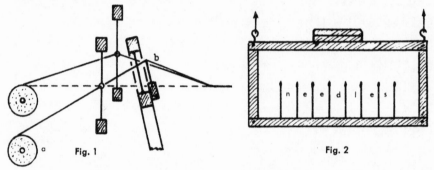

Fig. 1   Fig. 2

The embroidery warp (corresponding to the "Whip" in cross-weaving) is wound on a separate warp-beam which is only slightly braked ("a" Fig. 1). The embroidery yarns pass between the heddles and through the reed anywhere near the centre of the pattern to be made. Then they are threaded through special heddles placed on the batten very close to the reed (b). These heddles are made of metal exactly as sewing-machine needles, but they are several inches long. Their lower ends are set in a wooden frame, (Fig. 2) and the upper ends with eyes near the points are free. The frame can be moved several inches in the vertical direction, and it can move horizontally along the batten as well. The needles enter the warp from below, when the ground shed is open. Thus all embroidery yarns are in line with the upper part of the shed. After one shot of weft all pattern yarns are stitched to the ground, and the needles come down. Then they are moved horizontally to another place in the warp, where the same process is repeated. Between these two points the embroidery yarns form floats of a length equal to the displacement of the frame (Fig. 3).

The floats are nearly parallel to the weft, and come very close together, because two consecutive floats are separated only by one shot of ground weft. By changing the length and position of floats any small pattern can be executed. For more complicated patterns, or for patterns with more than one colour, more than one lappet frames are used, and each frame moves independently. The up-and-down movement of the needles is automatic. Whenever the batten is brought forward, the frame drops, and whenever it is released, the frame mounts. This is arranged by a system of cords and pulleys. After each shot of weft the frame must be moved horizontally, and this is done either by hand, or if the same pattern is repeated over and over again, by a special wheel mounted on the batten, so called Lappet Wheel.

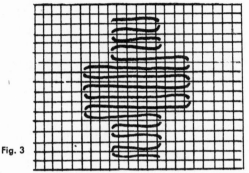

Fig. 3

The traditional Lappet can weave only a large number of identical small patterns, but at a very high speed. In modern weaving where more freedom is desired, the above described equipment is both too involved and unnecessary. Instead of lappet frames, individual large needles are hung from above, and each needle carries its own supply of yarn. The needles can move independently and the weaver has a complete freedom of design, but the process is much slower.

LAPPET WHEEL. A wooden disc several inches in diameter mounted on one side of the batten. It has a ratchet which turns it for a distance of one tooth after each shot of weft. On its front it has also a groove which guides the lappet frame. The shape of this groove depends from the pattern to be embroidered.

LASH (fr. old En. *lashe* = whip). Two picks of weft.

LASH. In a draw-loom, a bunch of Tacks (v) twisted together or tied to a short piece of cord. One Lash opens one shed of the pattern.

LASTING BEAUTY. A Colonial pattern of the Two-Block-Patch group. Short draft:

16 4 4 16 4 4 4 4 4 4 4 4 4 4 4 4

16 4 16 4 4 4 4 4 4 4 4 4 4 4 4 4

LATHE (fr. Icelandic *lodh*). The same as Batten (R).

LAWN (fr. *Laon* in France). Thin cotton fabric woven in tabby.

LAY (fr. AS *lecgan* = to lay).   1. The same as Batten.   2. The same as Lea.

LEA (fr. AS *lecgan*).   Three hundred yards of linen yarn.   Thus the number of leas in one pound of linen yarn indicate its count.   E.g.: linen yarn marked "18 lea" has 5,400 yards per pound.

LEA.   One-half of a Portee.   The total amount of yarn used for making a warp from one end to the other.   Thus when we warp from 8 tubes and the length of warp is 20 yards, one Lea will have 8 yarns each 20 yards long.   A Portee will have 16 yarns 20 yards long.

LEAF.   A set of heddles mounted on the same frame.   Up to the beginning of the revival of hand-weaving this was the only term used both in the British Isles and in North America.   Scandinavian influence in weaving introduced or rather re-introduced an old Anglo-Saxon term, "heddle," which at first was used indiscriminately for both "leash" and "leaf," possibly due to the fact that rigid heddles or leaves made of one piece of wood were used in Scandinavia.   Still later in Britain, "leaf" has been abandoned entirely, and replaced by "heddle," when what we call "heddle" was replaced by "leash."   In North America "leaf" died with the colonial hand-weaving, and after the revival has been called "harness" by mistake, when heddles remained and mean the same as British "leash."   See: Shaft.

LEAVED.   With a preceding number, e.g., "6 leaved" = made on six shafts.

LEASE (corruption of *Leash*).   Any place in the warp where the warp ends are crossed at regular intervals, most often singly, by pairs, or by fours.   The lease or leases are made during warping.

LEASE (Cross)

The purpose of a lease is to keep all ends of warp in the same order in which they were wound.   Some methods of beaming require one lease only at the beginning of the warp (Portee Cross), when other methods need another cross at the end as well (Porrey Cross).   When spreading is done with a reed instead of a raddle, the cross must be transferred to the back of the reed before the latter is removed.   In coarse weaving the lease may be removed (by pulling out the lease-rods) after threading, but otherwise the lease-rods should be kept in warp at the same distance from the harness, as the front shed. This is done to prevent unnecessary friction between the warp and the heddles, which is particularly important with steel or wire heddles. Synonym: Cross.

LEASE RODS. A pair of flat, wooden laths with rounded edges and a very smooth finish. They are inserted into the Lease of a finished warp and tied together at both ends. If they are left in the warp during weaving they should be tied to the loom frame to prevent their moving forward with the warp. Synonyms: Lease-sticks, Cross-sticks.

LEASH (fr. L. *laxus* = loose). The same as heddle. In old English, the same as Lease.

LEASH ROD. The same as Heddle-stick or Shaft.

LEE'S SURRENDER. Colonial pattern (v) of the Sunrise group. Short draft:

```
        8  8 2  2 8  8                    3
2 2 2 2 8  8      8  8 2 2 2 2 5 5     5 5
        8  8 2 2 8  8              6 3 6  6 3 6
7 6 6 6 7 8    3    8  7 6 6 6 7      4 4
                              5x
```

LENO WEAVE (fr. Fr. *linon*). 1. A cross-weave (v) in which one pick of weft made with crossed warp ends is followed by an odd number of tabby: 3, 5, 7, etc. Leno can be woven on the same set-up as Gauze. 2. In industrial terminology Leno means sometimes any cross-warp technique higher than Gauze. 3. In colloquial language of hand-weavers Leno may mean any cross-weave, and even Net Weave.

LEOPARD SKIN. Colonial pattern (v) of the Three-Block-Patch group. Short draft:

```
6 5 5 5 5 5 5 6  6 6  6 6
            13  13  13
5 5 5 5 5 5 5    5    5
```

LET-OFF. Any mechanism used in connection with Take-Up Motion (v), which releases the warp from the warp beam in a continuous way, keeping it always at the same tension. The simplest Let-Off is an adjustable frictional brake, but it must be very precisely built, which is seldom the case. A better mechanism is the old fashion brake with counterweights (v Brake, Fig. B), but it must be reset from time to time.

LEVER. A general term which may mean a Lamm, a Couper or a Horse.

LEY. Alternative spelling of Lay (v).

LIESH (prob. corruption of *Leash*). Silk cord used for making heddles, particularly Doups, and Bead-lams in Cross-Weaves.

LIFTING PLAN. A diagram which shows the order in which the shafts are lifted in a weaving loom. It is used in power weaving, and in all drafts for looms without tie-up (table looms) or with a direct tie-up (one

95

frame to each treadle). The lifting plan corresponds to the treadling draft, and it can be either graphical or numerical:

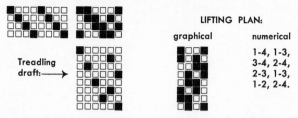

LIFTING PLAN:

graphical   numerical

1-4, 1-3,
3-4, 2-4,
2-3, 1-3,
1-2, 2-4.

Treadling
draft:——►

We have no convention in hand-weaving as to the direction in which the sheds open, thus a lifting plan may mean a rising or a sinking shed, although it should mean only rising shed. Synonyms: Looming Plan, Peg Plan.

LILY OF THE VALLEY. Colonial pattern (v) of the Diamond-and-Table group. Short draft:

LINAU, LINO. The same as Leno (R).

LINE (fr. AS *lin* = linen). Long fibres of Flax.

LINED WORK. Old English term for Pattern Twills (v).

LINEN. Anything made of Flax fibres, as linen yarn, linen fabrics.

LINENE. Cotton fabric imitating linen one.

LINGO (fr. Fr. *lingot*). A leaden weight tied to the lower end of a heddle in the Draw-Loom.

LINSEY-WOOLSEY (fr. Old En. *linsel* = linen; *wolsey* = wool). Fabrics made of linen and wool.

LISBON STAR. Colonial Summer-and-Winter pattern. Short draft:

LIST (fr. Fr. *liste* = border). The same as Selvedge (R).

LOADED FABRIC. The same as Weighted Fabric (v Weighting).

LOCKED WEFTS. A weaving technique which gives comparatively free patterns without picking-up and with any number of shafts (from 2 up). The fabric may be woven in any basic weave from tabby to satin. The pattern does not depend from the threading. There are as many shuttles as colours to be used, and they are all kept on the right hand side of the weaver. The same colours are wound on a number of bobbins which are put on a bobbin rack on the left hand side of the weaver. If, for instance, red colour is required on the right and black on the left, the weaver picks up the shuttle with red, opens a shed, throws the shuttle from the right, catches it on the left and passes it under the black yarn which comes from the rack. Without changing the shed the shuttle is thrown back to the right. Both wefts, red and black, are now interlocked and by pulling

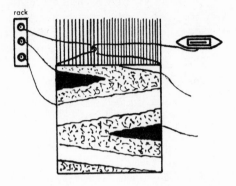

the shuttle we can move the point of interlocking as far to the right as required. Only then comes the beating and changing of sheds. This method is nearly as fast as plain weaving. The patterns are limited to two colours in the horizontal direction, although more elaborate set-ups give three colours (double weaves).

Locked Wefts can be used in any kind of weaving where comparatively large patterns are required. Application of this method to the twice-woven rugs (v) gives particularly interesting results.

Synonym: Clasped Wefts.

LOG CABIN WEAVE. 1. The same as Rep Weave. 2. Patterns woven in Tabby by alternating two colours in weft and warp (v Tabby).

LONGCLOTH. Light, soft cotton fabric woven in tabby.

LONG MARCHE. The long lever or lamm under the loom in a Double Tie-up. Compare: Independent Action Loom.

LOOM (fr. AS *geloma* = tool). An arrangement which keeps the warp in proper position during weaving. Thus the simplest and probably the oldest loom consists of a horizontal stick longer than the width of warp suspended a few feet above the ground. One end of the warp is attached to this stick. The other may be weighted and stretched vertically (as in old Greek looms), or tied to the weaver's belt and stretched horizontally (Latin America). The next step in the construction of a loom is to wind or stretch the warp on a frame (Frame Loom). When longer warps were required, two rollers were added: one on each end of the frame (Egypt). Still there was nothing to help the weaver in opening a shed. The first such mechanism appears in India long before our era. It had two frames with heddles operated by stirrups. It was probably preceded by a simpler shedding motion, such for instance as we use now in tapestry looms. The further development of the loom consisted mostly on increasing the number of shafts. This resulted in more and more complicated machinery for selecting shafts for each shed, from treadle-and-lamm combination to the Jacquard's machine. Eventually the loom reached its highest form in which every heddle could be operated independently (Draw-Loom).

Hand looms can be classified according to their size, position of warp, shedding motion, number of shafts, the way in which they are operated, purpose for which they are built, and their origin.

The simplest looms without rollers, i.e., for a limited length of warp, are: Board Loom, Box Loom, Cradle Loom, Frame Loom, Inkle Loom. They all have either no shedding motion or a very simple one with a Rigid Heddle or a Heddle-Stick.

The size of a loom means the greatest width of warp used in this loom. Table looms have usually from 8 to 25 inches. Foot-power looms from 20 to 90 inches. Wider looms are built occasionally for large pieces of tapestry, rugs, etc. Looms narrower than 8 inches are either Inkle Loom or Sample Loom.

Nearly all looms are Horizontal. Vertical looms are used exclusively for tapestry and rug weaving.

Looms operated entirely by hand are: Inkle, Table Looms and all small frame looms. Those operated by hand and foot are called: Treadle Loom or Floor Loom or Foot-Power Loom. When the shuttle is not thrown by hand, but by a special mechanism, we have Fly-Shuttle or Flying Shuttle Loom.

As far as the Shedding motion is concerned, we have: Counter-balanced Loom, Jack Type Loom, Independent Action Loom, Double Tie-Up Loom, Table Loom and Draw-Loom.

Any number of shafts from 2 to as many as 90 can be used in one loom. The usual numbers are 2, 4, 6, 8, 12, 16; less common, 5 and 10. The looms are called accordingly: four-frame loom or four-leaf or four-shaft. The English term, four-heddle loom, is rather confusing in North America, and the American term, four-harness loom, is as confusing in the British Commonwealth; both should be avoided. Looms with so many shafts that they cannot be operated directly by treadles are called Multi-frame or Multiharness (abbreviation of "Multi-frame Harness"). In a class by itself stands the Draw-Loom, without shafts, but with practically an unlimited number of sheds.

Most of the looms have one harness (set of shafts) only. But there are Two-Harness Looms, and even Three-Harness Looms were used in the past.

Looms built for special purposes are, for instance: Velvet Loom, Cross-Weave Loom, Lappet Loom. They all belong to the Industrial hand-weaving as well as looms built only for one particular yarn like linen, wool or silk. Looms made now are all more or less universal.

Certain types of looms are ascribed to the countries where they were originally used, but since nearly every type of loom is used in every country, such classification is often misleading. Thus Scandinavian Loom means a Double-Tie-Up Loom; Danish Loom, a partly folding one, etc.

LOOM-COMB. The same as Reed (R).

LOOM FRAME. All immovable parts of a loom. Usually the frame is made of 6 vertical pieces, and 6 or 7 horizontal ones. Of these, only 2 are working parts: the Breast Piece and the Slabstock. All other components of the frame only support the working parts. The frame should be resistant to shock and tension, and the wood free from any tendency to warp.

LOOMING PLAN. The same as Lifting Plan or Treadling Draft.

LOVERS' KNOT. A Colonial pattern or part of a pattern. Short draft:

```
5  4 4  5 5         5 5  4 4
 4    4      9 5 9      4   4
 4    4    8 5 5 8      4   4
 4   5  6 5 6     6 5 6   5   4
```

LOVITT. Light shade of Heather.

LOW WARP. In Tapestry weaving, any weave or technique which requires an ordinary reed and batten for beating the weft, as opposed to High-Warp (v). The weaving proceeds upwards in horizontal lines, i.e., the whole width of the fabric is filled with weft before every beat. The patterns most suitable for Low Warp are the geometrical ones, although any pattern may be made in this way. Curved lines in Low Warp have more rigid appearance due to the fact that the texture does not follow the pattern as it does in the High Warp. Low Warp tapestry can be woven on any horizontal or vertical loom with a batten.

LUSTRINE. Cotton satin fabric, polished with chemicals, heat and pressure.

LUSTRING. The same as Lutestring.

LUTESTRING. Very heavy yarn used for weft (R).

M'S-AND-O'S. A weave which may be considered as a texture weave, when small regular blocks cover the whole fabric, or as a pattern Lace weave when blocks of M's-and-O's are woven on a background of tabby.

Larger blocks of pattern have a peculiar untidy appearance which may be desirable or not.

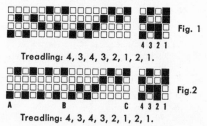

Treadling: 4, 3, 4, 3, 2, 1, 2, 1.

Fig. 1

Treadling: 4, 3, 4, 3, 2, 1, 2, 1.

Fig.2

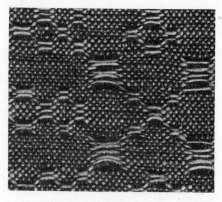

M's-&-O's

Fig. 1 shows the traditional draft, and Fig. 2 a modern draft. The first does not give tabby either in the vertical or horizontal direction. The second gives tabby in both directions, and can be used for pattern weaving. M's-and-O's can be woven on practically any draft by alternating two Opposite sheds (v) for a while and then changing to another pair of opposite sheds. For instance, the treadling for Overshot will be 12, 34, 12, 34, 13, 24, 23, 21, 23, 21, 13, 24 (numbers indicate the shafts). The same for Crackle. For Summer-and-Winter: 13, 24, 13, 24, 12, 34, 23, 14, 23, 14, 12, 34. For Huckaback: 12, 34, 12, 34, 13, 24, 12, 34, 12, 34, 13, 24. For Bronson: 1, 234, 13, 24, 13, 24, 1, 234, 14, 23, 14, 23, 1, 234, 134, 2, 134, 2. Swedish Lace: 13, 24, 123, 4, 123, 4, 13, 24, 1, 234, 1, 234, 13, 24, 12, 34, 12, 34. The best drafts to be used with M's-and-O's are Bronson Lace and Swedish Lace.

M'S-AND-W'S. The same as Double Point Twill (v).

MACKINAW (fr. *Mackinaw Island*). Thick, strong woollen or wool-and-cotton fabric. Woven in Stitched Double Cloth and napped.

MADRAS (fr. *Madras*, India). Cotton or rayon shirting.

MAIDEN. One of the supports of the spindle in a Spinning Wheel.

MAIL (fr. Fr. *maille* = link). The eye of a heddle, particularly when made of metal, glass or plastic. Synonym: Niece.

MAIL NET. A net weave (v) similar to Spider Net (v) but with tabby between crossings.

MAITLAND CORDS. Part of old heddle-frames. Two cords to which the heddles are tied, or on which they slide. Synonyms: Muddling Cord, Backing.

100

MALTESE CROSS. Colonial pattern (v) of the Wheel-and-Rose group. Short draft (one of several):

$$4 \quad 4 \quad 777 \quad 4$$
$$5 \quad 6 \qquad 6 \quad 5$$
$$4\,4 \quad 6\,3\,3\,6 \quad 4\,4$$

MANILA. Fibre of the plant *Musa Textilis* (Philippines). Extremely long (up to 10 feet) but coarse.

MAPLE LEAF. Colonial pattern (v) of the Bow-Knot group.

$$2\,2\,4 \quad 6 \quad 8 \quad 4\,2\,2 \qquad 2\,2\,4 \quad 8 \quad 6 \quad 4\,2\,2\,5$$
$$2\,2\,4 \quad 8 \quad 6 \quad 4\,2\,2 \quad 2\,2\,4 \quad 6 \quad 8 \quad 4\,2\,2$$
$$4 \quad 6 \quad 6 \quad 4 \qquad 4 \quad 6 \quad 6 \quad 4$$

MARCHE (Fr.). The same as Lamm or Lever.

MARQUISETTE (Fr.). Light cotton fabric woven in Gauze (v).

MATCHING (About drafts or patterns). When several drafts are used in the same piece of weaving (for instance: main pattern, borders and selvedge) they must be matched so that there will be no break either in the weave or in the pattern. When two drafts to be matched are both for the same weave, the same unit (v) of weave should be taken for both, and each should have a full number of units. E.g.:

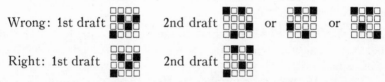

When the weaves are different, we must first check whether they can be woven simultaneously at all, preferably by making a draw-down (v). For instance, 2:2 twill, crackle and overshot can be mixed in the same draft, while damask and spot weave cannot, except on a draw-loom. Another reason why two weaves may not go together is that each of them takes up a different amount of warp, e.g., tabby and satin; consequently such a combination should be abandoned, or two warp beams provided: one for each weave. As a rule we can combine only weaves which have the same length of floats in warp.

Matching of patterns is more a question of good taste than of any strict rules. Every pattern should end at one of its centres of symmetry. E.g.: A and B are both right, but C is wrong. When there is a definite and rather complex figure, like circle (Wheel), it is better not to cut it in

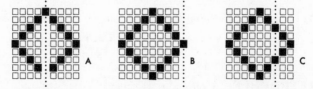

half even at its centre. When there are two or more components of one pattern it is better to cut the smaller or the less conspicuous one. Joining diagonals of different pitch should be avoided, but when necessary reverse

101

the direction of the diagonal at the point of joining. Finally, the last block of the first draft should never be on the same shed as the first block of the second draft.

MATELASSÉ (fr. Fr. *matelas* = mattress).   Brocade with raised design.

MATT WEAVE (fr. AS *meatta* = mat).   The same as basket weave.

MELTON (fr. *Melton* in England).   Heavy woollen twill with a short nap.

MERCERIZING (fr. *John Mercer*, the inventor).   Treatment of cotton or linen yarn.   The yarn is subjected to the action of alkalis and becomes silky and shiny.   The solution used acts also as a mordant.

MERINO (fr. Sp. *merino* = shepherd).   A breed of sheep which gives one of the finest wools.   A fabric woven from Merino wool, or imitation of such fabric.

METALLIC YARNS.   Yarns made of metal: pure (usually flat) or mixed with natural fibres (twisted together or metal powder painted or sprayed on a natural core).

METRIC COUNT OF YARN.   The count is the same for all yarns. Number one is one meter per gram (or one kilometer per one kilogram). This corresponds to 500 yards per pound (approximately).   To find yds/lb we multiply the metric number by 500.   The relationship between the English and the Metric count is given by the following formulas:

$$M = 1.7 \times Nc; \qquad Nc = 0.6 \times M;$$
$$M = 0.6 \times Nl; \qquad Nl = 1.7 \times M;$$
$$M = 1.1 \times Nw; \qquad Nw = 0.9 \times M;$$
$$M = \frac{9000}{D}; \qquad D = \frac{9000}{M};$$

where: M—metric number; Nc—number of cotton; Nl—number of linen; Nw—number of wool; D—number of silk in deniers.

MINIATURE PATTERN.   Any small pattern made by reducing a larger one.   In Colonial weaving overshot patterns transcribed for short floats only, or partly for overshot and partly for diamond twill.   Used for borders or for small pieces of weaving.

MISSOURI CHECK.   Colonial pattern (v) of the Four-Block-Patch group.
Short draft:

```
          8 8 8 8 8 8 8 8 8 8 8 8 8 8 8 8      8 8 8 8 8 8
                                    3 3 3               3 3 3
          5                       5  9 9 9 9  5   5   9 9 9 9
          3   3 3 3 3 3 3 3 3 3 3 3  3          3   3   3
```

MISSOURI TROUBLE.   Colonial pattern (v) of the Star-and-Table group.
Short draft:

```
          4       4     |10 10          |10 10      4     4| 3|
            5   4        3      3 3 3     3      4   5    |7 |7
            4 4   10          10 3 3 10         10    4 4 |
          4     4    10       10          10   10    4   4|
                        |◄——————2x——————►|              |9x|
```

102

MISTAKES IN WEAVING.

Warping:

Too many portees. Remove the surplus gradually during beaming, not before.

Too few portees. Make an additional warp of the missing portees, chain it, and beam together with the main warp.

One portee is too short. Unwind it, cut off, and tie the ends together at the lease. If unwinding impossible, remove during beaming. An additional portee must be made in both cases, and beamed as before.

One portee is too long. Bring the extra length to the end of warp, and cut it off there.

Only half of the lease made on one portee. Break the ends, correct the lease, and tie again.

One portee without cross. Remove the whole portee, or break the ends and make the lease in the most likely place in the warp.

Threading:

One end in a wrong heddle. Cut the heddle (not the end) if the mistake is noticed during weaving, and tie a new cord heddle around the end.

One end and heddle missed. Tie a new heddle in the proper place, and add one end (spool with warp yarn hanging behind the loom). Or re-thread one part of the warp.

Two ends crossed between heddles. Break one end (find out first which), straighten, and retie.

Sleying:

Too many ends in a dent. Repeat sleying between the mistake and the nearest selvedge, starting with the edge.

Too few ends in a dent. Repeat sleying *from* the mistake to the nearest edge.

Crossed ends (shed does not open in this particular place). Untie the offending end, pull it from the reed, then straighten it and pass through the reed again.

Weaving:

Broken ends. Cut off the end close to the fabric, then take a piece of warp yarn and pin it to the cloth in line with the broken end. Darn it into the cloth for about half an inch parallel to the broken end, pull through the reed and harness and tie to the other end at such a distance that the knot will come at the end of the woven piece. Or better: make the knot or knots anywhere, and mend later on.

Possible causes of breaking: shed not clear—correct the tie-up;

103

too much tension, ends break near edge—release the warp; the batten is rubbing the warp—correct the upper tie-up or the batten.

Blotches (dropped warp ends). Unweave or mend later with a darning needle. Correct the tie-up to get clear shed.

Wrong treadle, or wrong colour of weft. Unweave or mend later on, removing the wrong pick gradually, and introducing a new one.

One line of pattern missing. Unweave.

Jisps (uneven beating). Unweave and find the cause before starting again. Take shorter bores (v), keep always the same tension of warp. Hold the batten right in the centre. Check the winding of bobbins, particularly when jisps are more visible at the edges.

MIXED WARP. Warp made of two or more different yarns. The main problem in making such warps is to get the right tension for each yarn. Tension boxes are used. Layers of warp on the warp beam should be separated with very heavy paper (even corrugated paper) or paper and warp sticks.

Sett of warp is figured out as an average sett corresponding to the average number of yards per pound. E.g.: 4 ends 300 yds/lb, 10 ends 3,000 yds/lb give an average of: 840 yds/lb from the formula:

$$Y = \frac{N}{\dfrac{n'}{y'} + \dfrac{n''}{y''}} \quad ;$$

where: Y is the average No. of yds/lb; N—number of warp ends in one repeat of warping (the same as $n'+n''$); n'—number of warp ends of the first yarn; y'—yds/lb of the first yarn; n''—number of warp ends of the second yarn; y''—yds/lb of the second yarn.

MOCK LENO. Imitation of cross-weaving, particularly of Gauze or Leno. Thus 6 x 6 huckaback lace woven on tabby ground is often called Mock Leno. Uneven sleying may produce similar effects, but it must be done with wool or other non-slippery yarns. E.g.:

Sleying: A—continuous,
B—3+0+1+0+3.
Treadling: 1, 2, 3, 2.

MODERN OVERSHOT. Overshot weave (v) with uniform texture. All floats in the fabric are of the same length: 3 and 5, 3 and 7, or 3 and 9. The threading draft has 4 units corresponding to 4 blocks of pattern and incidental heddles between the blocks. E.g.:

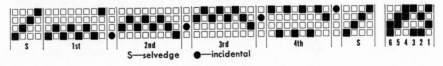

S—selvedge   ●—incidental

104

Each unit can be repeated any number of times, and the blocks of pattern can be of any size. The treadling can be conventional as in colonial overshot, or the same as for bound weaving: 3, 4, 5, 6. In the latter case the weft must be at least in two colours, but three or four colours may be also used.

MODERNIZING. Adapting traditional weaves or patterns to modern requirements. This usually implies: simplifying the pattern, making the weave more practical (see Modern Overshot), changing the draft in such a way as to produce texture effects only, without any pattern, and so on.

MOHAIR (fr. Arabic *mukhayyar*). Wool from Angora goat, and pile fabric woven from this wool. Usually only the pile is of mohair, when the ground is of cotton, wool or linen. Imitation of genuine mohair.

MOIRE (Fr.). Fabrics made of natural or artificial silk with design resembling wood grain, made by embossing (v Embossed Fabrics).

MOLESKIN (fr. *mole's skin*). The same as Terry Velvet (loops in pile left uncut) but the fabric is made for clothing. Heavily napped cotton twill.

MOMME (fr. Japanese). Unit of weight of silk fabrics.

MONK'S BELT. Two-Block weaving pattern. Short draft: $^{2\ \ 2\ \ 8\ \ 3\ \ 8}_{2\ 2\ 8\ 8\ 2}$

MONK'S CLOTH. The same as 2:2 Basket Weave. Upholstery fabrics woven in cotton, jute or flax.

MONTURE (Fr. = mounting). Part of a draw-loom composed of heddles, comber board, necking cords, pulley box, pulley cords, tail, and simple. Corresponds roughly to the Harness in ordinary looms.

MORDANT (fr. Fr. *mordre* = to bite). Any chemical compound which makes dyeing easier, applied before dyeing or together with the dye.

MORNING GLORY. Colonial pattern of the Rose-and-Table group. Short draft: $^{8\ \ 3\ 3\ \ 8}_{7\ 3\ 7}\ ^{8\ 8\ 8\ 8}_{8\ 2\ 2\ 2\ 2}$

MOSAICS. Colonial Summer-and-Winter pattern. Short draft:

$$^{2\ 1\ 2}_{2\ 2}\qquad ^{2\ 1\ 2}_{2\ 2}$$
$$^{2\ 2}_{2\ 2\ 2}\quad ^{3\ 1\ 1\ 5\ 5\ 1\ 1\ 3}_{3\ 1\ 1\ 1\ 2\ 1\ 1\ 1\ 3}$$

MOSQUITO BAR. Rough cotton fabric woven in cross-weave.

MOTHER-OF-ALL. The horizontal part of the spindle frame in a spinning wheel.

MOUNTERS. The same as justers.

MOUNTING. All adjustable parts of a loom, i.e., harness or harnesses, lower and upper tie-up, lamms, treadles and shedding machinery, if any.

105

MOVE. In satin weaving, the nearest distance between two warp ends lifted on two consecutive sheds. Move is expressed in number of ends. It should be constant all through the fabric.

move = 3

MUDDLING CORD. Probably corruption of Maitland Cord (v).

MULTIHARNESS LOOM. Any loom with a large number of shafts. Sometimes any loom with more than 4 shafts. Looms of this kind reached as many as 90 shafts. Above 16 shafts the loom must be operated by some kind of Shedding Machine (v) since there is no room for so many treadles. The shafts above 16 are of special construction, sometimes as thin as $\frac{1}{8}$ of an inch. Synonyms: Multiframe, Multishaft, etc.

MULTIPLE WARP. The same as Mixed Warp (v).

MUMMY CLOTH. Cotton or linen fabric woven in broken twill, or similar weave which gives rough texture. The same fabric made of wool is called Granite Cloth.

MUNSELL'S THEORY OF COLOUR. The colour has three components: *Hue*—or its position in the rainbow, or spectrum; *Value*—its lightness or darkness; and *Chroma*—its purity. Each colour is designated by corresponding 3 symbols: one for Hue, one for Value and one for Chroma. Hues are divided into 10 groups: R (red), YR (yellow-red or orange), Y (yellow), YG (yellow-green), G (green), BG (blue-green), B (blue), PB (purple-blue), P (purple), RP (red-purple). Each group has decimal subdivisions. Thus 5P means average purple, where 2.5P means halfway between purple and red-purple. This division of Hues is based on psychological and not on physical properties of colours. Value ranges between black and white and has 10 steps, so that any colour with value 10 is pure white, and any colour with value 1 is pure black. Chroma starts with 1, where it is nearly grey (light or dark), and reaches 14 or 16 for the purest colours. The highest Chroma depends entirely on the technique of dyeing.

Besides classifying colours Munsell's theory gives formulae for colour combinations, based on statistical data. These formulae are supposed to work well in conservative colour schemes of the Western civilization. They are excellent for designers satisfied with traditional colour effects, and they certainly protect an amateur from an abuse of colour.

A project in weaving must be divided into four main areas: the largest is the Dominant; the second large, a Subdominant; a small area is an Accent on the Dominant; and the smallest, the accent on the Subdominant. Only the Accents can have pure (high Chroma) colours.

The theory works in practice very well, but it cannot be used as a criterion of good and bad design.

NAIL (fr. AS *noegel*).   Unit of measure of cloth, $\frac{1}{16}$ of a yard.

NAINSOOK (fr. Hindu *nainsukh* = muslin).   Light cotton fabric, white, woven in tabby.   Glossy finish on one side.

NAP (fr. AS *hnoppa*).   Fibres or hair on the surface of a fabric.   Nap may appear during weaving as a result of friction between warp and the reed, or when very fluffy weft is used.   As a rule, however, it is raised artificially after weaving with wire brushes, flat or cylindrical.

NAPERY (fr. Fr. *nappe* = table cloth).   Table linen.

NAPPING.   Action of raising the nap on a fabric.

NAVAJO WEAVING.   Weaving made by Navajo Indian tribes of New Mexico and Arizona.   In its original form it is made on simple vertical looms in flat tapestry technique.   The only weave used is tabby, and since vertical lines are avoided, there are neither slits nor interlocking.   Patterns are simple, geometrical.   The material used has been cotton and, after the arrival of Spanish colonists, wool as well.

NECK TWINE.   The same as Necking Cord.

NECKING CORD.   The cord which connects heddles with pulley cords in a draw-loom.

NEEDLE.   1. The same as heddle, particularly a special heddle used in Lappet weaving.   2. One of the horizontal steel wires which penetrate the holes in cards of a Jacquard's Machine.

NEEDLE FRAME.   In Lappet weaving, a heddle frame mounted on the batten in front of the reed.   The heddles, called needles, are made of strong brass or steel wire and are set vertically in the lower shaft of the frame.   They have eyes near the top.   This frame is set in another, slightly larger one, and can slide in it up and down.   Finally both frames move horizontally on the batten.   See Lappet.

NET WEAVES.   Cross-weaves (v) which produce a web similar to nets.   As some of the warp threads cross so many others that they could not all be put into the same dent of the reed, the crossing must take place in front of the reed.   The heddles used for this purpose are doupes with beads on the end, called beadlamms.   The beads are perforated and the holes highly polished to reduce the friction.   They are mounted in a frame hung on the batten.   The frame moves together with the batten and is operated by a treadle.   When the frame is in neutral position, plain tabby can be woven—when it is raised the crossing takes place.   For very complicated Net Weaves more than one such frame is used.

   The principal Net Weaves are:

   Whip Net.   Each warp thread crosses alternately the next thread

107

to the right, then the next to the left.   The weft shots pass through the crossings.

Spider Net. It differs from the Whip Net inasmuch as there are additional pairs of Gauze Weave between pairs of Whip Net.

Mail Net. The same as Spider Net, but with shots of tabby between crossings.

Patent Net. The Whip (v) form hexagons on a background of Gauze.

Princess Royal Net. Similar to the above, but the pairs of gauze and the shots of weft are so spaced that the Whip forms circles.

NIDDY-NODDY (fr. *nidnod* = because of the characteristic movement made by the instrument when in use).   A simple implement for winding the yarn into skeins.   It consists of one long vertical stick with a handle at its lower end, and two transverse sticks set at right angles to each other and to the main stick.   The size of the skein can be changed by moving the upper horizontal stick up or down.

NIECE.   The same as Mail.

NINE SNOWBALLS.   Colonial pattern, the same as Scarlet Balls.

NO-HARNESS LOOM.   Any loom without proper shedding motion. The shed in such a loom is opened either with a needle, fingers, heddle-stick, or rigid heddle.   See Board Loom, Box Loom, Cradle Loom, Frame Loom.

NOILS (fr. Lat. *nodus* = knot).   Short fibres rejected in manufacturing quality yarns.   Used for making felt and low-grade yarns.

NON-SLIP KNOT.   The same as Snitch Knot.

NO-TABBY WEAVE.   Any weave which requires tabby binder but woven without it.   For instance, Bound Weaves.

NOVELTY YARNS.   See Three Dimensional Yarns.

NUB or **NUBBY YARN.**   A texture yarn with small lumps irregularly distributed along the core of the yarn.   The nubs (lumps) are often of a different colour than the core.

NUMBER (En.).   840 yards of yarn.

NYLON.   Synthetic fibres of different chemical composition, but all belonging to linear polymers.   The single filament of nylon had a count of about 1,500,000 yds/lb.   Nylon is very strong, very elastic, resistant to friction, and does not absorb water (dries fast).

OCTAGON. Element of patterns. May be executed on any draft which has a horizontal line between two diagonals of opposite direction.

ODDS - AND - EVENS. A method of tying the two tabby treadles, one to all shafts with odd numbers, the other to the ones with even numbers. E.g.: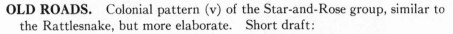

OLD ROADS. Colonial pattern (v) of the Star-and-Rose group, similar to the Rattlesnake, but more elaborate. Short draft:

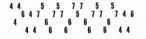

OLD SOUTH COUNTRY. Colonial pattern of the Diamond-and-Table group. Short draft:

OPEN (about the warp). A warp which has ends set widely apart.

OPEN (about a fabric). A fabric with a low count, i.e., with few yarns to the square inch. This feature is highly desirable in such goods as shawls, scarves, curtains, and so on, but it is very difficult to achieve with ordinary weaves. The best of them is plain tabby, and the best yarn wool. But every open fabric thus made presents a certain amount of slippage (v). Only Cross-weaves (v) overcome this difficulty.

OPPOSITES. 1. "Drawn on opposites," or draft written on opposites. In Overshot weave, this means drafts which give patterns without the "half-tones" or half-shaded areas around blocks. E.g.:

Two shafts are needed for every block of pattern. In patterns written entirely on opposites the pattern weft does not tabby with the warp at all, and is very loosely bound to the fabric.

2. "Partly on opposites" means an overshot draft which has portions written as above, and other parts in plain overshot. E.g.:

3. "Woven on opposites." Usually Crackle or Summer-and-Winter weave executed so that, after every pick of pattern, another pick of contrasting colour is made on opposite shed (v). This kind of weaving (called sometimes Bound Weave) is best adapted for heavy fabrics, bedspreads or even rugs. Its purpose is two-fold: to do away with the binder,

which necessarily thins the fabric, and to obtain solid blocks of colour by covering the warp completely with pattern weft.   Since the weft is only lightly bound to the warp, due to the large number of floats, a very heavy

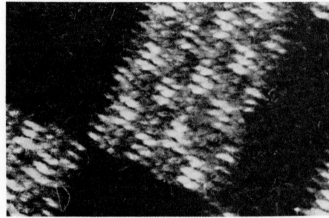

FABRIC
WOVEN
ON
OPPOSITE
SHEDS

beating is necessary to prevent the slippage.   When two opposite sheds are used alternately for several shots, the warp has a tendency to gather into small bundles inside the floats.   Shot of binder made from time to time will keep the warp spread evenly.   The same effect may have a pattern shot made on any of the remaining sheds.   E.g.:

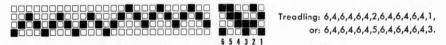

Treadling: 6,4,6,4,6,4,2,6,4,6,4,6,4,1,
or: 6,4,6,4,6,4,5,6,4,6,4,6,4,3.

OPPOSITE SHED.   A shed which raises all warp ends formerly sunk, and sinks all that were raised.   E.g.: B is opposite shed to A.

ORANGE PEEL.   Colonial pattern of the Cross-and-Table group.   Short draft:

ORGANDY or **ORGANDIE** (fr. Fr. *organdi*).   Very thin and stiff cotton fabric woven in tabby.

ORGANZINE (fr. It. *organzino*).   Silk thread composed of several singles (each single of 12 or more filaments) and twisted in the opposite direction to the singles.

110

ORLON. A synthetic fibre closely related to Nylon. Chemical name: polyacrylonitrile. It resists sunlight better than nylon, but is weaker in general. Orlon filaments resemble silk. The filaments can be cut up and spun, and then give a poor imitation of wool.

OSTWALD'S METHOD. Classification of colours (v) according to W. Ostwald.

OTTOMAN (fr. the name of a Turkish dynasty). Corded fabric of Turkish origin. Silk warp and cotton weft. The weft covers the warp.

OXFORD. Cotton fabric woven in basket weave.

OXFORD GREY. Grey colour of any fabric (particularly woollen) obtained by mixing white and black yarns in weaving.

OVERHEAD BATTEN. A batten (v) suspended from the Capes (v) of the loom frame. In its original form this type of batten is particularly well adapted to weaving with one shuttle. When the speed of weaving is the same as the swing of the batten, the beating becomes effortless, and the rhythm of weaving particularly easy to achieve and maintain.

OVERSHOT WEAVE. This weave is or has been known in every country where hand-weaving reached a fairly advanced stage, but it has been developed to the highest degree in Colonial weaving (v).

OVERSHOT
WEAVE

Overshot is essentially a 4-shaft weave, although it can be woven on a higher number. The pattern is produced by floats (nearly always in weft) on a plain tabby ground. There are four blocks of pattern: 1st, threaded on shafts 1 and 2 (e.g., 121212); 2nd, on shafts 2 and 3; 3rd, on 3 and 4; and 4th, on 4 and 1. Each block can be of any size, that is, produce floats of any length from 2 to about 16. Longer floats would not be practical. The blocks are joined so that the tabby order is preserved (no gaps between 1 and 3 or 2 and 4). Each shot of pattern is followed by a shot of tabby binder. In its classical form the pattern weft is slightly heavier than the warp or the binder, and of a different colour.

Typical overshot draft: Short draft:

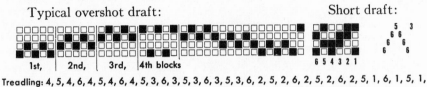

1st, | 2nd, | 3rd, |4th blocks   654321

Treadling: 4, 5, 4, 6, 4, 5, 4, 6, 4, 5, 3, 6, 3, 5, 3, 6, 3, 5, 3, 6, 2, 5, 2, 6, 2, 5, 2, 6, 2, 5, 1, 6, 1, 5, 1, 6, 1, 5, 2, 6, 2, 5, 2, 6, 2, 5, etc.

Overshot is woven either as-drawn-in (see Woven-as-drawn-in) or in Rose-fashion (v), or finally with a completely fancy treadling.

Overshot can be woven so that the colours and floats are in the warp only. Then the weaving is done with one shuttle. This method is used often in industrial hand-weaving. The warp has two colours which alternate in threading (see Turned Overshot).

The overshot in warp can be combined with overshot in weft to get borders on all sides of a tabby ground.

Overshot woven on more than four shafts is rather rare. E.g.:

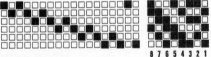

87654321

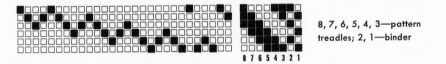

87654321

8, 7, 6, 5, 4, 3—pattern
treadles; 2, 1—binder

The elements of pattern used in overshot are: Cross, Diamond, Star, Rose, Table, Wheel, Hexagon, Octagon. The last two seldom found in Colonial weaving.

Overshot weave is very important from the historical point of view, but seldom used now in its classical form. See Modern Overshot.

112

PACE (fr. Lat. *passus* = step). A friction brake on the warp beam used in old looms (see Brake, Fig. 2).

PADDLE. A flat piece of wood used in warping when one portee has more than 4 ends. Its purpose is to make single crosses, although several ends are warped at a time. The paddle 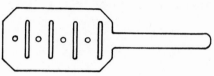 may have two rows of holes, or slits and holes alternately. A sleight of hand difficult to describe is necessary to produce the cross. The paddle is replaced by a Heck-Block in a Warping Mill (v) where two sets of small heddles are used.

PAISLEY SHAWLS. Imitation of Cashmere shawls made in Paisley, Scotland. The original Cashmere fabrics were brocaded, but the Paisley shawls were made on draw-looms of special construction.

PANAMA. Originally hats made in Central America. Later, very stiff cream-coloured cotton fabric woven in basket weave.

PAPER SPOT WEAVE (En.). The same as Dropped Tabby, but for a higher number of shafts. The weave belongs to a class of Double Spot Weaves, where the ground is woven on two shafts, but it also may be considered as a development of the Bronson Spot. E.g.:

In treadling, an even numbered treadle comes after an odd one, and *vice versa*. The higher the number of shafts, the finer are the patterns in paper spots.

The name of this particular weave remains a mystery, and probably has nothing to do with paper. An attempt has been made to compare the smoothness of the pattern blocks to the texture of paper, but it is not convincing.

PARROT. A shedding machine, operated by two treadles, and in turn controlling a large number of shafts or cords in a draw-loom.

PATCH PATTERNS. Very simple Colonial patterns of 2, 3 or 4 blocks. The most typical are two-block patterns such as Window Sash, Monk's Belt or Four o'Clock. They can be executed in any weave, and are best adapted for weaves which require a large number of shafts per block of pattern (Summer-and-Winter, Turned Twills).

PATENT HEDDLE. A steel wire heddle for Cross-Weaving.

113

PATENT NET. A Net-Weave (v) in which the Whip (v) forms hexagons on a background of Gauze (v). It has four whip ends, and four plain ones in each repeat. The hexagons are staggered.

PATTERN DRAFT (En.). The same as Draw-Down.

PATTERN HARNESS. In Two-Harness Method (v) the harness which weaves the pattern. Usually this function is performed by the second or back-harness, but for certain weaves such as Spot or Dropped Weaves it may be hung in front. When a pattern harness is mounted at the back it has ordinary heddle-eyes but longer heddles, when it hangs in the front it has shorter heddles with long eyes. Synonyms: Caam, Figure Harness.

PATTERN TWILLS. Twills of any kind which can produce a pattern (see Diamond Twills). With a higher number of shafts the number of possible patterns increases to a point where it defies all description. Pattern twills can be roughly divided into three classes: 1st, pattern in threading and treadling, biased twill in the tie-up; 2nd, plain threading and treadling, pattern (not necessarily symmetrical) in the tie-up; 3rd, pattern in threading, treadling, and the tie-up. E.g.:

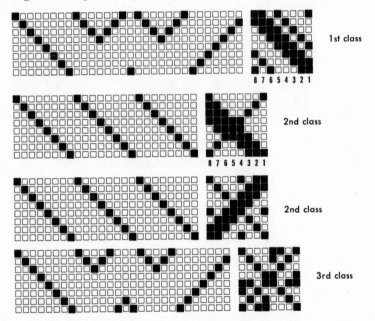

In all these examples the threading is identical with treadling, and no binder is used although tabby can be woven if necessary. As a rule the weft should be of the same count as the warp and of the same colour, or only slightly different. Contrasting colours make the pattern too obvious.

114

PATTERN VARIATIONS. Different symmetrical patterns obtained from the same threading draft. This is done by squaring (v) different combinations of pattern blocks, either with a diagonal (woven-as-drawn-in) or without it (Rose-fashion treadling). In weaves which permit weaving of two or more blocks at the same time (spot, lace, turned twills), two blocks give 4 combinations, three 16 variations, four 64, and so on. With other weaves, such as overshot or crackle, the number of variations is smaller: 6 for 4 blocks of pattern.

PATTERN WEAVING. Properly speaking, every weave has a certain pattern. Usually, however, this term is reserved for comparatively large and elaborate patterns only. A pattern may be obtained by combination of colours or texture, or both.

Patterns in colours only are: Stripes, Checks, Plaids, Two-Block patterns in Rep Weave, Log Cabin, small designs in tabby, and all tapestry weaves. In all the above cases the pattern would not be visible if not for different colours used.

Patterns in texture only are: Turned Twills (Dimity, Dornick, Diaper, Damask), Lace, Cross and Net Weaves, and Pile Weaves with different length of pile, or with cut and uncut pile. In these weaves the difference in colour between warp and weft is not only unessential but should be avoided.

We find combined texture and colour in such weaves as Overshot, Spot Weaves, Barley Corn, Summer-and-Winter, Pile Weaves, Lappet and all Tissue Weaves. They all will show a trace of pattern even without colour.

The more complicated the pattern, the more complicated the weaving equipment. Two-Harness Method, Draw-loom, and both combined are best suited for complex pattern weaving. Whenever the time element is of no importance Free Weaving has the largest possibilities and it requires hardly any equipment.

PAWL. See Ratchet Wheel.

PEARL COTTON. Loosely twisted two-ply mercerized cotton.

PECKER. The main part of a Parrot (v).

PEDAL (fr. Lat. *pedalis*). The same as Treadle.

PEG PLAN. The same as Lifting Plan.

PENCE (En.). 16,800 yards of yarn.

PERCALE (Fr.). Cotton fabric woven in tabby, rather fine (60 to 80 threads per inch), usually printed on one side.

PERLE COTTON. The same as Pearl Cotton.

PERLON. Synthetic yarn similar to Terylene; nearly as strong but less resistant to heat.

PERRY'S VICTORY. Colonial pattern of the Table-and-Cross group. Short draft:

```
6     6     6    6 4 3 4 4 3 4 4 3 4
  7  6 5 6   7 7   7     7     7   7
  6 6   5 5   6 6
  6   6     6   6   3 3   3 3   3 3
```

PHILADELPHIA PAVEMENT. Colonial Summer-and-Winter pattern. Short draft:

```
  2       2       2      6 1 1 1 1 1 1 6     2       2       2
  1 1     1 1     1 1    6 1 1 1 1 1 1 6     1 1     1 1     1 1
    1   1   1   1 1   4 1 4              4 1 4   1 1   1   1   1 1
  2       12      2      4 4              4 4     2       12
```

PICK (fr. AS *pecan* = to pull). One thread of the weft. Synonym: Shot.

PICKER. A part of the Fly-Shuttle equipment. Synonym: Driver.

PICKETS. A cross-weave (v) in which some of the warp threads are twisted together, when the others are woven in tabby. This weave is similar to Leno (v) with the exception that the rows of Gauze (v) are vertical instead of horizontal.

PICKING STICK. A part of the Fly-Shuttle equipment.

PICK-UP STICK. A flat, very smooth and pointed piece of wood, a little longer than the width of the warp, and about $1\frac{1}{2}$ inches to 2 inches wide. It helps picking up warp ends in certain classes of free-weaving. It is also used to enlarge the shed in cross and net weaves. The stick is inserted in the warp horizontally and then turned on edge.

PICK-UP WEAVING. Whenever the shed or a portion of a shed is opened not by the harness itself, but with fingers, a needle or a shuttle, the weaving is called "pick-up." This method is used in two cases: 1st, when the weave to be executed calls for more heddle-frames than the loom is supplied with, and 2nd, in Free Weaving, i.e., when the weft does not pass the shed from end to end in one straight line. The pick-up is a very slow method, and consequently it is justified either in high-quality work such as tapestry, or when a small but complicated pattern is woven on a large piece of plain weaving. The shed is seldom opened with fingers only. Usually the ground shed (for tabby, twill, etc.) is opened first, and only then the warp ends required for the pattern are picked by hand.

PIECE (of cloth). The same as Bolt.

PIECE DYEING. Dyeing of fabrics after weaving.

PILE (fr. Lat. *pilus* = hair). Loops of weft or warp on the surface of a fabric. The loops may be left uncut, or all of them cut in two, or just a part of the loops is cut. Long floats either of weft or warp cut in the middle will form a pile. Special weft (chenille) will give the same effect in plain weaving.

116

PILE WEAVES. There are at least five different techniques of weaving pile fabrics:

1. Chenille (v). The pile weft is woven separately, and then introduced in the shed.

2. Rows of alternate floats are made on tabby ground, exactly as in overshot, provided that the pile weft will tabby with several warp ends between two floats. When the fabric is taken off the loom, the rows of floats are cut in the middle with a special knife called Plough. Neither thick nor long pile can be made this way. See: Corduroy.

3. The same as 2 with floats in warp instead of weft.

4. The weft is pulled up at regular intervals above the shed, and a rod is inserted in thus formed loops, in the same way as in Tufted weaving. The length of loops depends on the diameter of the rod. The loops may be cut, or left uncut. Since the loops are made by pick-up, the work is very slow, but on the other hand it is the easiest way of weaving complicated patterns in pile.

5. The Warp-Pile Weave (called also Velvet Weave) requires at least two warps, one for the ground, and one or more for the pile. The pile warp must be wound on a separate warp beam or beams, since it is much longer than the ground warp (5 to 10 times). If the fabric has any pattern, one additional warp beam is necessary for each block of the pattern. In old "figured velvets" hundreds of small independent warps were used. The harness has two sections: one for the ground of at least two shafts, and one for the pile with as many shafts as blocks in the pattern. These two sections can be set quite close together.

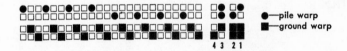

●—pile warp
■—ground warp

4 3 2 1

The treadles 4 and 3 are used to weave the ground and at the same time to bind the pile to the ground. After several picks of weft on 4 and 3, treadle 2 is depressed for the first block of the pattern in pile. In this shed, instead of weft, a metal rod is introduced. On its size depends the length of pile. Since the pile-warp beam is only slightly braked, the pile-warp will go around the rod, after the shed 2 is changed for the shed 3. Several picks of ground are woven again, then treadle 2 used once more, and a new rod put in place. When 5 or 6 rods are thus in the fabric, the first of them may be pulled out. If cut pile is desired, the loops are cut

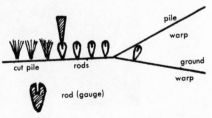

cut pile   rods

rod (gauge)

pile
warp

ground
warp

when the rod is still in place. To make the cutting easier, the rod has a groove in its upper surface, and a special cutting tool, called trevette, fits into this groove, thus making all pile ends of the same length. The second block is woven in exactly the same manner on the first treadle. When the whole fabric is to be covered with pile the pattern may be formed by: two piles of different length, cut and uncut pile, or pile of different colours. In the first case treadles 2 and 1 will be used alternately, e.g.: 43434321, and rods of two different sizes—one for treadle 2, another for treadle 1. With the same treadling, and rods of one size, the pile may be cut on treadle 2, and left uncut on treadle 1.

Patterns in colours require a different threading:

r—red pile warp
w—white pile warp
■—ground warp

4 3 2 1

The treadling will be 4343432 for the first block, and 4343431 for the second.

PILE-ON-PILE. A velvet with two piles of different length.

PILE WARP. Additional warp much longer than the ground warp. It forms pile in such fabrics as Velvet.

PINE TREE. A component of Colonial patterns (v) suitable for weaves in which blocks of pattern can be combined (Summer-and-Winter, Double, Turned Twills).

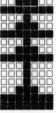

Pine tree

PIQUÉ (Fr.). Corded cotton fabric. Cords parallel to the warp.

PIRN (origin unknown). The same as Bobbin (R).

PLAID

PLAID (fr. Gael. *plaide* = blanket). Fabric with identical stripes of colours in warp and weft.

118

PLAIN THREADING. The simplest diagonal threading which can be made on any number of shafts. E.g.:

 or:

PLAIN WEAVE. The same as Tabby weave.

PLAIT (fr. Lat. *plecta* = rope). See Braid.

PLISSÉ (Fr.). Cotton crepe chemically treated.

PLUG. In a fly-shuttle the weft is wound on a plug which does not turn on the shaft. The weft comes off one end of the plug.

PLUG-WINDER. A bobbin winder (v) with a shaft fitting the plugs.

PLUSH (fr. Fr. *pluche*). A pile fabric similar to velvet but with longer pile.

PLY (fr. Fr. *plier* = fold). One strand of fibres twisted together. Yarn may have one or more plies, and is called accordingly: single, two-ply, three-ply, etc.

PLYING. The action of twisting together several single threads. It may be done on a Doubling Stand, which gives a very slight twist, or on a Spinning Wheel.

POINT REPEAT. Part of a draft which is symmetrical to a former part. E.g.:

A is point repeat of B

The term is usually applied to the threading draft, but it may be used in connection with a treadling draft as well.

POLE (prob. fr. Fr. *poil*). The same as Pile-Warp (R).

POMEGRANATE. Colonial pattern (v) of the Bow-Knot group. Short draft:

$$9\ 9\ 9\ 9 \quad\quad 6\ \ 10 \quad\quad 9 \quad\quad 10\ \ 6\ \ 4$$
$$4\ \ 6\ \ 10 \quad\quad 10\ \ 6\ \ 4$$
$$2\ 2\ 2\ 2\ 2\ \ 4\ \ 8 \quad\quad 10 \quad\quad 10 \quad\quad 8\ \ 4\ \ 2$$
$$4\ \ 8 \quad\quad 10\ 10 \quad\quad 8\ \ 4$$

POND LILY. Colonial pattern (v) of the Wheel-and-Rose group. Short draft:

$$4\ \ 10\ \ 5\ 5\ \ 10\ \ 4$$
$$4 \quad\quad 4\ \ 6\ 3\ 6$$
$$4 \quad\quad 4\ \ 7\ 7$$
$$4 \quad\quad 11\ 5\ 11 \quad\quad 4$$

PONGEE (fr. Chinese). Silk yarn or fabric made of natural, not cultivated silk.

POPLIN (fr. Fr. *popeline*). Fine, corded fabric made of silk and worsted, or of fine cotton and worsted. Ribs in weft.

PORREY CROSS (fr. Gaelic *porr*). The cross or lease at the end of a warp, i.e., the end coming last in beaming. Compare Beaming.

PORRY or **PORREY.** Part of warp between the harness and the lease (R).

PORT (En.). 280 yards of yarn.

PORTEE (fr. Fr. *portée*). In warping, the total number of threads taken from one end of the warp to another, and back. E.g., if four threads are wound simultaneously, the portee will consist of eight threads or ends. Synonyms: Bout, Gang.

PORTEE CROSS. The cross or lease made at the beginning of a warp, i.e., at the end which comes first in beaming.

PORTER (prob. fr. Fr.). 1. The same as Beer. 2. 50 yards of linen yarn.

POWER LOOM. Any weaving loom operated by power (other than the weaver's hands and feet) entirely or partially.

PRESSER HARNESS (origin unknown). The same as Double Harness. See Two-Harness Method.

PRIME WOOL. Short and weak wool from the part of the fleece lying just above the hind legs of a sheep.

PRINCESS ROYAL NET. A Net-weave similar to the Patent Net (v), but in which the pairs of Gauze and the shots of weft are so spaced that the whip forms circles instead of hexagons.

PRINCIPAL WEAVES. The same as Basic Weaves.

PRINTED FABRICS. Fabrics on which the pattern is printed, usually after weaving. This is done either with carved cylinders which print in a continuous way, or with flat blocks (Block Printing).

The warp may be printed before weaving (v Warp Printing), or the weft is printed. The latter method is used only in industrial power weaving to make imitation of tapestry.

PROCESSING. The same as Finishing.

PROFILE. The same as Graphical Short Draft. See Short Draft.

PULLEY BOX. In a Draw-Loom a box placed directly above the Comber Board, with as many small pulleys as there are cords in the Tail.

PULLEY CORDS. In a Draw-Loom cords between the Pulley Box and the Necking Cords.

PURLES (fr. Fr. *pourfiler* = to embroider). A cross weave in which blocks of gauze alternate with blocks of tabby.

120

QUADRILL. Overshot pattern. Short draft:

```
6  6 4              4
    5     3     5
  3   7 4 4 7
4 4   4 7   7 4
```

QUARTER (En.). Nine inches of yarn, or of warp.

QUEEN'S DELIGHT. Colonial pattern (v) of the Star-Rose-and-Table group. Short draft:

```
6 5 5 5 5 5 5 6     4       4       4       4
              6 3 6   7 7   6 3 6   7 7   6 3 6
                  7 7   6 3 6   7 7   6 3 6   7 7
        5 5 5 5 5 5 5 5     4       4       4       4
```

QUEEN'S FANCY. Colonial pattern (v) of the Star-and-Table group.

```
9 9 9 9 9 9 9 9 9         7 7
              7       7   7       7
                6 3 3 6       6 3 3 6
        3 3 3 3 3 3 3 6   3 3 3   6 5 6   3 3 3   6
```

QUEEN'S VICTORY. Colonial Two-Block pattern.

```
10 10 10 10 10 10 10 10 10 2 2 2 2 2 2 2 2 2 2 2 2
   2 2 8 2 2 8 2 2 8 8 2 2 2 2 2 2 2 2 2 8 8
```

QUILL. A tiny paper cylinder used in the hand shuttle instead of a bobbin. Originally quills (feather shafts) were used for this purpose.

QUILL WINDER. The same as Bobbin Winder.

QUILLED FABRIC. The same as Corded Fabric (v).

QUILT WEAVE (fr. Fr. *cuilte* = mattress). A double weave (v) in which two layers of fabric, usually of different count, are stitched together. Between these two layers are inserted shots of very heavy weft (wadding). Four-shaft quilt weave:

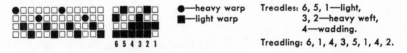

●—heavy warp   Treadles: 6, 5, 1—light,
■—light warp   3, 2—heavy weft,
                   4—wadding.
6 5 4 3 2 1   Treadling: 6, 1, 4, 3, 5, 1, 4, 2.

With more than four shafts, the stitching may form a pattern:

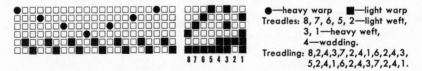

●—heavy warp   ■—light warp
Treadles: 8, 7, 6, 5, 2—light weft,
            3, 1—heavy weft,
            4—wadding.
8 7 6 5 4 3 2 1   Treadling: 8,2,4,3,7,2,4,1,6,2,4,3,
                     5,2,4,1,6,2,4,3,7,2,4,1.

The stitching will form a diamond. The shafts Nos. 3, 4, 5, 6 are called Stitching Leaves. Compare: Turned Quilt Weave.

RACE. The lowest horizontal piece in a batten. It has a groove in its upper surface and it supports the reed. In some looms (and in all fly-shuttle looms) the race extends forward, and is slightly inclined to form a support for the shuttle, which "races" over it. It is inclined outwards for a hand-shuttle, and inwards for a fly-shuttle. In most modern looms, the "race" proper is entirely lacking, and the shuttle travels on warp alone. Synonyms: Race-Block, Race-Board, Race-Plate, Race-Rod.

RADDLE (fr. AS *hriddle* = sieve). A long wooden lath with vertical pegs or rods, usually set on the slabstock during the beaming, to keep the warp uniformly spread. The distance between pegs of a raddle may be anything from ¼ of an inch to 2 inches. Sometimes the pegs are covered with another piece of wood (cape) after the warp is spread and before beaming starts. This cape has either a groove or a row of holes in its lower face.

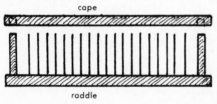

cape

raddle

A spare reed can be used instead of a raddle, but a reed is much less satisfactory since it cannot be fixed firmly to the slabstock, and since it requires an additional operation of transferring the lease in warp from one side of the reed to the other. Synonyms: Spreader, Evener, Raith, Ravel.

RAG RUGS. Rugs which have strips of cloth of any kind for weft. Long band torn from a piece of fabric is wound between two fingers to form figure 8, and then put loosely in the shuttle.

The simplest rugs thus made have no pattern except for hit-and-miss effects, when different colours of weft are used. Stripes are easy to obtain, and plaid effects can be produced as well since the warp is not covered by weft. Two-block warp patterns (compare Rep) can be made on the condition that the warp is closely set. Finally, flat tapestry technique may be adapted to rag rug weaving. The warp should be of a neutral colour and comparatively open. Low-Warp (v) is better here than High-Warp. Interlocking should be avoided; wefts of two different colours may be linked on two alternate warp ends (See Interlocking).

RAISED PATTERN. Any pattern which is woven so that it rises above the ground. This effect is obtained either by using heavier and softer yarn for the pattern than the one for the ground (overshot, crackle, lined work) or by giving different tension to the pattern, and ground threads, both in warp and weft (double weave, tissue weaves). In double weave and tissue weaves the ground warp is wound on a separate warp beam, and consequently the difference in tension is easy to maintain.

RAITH. The same as Raddle.

122

RAMIE or **RAMEE** (fr. Malayan). A perennial nettle native of Asia. Fibres and yarn made of this plant resemble linen.

RATCHET WHEEL. A wheel used both on warp and cloth beams, which turns freely in one direction but is prevented from turning back by teeth inclined all in one direction, and a pawl which engages these teeth.

RATINÉ (Fr.). A texture yarn with one ply wound in a loose spiral around the core. In weaving it gives an effect similar to both: boucle and nubby yarn. Fabric woven with this yarn.

RATTLESNAKE. Colonial pattern (v) of the Star-and-Rose group.

Short draft:

$$\begin{matrix} 8\,3\,8 & & 4\,5\,\,4 \\ & 8\,3\,8 & 4 & 5\,4 \\ & 7\,7 & 4 & 4\,5 \\ 7\,7 & & 5\,4\,\,4 \end{matrix}$$

RAVEL (fr. Dutch *rafelen* = disentangle). The same as Raddle (R).

RAYON (fr. Fr. *rayon* = ray, beam). Artificial fibre obtained chemically from cellulose. Imitates silk (gloss and continuous filament), or wool, when cut into short fibres and spun. It has less resistance to friction than wool or cotton, and less tensile strength.

READS and **UNREADS.** In the texture of a fabric the portions of weft covered by warp are called "unreads," and those which are not covered, "reads." A weave may be shortly described by the number of reads and unreads in one repeat. E.g.: tabby is one read, one unread; 1:3 twill, one read, three unreads, etc. (R).

REED. A straight row of evenly spaced metal blades set between two shafts. Originally reeds were made of split reed stalks, hence the name. The blades used now are either steel or brass. The distance between two blades is always the same in one reed, except sometimes at the edges, where it is slightly greater to overcome the tendency of warp to form thick edges (v Selvedge), but such an arrangement of blades will work only when the whole width of the reed is used. Even spacing of blades is obtained by a wire or cord being wound around the shafts of the reed. The thickness of wire plus the thickness of blade gives the distance between blades.

The width (or length) of a reed may be anything from 12 to 90 inches. The height is from 3 to 5 inches. The number of dents per inch (or Sett, or Dentage) most widely used is between 8 and 20.

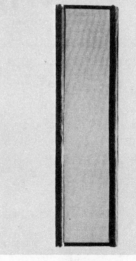

REED

123

When the sett of a reed is designated by a number it may correspond to the number of "beers" (v) in 24 inches, or the number of hundreds of dents in 34, 37 or 40 inches, or the number of dents in 2 inches. In metrical system the number of a reed means the number of dents in 10 centimeters (roughly 4 inches). Synonyms: Sley, Slay, Comb, Loom-Comb.

REED HOOK. The same as Entering Hook (v).

REEDING. The same as Sleying.

REEL (fr. AS *hreol*). A simple wooden frame or wooden cross with pegs on the four ends. It may serve to make the skeins (see Swift), or to unwind them (compare Bobbin Winder). Large reels are used for warping (see Warping Reel).

REP or **REPP** or **REPS** (prob. fr. *Rib*). Corded upholstery fabric made of wool, cotton, silk or their mixture. Ribs in warp.

REP WEAVE. A derivate of Tabby with warp set so closely that it covers the weft. Two wefts are used alternately: one very heavy and another very fine. The fabric has ridges parallel to the weft. If the warp has all odd numbered ends of one kind of yarn, and all even ends of another, the fabric will have its two sides woven in two different yarns.

Cross-section of Rep along the warp

The same applies to the warp made of two alternating colours: the fabric will have one colour on one side and the second colour on the other.

Two-block pattern can be woven on 2 shafts (**O** and ■ colours):

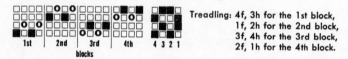

1st · 2nd blocks · 2 1

Treadling: 1f, 2h for the 1st block,
1h, 2f for the 2nd block.
(f—fine weft, h—heavy weft)

With 4 shafts we can have 4 blocks of pattern:

1st · 2nd · 3rd · 4th · 4 3 2 1
blocks

Treadling: 4f, 3h for the 1st block,
1f, 2h for the 2nd block,
3f, 4h for the 3rd block,
2f, 1h for the 4th block.

Six blocks are also possible with 4 shafts, but then at least a part of the fabric will not be woven in true tabby:

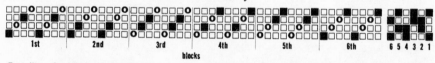

1st · 2nd · 3rd · 4th · 5th · 6th · 6 5 4 3 2 1
blocks

Treadling: 1st block: 6f, 5h; 2nd block: 4f, 3h; 3rd block: 2f, 1h; 4th block: 5f, 6h; 5th block: 3f, 4h; 6th block: 1f, 2h.

For this last rep the warp must be set much closer than usual to cover the weft. See also: Corded Fabrics, Two-Warp Corded Fabrics.

REPAIR HEDDLE. A cord heddle made on the loom, when a mistake is found in threading. A special steel wire heddle, which can be snapped on the shaft, and which serves the same purpose.

124

REPEAT. In threading or treadling drafts, the smallest number of ends or picks which form one complete pattern. E.g.: in diamond twill:

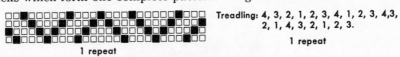

Treadling: 4, 3, 2, 1, 2, 3, 4, 1, 2, 3, 4,3,
2, 1, 4, 3, 2, 1, 2, 3.

1 repeat

1 repeat

Whenever drafts of more complicated patterns are given without any further explanations, they are drafts of just one repeat. Compare: Comber Repeat, Point Repeat, Turnover and Drop-Turnover Repeat.

RETTING (fr. old En. *retten*). A process of fermentation which separates the fibres in flax stalks. See Flax.

RETURN. To reverse the pattern in weaving as in a Point Repeat (v).

REVERSED. About a weave means that either the direction of a pattern is reversed in threading or treadling, or that the ratio between the weft and warp is reversed (3:1 instead of 1:3 twill). In the latter case the weave is said to be Turned.

REVERSED TWILL. 1. Any twill reversed in treadling. The same as Wave Weave. 2. In England, the same as Turned Twill (v). 3. In U.S.A., the same as Double Twill, i.e., double cloth woven in twill.

RHYTHM. The sequence of movements during weaving. This includes: opening the shed, throwing the shuttle, beating and closing the shed. In normal weaving opening and closing of sheds is done in one movement. Beating comes usually at the time when the first shed is just closed, and before the second shed opens. On the timing of these two operations (changing the shed and beating) depends the quality of the fabric. If beating comes a fraction of a second *before* the changing of sheds, the edges will have a tendency to draw-in. They will spread more if beating comes *after* changing the sheds. The rhythm may be different for different weaves (e.g., basket) and fabrics, but in one piece of weaving it must be always the same. The rhythm includes also the speed of weaving which should never be changed in the same fabric.

RIB WEAVE. Term used in industrial weaving, no corresponding term in hand-weaving. A cross between basket weave and tabby. Should be called: half-basket. Examples:

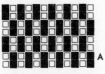 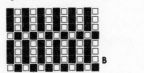 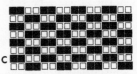

The weave produces faint corded effect in weft (a) or warp (c), or a rep (b).

RIBBED FABRICS. The same as Corded Fabrics.

125

RIDDLES (fr. AS *hriddel* = sieve).   A cross-weave with the same threading as Pickets (v), but woven as Leno (v).   As a result, squares of Gauze appear on a solid tabby ground.

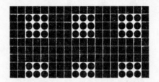

RIGID HEDDLE.   A heddle-frame made all in one piece, whether of wood or metal.   It has alternate holes and vertical slits.   It is used as an ordinary shaft for narrow fabrics.   In most cases rigid heddles were not

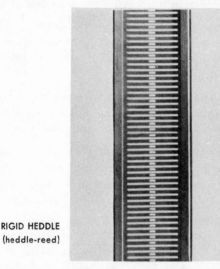

RIGID HEDDLE
(heddle-reed)

hung in a harness but held in hand.   Since not only every sett of the warp, but nearly every pattern would require a separate set of rigid heddles, they have at the present only historical value.   Similar heddles made of steel are used now in teaching and occupational therapy in connection with "no-harness" looms (v), and are known under the name "heddle-reed."   They replace the batten, as well as the shafts.

RIPPLING (fr. G. *riffeln*).   The action of separating the flax seeds from the stalks (see Flax).

RISING SHED.   A shed in which the upper part corresponds to the shafts tied to the working treadle, when the unconnected shafts form the lower part.   Independent action looms with single tie-up have rising shed, as well as table looms.   Compare: Shedding Motion, Sinking Shed.

ROCKER.   The same as Rocking Shaft in a hanging batten.

126

ROCKING SHAFT. 1. A shaft on which the Pecker slides in a Parrot (v). 2. The cross piece on which hangs the batten. The shaft is supported by the capes of the loom. There are two different ways of setting it. It may have two steel rods inserted horizontally, one at each end, and there are corresponding notches in the capes. Or two steel prongs project vertically from the lower face of the shaft. They rest in depressions made in small steel plates fixed to the capes.

ROCKING TREE. The same as Rocking Shaft in a Batten.

ROLAG (fr. Fr. *rouler*). The yarn ready for spinning, after it has been carded. Synonyms: Cardings, Rove, Slub, Roving.

ROLLER. Any of the rotating, cylindrical parts of a loom. In counter-balanced looms the harness is often hung on long wooden shafts, and these are invariably called rollers. But the same name is often given to the warp-beam (Cane-Roller) and cloth-beam (Breast Roller).

ROSE (Colonial term). A component of a larger weaving pattern, not necessarily Colonial. E.g.:

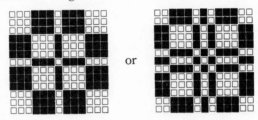

or

ROSE OF SHARON. Colonial pattern (v), the same as Indian War.

ROSE FASHION TREADLING. In Colonial overshot, such a treadling which will produce a symmetrical pattern without a diagonal. Thus it is the opposite of "woven-as-drawn-in" (v). To figure out this treadling we take the original (or basic) treadling draft which gives a diagonal, and turn it, i.e., in a standard tie-up we replace the treadle 1 with 4, 2 with 3, 3 with 2, and 4 with 1, leaving the number of shots for each block unchanged.

ROSENGANG. A small weaving pattern usually in Diamond Twill, with or without binder, but suitable for any other weave. Draft:

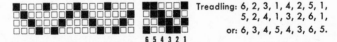

Treadling: 6, 2, 3, 1, 4, 2, 5, 1,
5, 2, 4, 1, 3, 2, 6, 1,
or: 6, 3, 4, 5, 4, 3, 6, 5.

ROSEPATH. The same as Rosengang.

ROUNDEL (fr. Fr. *rondel*). A component of weaving patterns of Persian origin. It is an oval in which one or two symmetrical figures are enclosed.

ROVE, ROVING (origin unknown). 1. The same as Rolag. 2. Very slightly twisted cotton yarn.

RUG FILLER. The heaviest weft used only in tapestry and pile rugs. The best rug filler is made of wool, which does not need to be of a very high quality. Cotton is the second best. Rug filler, to be of any use, must have a very large range of colours.

RUG WEAVING. Rugs differ from other fabrics inasmuch as they are much heavier and more resistant to wear. Any weave which permits very close weaving and hard beating may be used here. Long floats are to be avoided. If pile is used, it must be a thick one. In most cases large patterns are preferable to the small ones. Weaves which satisfy all these demands are:

For flat rugs: Crackle and Summer-and-Winter when woven on opposites, Rep Weave with warp patterns, Quilt Weave (only for plaid patterns), Turned Twills with short floats (1:2, 1:3). The best of all, however, are Tapestry Weaves (v) since they permit a complete freedom of design.

For pile rugs: Warp Pile Weaves (v Pile Weaves) are very simple, but the proper thickness of pile is not easy to obtain. The best technique is knotted pile, which although very slow gives the highest quality in pile rug weaving. This kind of weaving may be done either on a frame

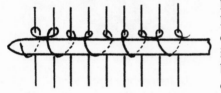 loom of proper size, or on any horizontal loom. The warp is heavy cotton or linen set at 5 to 10 ends per inch. The same or lighter yarn for binder, and very heavy wool, silk, or cotton for pile. A rod similar to Velvet rod (v) but much wider is necessary to secure a uniform pile. Several shots of binder are woven in plain tabby (seldom in twill) after every row of pile. The pile weft gets around the rod, then makes a knot and again a loop around the rod, and so on. Whenever the colour changes, the pile weft is cut off and another is used for the next knot. When one whole row is finished, the pile is cut and the rod removed. The knots may be tied always on the same pairs of warp ends, or staggered. In the second case the vertical lines are slightly blurred. There are many variations of the above technique, and several knots used, but the principle remains the same. Compare: Ghiordes, Sehna, Single Warp Knots.

The second best and much faster method of weaving pile rugs is chenille. See: Twice Woven Rugs.

RUSSIAN DIAPER. A simple diamond pattern in Overshot Weave.

RYA. Norwegian pile rugs.

128

SAMPLE FRAME.   Very small Frame Loom (v).

SAMPLE LOOM.   A small table loom, with a large number of shafts. The width of warp does not need to exceed 8 inches. As the name indicates, the loom is designed to make samples only, and is entirely unsuitable for any other kind of weaving.

SAMPLER.   A piece of weaving which shows variations of pattern executed on the same threading, by changing the order of treadling, the colour, and the grist of weft.

SAMPLER

SARAN.   Synthetic yarn made from resin.   More resistant to heat than Vinyon but weaker.

SATEEN or **SATINE.**   Imitation of Satin Fabric, made of other yarns than silk, or a weft-face satin fabric (more picks than ends per inch).

SATIN FABRIC (fr. Lat. *setinus* = made of silk).   A heavy silk fabric in Satin Weave. It has silk both in warp and in weft and then it is woven 50:50, or just silk in warp (proper satin, or warp face) with more ends than picks to the inch, or silk only in weft (satine, or sateen, or weft-face) with more picks than ends.

SATIN WEAVE.   Broken twill of the type 1:N (from 1:4 to 1:15) with ties placed so that the distances between them (moves) are nearly or quite

129

equal in all directions. Since this condition is not easy to fulfil with any number of heddle-frames, some satins are considered to be better than others. The best are: 1:4, 1:7 and 1:9. In Britain "full satin" is 1:15 and "Half-Satin" 1:7. E.g.: 1:4 satin:

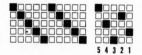 Treadling: 1, 2, 3, 4, 5.

The main object of satin weave is to have nearly all weft on one side and nearly all warp on the other side of the fabric. At the same time the diagonal or diagonals formed by the ties should show as little as possible. The texture thus obtained is extremely soft and smooth. The weave may be executed with any yarn or yarns, but silk and other soft and shiny yarns are most effective. The satin weave is the basis of all damasks, and of many Tissue Weaves.

SATINET or **SATINET TWILL.** Imitation of satin made in 1:3 broken twill. E.g.

 Treadling: 4, 1, 3, 2,
or: 3, 1, 3, 2, 4, 2, 1, 3, 1, 4, 2, 4.

To get the right effect the warp should be set not as for 1:3 twill, but much more open. The weft should be heavier than warp, soft and glossy.

SCARLET BALLS. Colonial pattern of the Rose-and-Table group. Short draft:

```
3 3 3 3 3 3 3 3 3 3 3 3        6 6        6 6
                         8 5 8     8 5 8     8 5 8
                           9 9       9 9       9 9
3 3 3 3 3 3 3 3 3 3 3 3        5         5       3
```

SCOBB (prob. fr. Lat. *scobis* = sawdust). The same as Blotch (R).

SCOURING (fr. Lat. *excurare*). Removing grease and dirt from cloth or raw wool.

SCUTCHING (fr. Lat. *excussare*). Cleaning the flax fibres (see Flax).

SECTIONAL WARP BEAM. A warp-beam usually of large diameter (up to 36 inches in circumference) with its length divided into a number of equal sections, separated with metal rods or wire loops. The width of one section is not more than 2 inches.

Each section of such a warp beam is beamed separately, and the warp is not prepared beforehand. A rather large bobbin rack is required for this technique, since as many bobbins as there are ends in two inches of warp must be placed on this rack. All ends of one section are wound simultaneously on the beam. A short raddle keeps them spread, and it is advisable (but not necessary) to pass the ends through lease rods, and secure the cross with a cord after each section is finished. When all sections are beamed, the lease rods are passed through the crosses again. With long warps it is well to use a revolution counter on the warp beam, so as to make sure that all sections are of the same length.

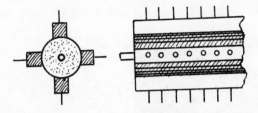

The advantage of sectional warping is that the whole operation may be performed by one person. The disadvantage—that the tension of warp may change from section to section [a Tension Box (v) helps here], and that it requires an extra large bobbin-rack for fine weaving. The time required for preparing the bobbins, and for the beaming itself, is rather longer than in standard warping and beaming.

SECTIONAL WARPING MILL. A warping mill used only in industrial hand-weaving for very long warps. It works on the same principle as a sectional warp beam. A large quantity of warp is prepared in this way and then transferred on the warp beams, which must be removed from the looms for this purpose.

SEEDING or **SEED WEAVE** (origin unknown). A weave based on the same principle as Turned Overshot (v), i.e., with floats of pattern in the warp. The floats may be so loose as to form loops, or even pile, or quite flat (dumb seed). In most cases one additional warp beam is required for every block of pattern, which seldom covers the whole fabric.

SEERSUCKER (fr. Hindu). A silk or linen and silk fabric with repeated rippled stripes running lengthwise. This effect is obtained by giving different tension to the alternate sections of the warp.

SEHNA KNOT (fr. *Sehna* in Iraq). A carpet knot used mostly in the Far East. It is made on two warp ends, circling only one-half of the first and the whole second end.

SELVAGE. The same as Selvedge.

SELVEDGE (fr. *Self+Edge*). The portion of a fabric nearest to the edges, and the edge itself. The selvedge should be straight and strong, particularly for loosely woven fabrics. Whenever possible it is woven in a simple weave, preferably tabby. With most weaves to have a tabby selvedge means two additional shafts and a separate warp-beam, because tabby requires more warp for the same length of cloth than any other weave.

131

The straightness of the selvedge depends on several factors, besides the skill of the weaver, probably the most important one being the way the weft is wound and held in the shuttle. Every time the weft catches, there is a dent in the selvedge. A too freely rotating bobbin may leave

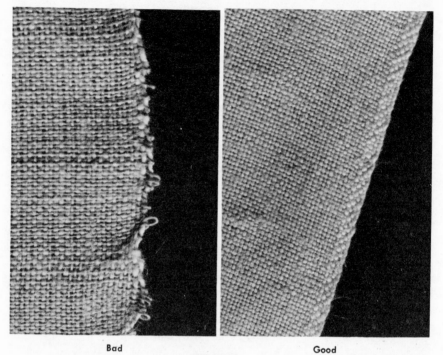

Bad   Good

SELVEDGE

loops on edges. The same effect will have a shed not sufficiently opened, or a rough and closely set warp. To get a good selvedge under all conditions the shuttle should have some kind of braking action on the weft. If not, the weft may be braked with the thumb, but this slows the weaving considerably.

Uneven tension of warp during weaving will make the edge wavy, it will be drawn-in more when the tension is greater. A smaller but still noticeable effect on the edge have: the distance between the harness and the cloth, the composition of yarn (e.g., stiff weft on soft warp), and the rhythm of beating.

The selvedge may be even, but still not satisfactory. This happens when the edge is thicker than the rest of the fabric, a very common phenomenon, due either to too much tension in warp or weft. Synonyms: List, Selvage.

132

SEMICIRCULAR WEAVE. The same as Double-Width Weave (v).

SERGE (fr. Fr. *serge*). Worsted fabric woven in twill.

SERGE WEAVE. The same as 1:2 or 1:3 twill.

SET OF LEAVES. Any number of shafts used for weaving one block of a pattern in such weaves as Turned Twills, Double Weaves, Turned Quilt Weave, and so on. E.g., one set for the simplest damask has 5 frames; for Double Weave, 4 frames, etc.

SETT. Alternative spelling of "Set," but in weaving used only when speaking about the warp, i.e., about the number of ends per inch. Thus a warp has a sett of 24 when there are 24 ends to the inch. The same applies to the reeds and raddles.

The sett of warp depends so much on the fabric woven that there are no general rules for figuring it out. The lowest sett should be such that, with a given weave, it does not show any slippage in a finished fabric, and the highest that the shed will still open without undue strain on the warp. The ratio between these two may be as high as 1 to 3. However, once the sett is established it is easy to figure out a sett for a different grist of warp yarn, provided that the weave is the same. In all circumstances the sett should be proportional to the square root of the count of yarn. E.g., when a satisfactory fabric has been obtained with linen No. 14 set at 24 ends per inch, a similar fabric will have 48 ends with No. 56, or 12 ends with No. 3½.

A practical way of establishing the Sett is to wind the warp yarn on a ruler so that the yarns hardly touch each other, and then count the number of turns necessary to cover one inch. This number is about right for double weaves and warp-face fabrics. It must be divided by 2 for tabby (and Swivel, Huck with tabby, Bronson, etc.), and by 1½ for twills. This rule is a very approximate one, and does not work with fabrics where the weft is much heavier than the warp.

In industrial hand-weaving the following formulas are used:

$$N = 0.9 \times \sqrt{yds/lb.}$$

which means: the highest possible number of ends per inch is equal to nine-tenths of a square root of the number of yards per pound of the yarn used for warp. This number must be divided by the coefficient given by the second formula:

$$S = \frac{R+T}{R} ;$$

where R is the number of ends in one repeat of the weave, and T the number of times the weft comes from the back to the front of the fabric and *vice versa*, also in one repeat. Thus S for tabby is 2; for 2:2 twill, 1½; for 3:3 basket, 1.3, etc.

133

SETTING-UP. About a loom, means either assembling a loom which has been dismantled, or Dressing (v) the loom.

SEVEN STARS. Colonial pattern of the Star-and-Table group. Short draft:

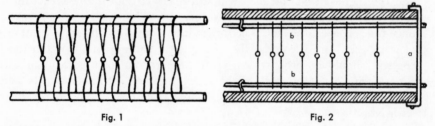

SEVENTH (Obs. En.). One-seventh of a Split (in warping) or about thirteen inches.

SHAFT (fr. AS *sceaft* = pole). A wooden bar with half-heddles hanging from it. One of the two bars in a Shaft (2) or frame on which the heddles are threaded. Synonyms: Maitland Cord, Heddle-Stick, Shed-Stick, Leash-Rod (to be distinguished from Lease Rod).

SHAFT (2). A shaft is a wooden or metal frame which holds a number of heddles. The simplest frame is made with two heddle-sticks or shafts which pass through the doups of the heddles (Fig. 1).

Fig. 1   Fig. 2

A better model has two strong cords (Maitland Cords) tied to the shafts; the heddles are threaded on these two cords. In both cases the heddles are fixed permanently to the frame so that a separate set of heddle-frames is required for every sett of warp. The heddles are then made in groups and not individually. This kind of shaft is excellent for extremely fine weaving, particularly with clasped heddles, because it reduces the friction between the warp and the heddles to a minimum.

When two upright pieces of wood or metal are fixed to the ends of shafts, the necessity of tying the heddles permanently to the shafts disappears and the heddles can be moved on the shaft, taken off or added at will.

A modern shaft, which can be used either with cord or steel heddles, has a frame made of two long strips of wood, and two vertical pieces of flat steel (a). Two steel rails (b) are held in place by two locks in the sides (a), and one hook in the centre. The heddles slide with hardly any friction on the rails, which makes the threading much easier. The heddles can be added or removed even during the threading.

Frames used in table looms are often of a much simpler construction. Sometimes even the number of heddles on each frame cannot be changed.

134

A different type of frame is used in special multi-shaft looms. Here the thickness of the frame is reduced to about ⅛ inch. Synonyms: Leaf, Harness, Harness-Frame, Heald, Heddle-Frame, Frame, Heddle, Stave.

SHAFT HARNESS. An optional part of a Draw-Loom which simplifies its construction. It replaces to a certain extent the Ground Harness in the Two-Harness Method (v). The heddles passing through the Comber Board can be operated either singly by the Simple, or in groups raised with treadles.

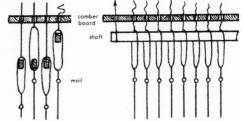

Each heddle has a loop above the Mail but below the Comber Board. The loop is about 4 inches long. A thin wooden shaft passes through all loops in one row of heddles. When the shaft is lowered it does not interfere with the normal operation of the Simple, and the pattern is woven in the usual way. But when making one pick of the ground, one of the shafts is lifted by a treadle, and all heddles in the corresponding row rise with it. Synonym: Split Harness.

SHAFTY WOOL (origin unknown). Long, strong and coarse wool (see Sorting).

SHAG (fr. AS *sceacga*). Coarse velvet.

SHANTUNG (Chinese). A tabby fabric of native nubby silk. Its imitation in rayon.

SHAPPE. Spun silk.

SHED (fr. AS *sceadan* = to separate). A triangle formed by the two parts of the warp and the reed when any of the treadles is depressed. The lower part of shed is *sunk*, the upper *raised*. In most looms the shed opens in both directions at the same time, because one part of the harness pulls it down when the other pulls it up. In other looms it is only raised.

Rising shed is a shed which opens in both directions but in which the shafts connected with a treadle rise, i.e., form the upper part of the shed. This action takes place in all single tie-up jack looms. Table looms also belong here, although they have no treadles, but the depression of a lever makes the corresponding shaft rise.

SHED

135

Sinking shed is the opposite of the rising one, i.e., the shafts connected with a treadle form the lower part of the shed. All counterbalanced looms have sinking shed, although the upper part of the shed rises, when the lower sinks.

Double tie-up jack-looms have both sinking and rising shed, since all treadles are connected with all shafts either through the short or the long lamms. Consequently it is necessary to distinguish between these two ties on the tie-up draft.

The number of different sheds possible with a given number of shafts is at least equal to the number of treadles, but often much larger. Thus a two-shaft loom has two treadles and two sheds. Four shaft looms are usually equipped with 6 treadles, but they have 14 different sheds. Six-shaft loom is operated either by 8 or 10 treadles, but the number of sheds is 64.

Opposite shed—See Opposite.

SHED REGULATOR. An optional part of a counterbalanced loom harness. It regulates the height at which the shed opens.

SHED STICK. The same as Heddle-Stick.

SHEDDING MACHINE. A mechanical appliance which permits selecting any required shed, and a large number of them, with two treadles only. The number of sheds, i.e., the number of all possible combination of shafts grows very rapidly with increasing number of shafts (see Shed) and it would be impossible to take the full advantage of all these combinations with treadles only. A number of different shedding machines was designed to overcome this difficulty: Dobby, Jack-in-the-Box, Jacquard, Parrot.

SHEDDING MOTION. The principle which operates the harness of a loom and which permits opening of different sheds. Compare: Counterbalanced Looms, Independent-Action Looms, Draw-Loom, Two-Harness Method.

SHEER FABRIC. Any light, transparent fabric.

SHEETING. Any fabric used for bed sheets. Mostly cotton or linen, woven in tabby, exceptionally in twill.

SHELL. In a batten, either hand-tree or race block, or both (R).

SHIFT (fr. AS *scyftan* = to divide). 120 yards of wool or cotton yarn.

SHIRE (in ME. thin and scanty). The same as Jisp (v).

SHOOT. 1. The same as Pick. 2. The same as Weft (R).

SHORT DRAFT (see Draft). Drafts written in full, particularly for large patterns and complicated weaves, would take too much space to be of any practical use. Consequently there are many ways of condensing the drafts, which are then called Short Drafts.

136

First of all, only one repeat of a weave or pattern is given, and a number placed underneath indicates how many times this repeat should be made. If the pattern is symmetrical it is sufficient to give the draft of the first half only, and mark the other as "point repeat." This applies both to the threading and treadling drafts.

In pattern weaving the binder if any is entirely omitted. Then the weave itself may be indicated at the beginning, and later only the blocks of pattern marked on the draft. Thus in Overshot it is quite sufficient to give the length and the relative position of blocks. E.g.:

In Spot Weaves, Bronson and Swivel the first shaft is omitted or marked by a continuous line. E.g.:

Full draft   Profile   Short draft

The second of the above drafts is called Graphical Short Draft or Profile. The third, Numerical Short Draft or simply Short Draft.

In all pattern weaves which have definite Units of Threading (v) one square in the profile means one unit (occasionally more than one but always the same number of units in the same profile). E.g.:

In this case the profile alone does not indicate the weave or the number of units in each square, and this information must be given separately.

Complicated tie-ups, particularly for Double Weaves and Turned Twills, can be also represented by short drafts (Binding Plans). E.g.:

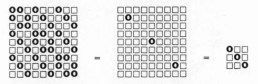

In the above tie-up for a three-block dimity (1:2 turned twill) the short draft has **o**'s to represent a block of 2:1 twill, when the remaining (not marked) blocks are 1:2 twill.

SHORT MARCH. The same as Lamm in a double tie-up loom.

SHOT. The same as Pick of weft.

SHRINKAGE. Reduction in width or length of the fabric during washing, processing and finishing in general.

The shrinkage in laundering depends not only on the weave but in a large degree on the yarn and count of cloth. Its amount may be only established in each case by experiment. In processing, i.e., in fulling and felting, the shrinkage is controlled at will and should be specified on the order.

SHUTE (prob. fr. *Shoot*). The same as Weft.

SHUTTLE (fr. AS *scytel*). An appliance which holds the weft, and which can be passed or thrown through the shed in the warp. The simplest

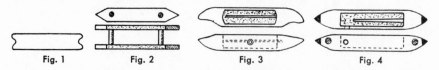

Fig. 1   Fig. 2   Fig. 3   Fig. 4

shuttle in a flat stick nearly as long as the width of the fabric. It has a notch for the weft on each end. It is put through the shed but it cannot be thrown (Fig. 1). A similar shuttle which, however, is thrown by hand, has two flat sides pointed at both ends, and connected with two round

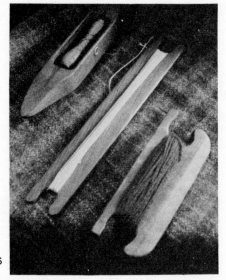

SHUTTLES

pegs (Fig. 2) on which the weft is wound. In both these shuttles the weft must be unwound before every pick. A shuttle in which the unwinding is continuous and automatic has a spool rotating freely on a spindle (Fig. 3). The shape, size and weight of a shuttle vary with the yarn used for weft, with the width of the fabric, and even with the weave.

138

A good hand-shuttle for all-around use should be from 8 to 12 inches long, 1 to 1¾ inches wide, and ¾ to 1½ inches deep. The weight 3 to 6 ounces. It is made of hardwood. Boxwood is supposed to be the best material. The points should be sharp and protected with metal caps, and the whole surface of the shuttle highly polished. The bottom may be smooth or with ridges parallel to its length. Sometimes it is provided with rollers to reduce the friction. The rollers are useful only when the shuttle runs on a race-board, which is seldom the case with modern looms.

The shuttle should have some arrangement to regulate the friction between the spool and the spindle, as the quality of the selvedge depends largely on this factor. Sometimes the spindle itself is composed of two thin steel wires, which can be bent more or less, thus acting as a brake on the spool.

Fly-shuttle (Fig. 4) is built more symmetrically than a hand-shuttle, has lead weights on both ends, the points are made of solid metal, and the weft comes off a plug which does not turn, but is set firmly on the spindle. The tension of weft is regulated by passing the thread through holes in the side of the shuttle.

SHUTTLE-BOX. A part of the Fly-shuttle equipment.

SHUTTLE-WOVEN. Any fabric which is woven entirely with the shuttle passing the whole length of each shed, as opposed to pick-up, inlay and other free techniques.

SILK (fr. AS *seoloc*). Silk filament is made by the caterpillar of the silk-worm (*Bombyx mori* and others of the same family). One cocoon contains two threads of about 1,000 yards. It undergoes only one operation, which consists of cleaning and twisting the thread at the same time. In most cases the silk-worm is cultivated. So-called wild silk comes from cocoons of wild silk-worms.

As a rule silk is not spun, since the filaments are of sufficient length to be used directly as yarn, after several of them are twisted together—this is called raw silk. Spun silk is made of short ends or broken filaments; it is carded and spun in the usual way. Thrown silk is made of several strands which have a different direction of twist than the whole thread. Boiled-off silk is obtained by removing the gummy substance which covers it in its natural state.

Silk yarn is very strong, smooth and glossy. It originated in China, and came to Europe through India and Persia. It is now cultivated in nearly every country of the world. See Count of Yarn.

SIMPLE (or Simblot, Symbolt—prob. fr. Fr. *simbleau* = cord). Part of a Draw-Loom.

SINGEING. Removing the nap from a finished fabric by passing a red-hot iron close to the surface. Compare Finishing.

SINGLE-WARP KNOT. A carpet knot used mostly in European carpets. The knots are made on all odd warp ends in one row, and on all even ends in the next.

SINKING SHED. See Shed.

SISAL. Fibres of the Sisal Plant (*Agave Sisalana*) growing and cultivated in Mexico, West Indies, East Africa and Java. Fibres are very coarse and are usually made into twine (about 300 yds/lb). Synonym: Sisal Hemp.

SIZE. A compound used for dressing (v) the yarn or fabrics. In hand-weaving used mostly in connection with warp dressing.

Size for wool: zinc chloride 1 part, beeswax 4 parts, gelatine 4 parts, flour 30 parts, water 2,500 parts.

For cotton: glycerine 1 part, suet 1 part, beeswax 1 part, zinc sulphate 2 parts, water 250 parts.

For linen: flax seed 1 part, water 20 parts. Boil and strain.

SIZING. The same as dressing the yarn.

SIZING MACHINE. Machine used in industrial weaving for sizing the warp.

SKEAN. The same as Skein.

SKEEN (En.). 120 yards of yarn.

SKEIN (fr. Ir. *sgainne*). A certain amount of yarn wound on a Swift or Skein-winder (v), then tied and removed. The skeins used to have standard size and weight; for instance, cotton—54 inches (in circumference), wool—54 inches, linen—90 inches. Now hardly any manufacturer keeps to these standards. The weight of one skein is often 8 ounces.

SKEIN WINDER. A cross of two wooden laths with pegs set near the ends. It turns either in the vertical or horizontal plan. It is essentially the same as Swift, and differs mostly by the use to which it is put. When a swift is used to unwind the yarn, the skein-winder serves to make skeins of yarn after spinning. It has usually a counter of revolutions.

SKIP. The same as Float.

SLAB BEAM. The same as Slabstock.

SLABSTOCK (prob. fr. AS *slipan* = to glide). The back horizontal beam in a loom. The warp passes from the warp-beam over the slabstock to the harness. Synonyms: Bearer, Thread Carrier, Slab Beam, Back Rest.

140

SLATE. A component of Colonial patterns with over-lapping blocks. Not suitable for Overshot.

SLAY. The same as Sley or Reed.

SLEEPER (prob. fr. Sc. *sleip* or AS *slipan*). In a Draw-Loom the cord which connects necking cords with mails.

SLEY (fr. AS *slean* = to beat). 1. The same as Reed. 2. The same as Batten (R).

Slate

SLEYING. 1. Passing the warp through the reed. This is done either after threading or in one operation with threading with a longer hook. As a rule sleying is a simple operation and does not require any indications on the threading draft, except for the number of ends to be passed through each dent. In exceptional cases (cross weaves, chenille, etc.) the sleying is given in a separate numerical draft, or the threading draft is spaced properly:

 = 2, 2, 2, 2, 0, 0, 2, 2, 0, 0, 2, 2, 2, 2.

Numerical sleying draft

2. Figuring out the sett (v) of warp.

SLIP. 1. One section of a Comber Board (v). 2. 1,800 yards of linen yarn.

SLIP KNOT. 1. The same as Snitch Knot (v). 2. Simple running loop.

SLIPPAGE. A fault in weaving due either to a too open warp or weft, or both. The threads of warp slip over the threads of weft, or *vice versa*. This defect is present in every fabric to a certain extent, but should not be noticeable. Slippage is the main difficulty to overcome when weaving open (v) fabrics. The best yarn from this point of view is rough wool. Fulling stops the slippage of even very open woollen fabrics.

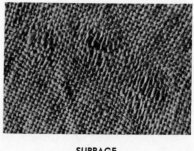

SLIPPAGE

SLUB (fr. Dutch = thick). 1. The same as Rolag. 2. The same as Tow.

SNAIL TRAIL. Colonial pattern of the Star-and-Rose group. Short draft:

SNAP (fr. Dutch *snappen*). 320 yards of woollen yarn.

141

SNITCH KNOT (prob. fr. snatch). A knot used for tying the treadles to the lamms. It does not slip unless the plain knot on the upper part of the tie is undone. The adjusting is done by tightening or loosening the plain knot. Synonym: Slip Knot.

SNOWBALL. Colonial pattern (v) or its component. Similar to the Rose (v) but with overlapping blocks. Not suitable for Overshot. Can be executed in all Spot Weaves, Double Weaves and Turned Twills.

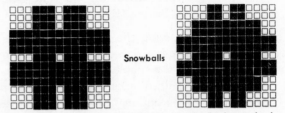

Snowballs

SNOWFLAKE. Colonial pattern (v) of the Star-and-Table group. Short draft:

$$\begin{smallmatrix} & & & & & 6 & 5 & 5 & 5 & 5 & 5 & 5 & 6 & 4 & & 4 & & & 4 & 5 & 4 & & 4 & 4 \\ & & 6 & 5 & 5 & 5 & 5 & 5 & 5 & 6 & 4 & & & 9 & 4 & & 9 & 9 & & 4 & & 4 & 9 & 9 & 4 & 9 \\ & & & & & & & & & & 4 & & 8 & 3 & 8 & & 4 & 4 & & 8 & 3 & 8 & 4 & \\ & & 5 & 5 & 5 & 5 & 5 & 5 & & 4 & 4 & & & 4 & 4 & 4 & & 4 & & 4 & 4 \end{smallmatrix}$$

SOLE. The same as Race Board (R).

SOLOMON'S DELIGHT. Colonial pattern (v) of the Star-and-Rose group. Short draft:

$$\begin{smallmatrix} & 4 & & & & 4 \\ & & 3 & 3 & & 4 & 5 & 4 \\ & & & 4 & 5 & 4 & & 3 & 3 \\ & 4 & & & & 4 \end{smallmatrix}$$

SOLOMON'S SEAL. Colonial pattern (v) of the Star-and-Rose group. Short draft:

$$\begin{smallmatrix} & 7 & & & & 7 \\ & & 7 & 3 & 3 & 7 & & 3 & 3 & 3 \\ & & & 3 & 3 & 3 & & 6 & 3 & 3 & 6 \\ & 7 & & & & 7 \end{smallmatrix}$$

SORREL BLOSSOM. Colonial Summer-and-Winter pattern. Short draft:

$$\begin{smallmatrix} & & & & & 6 & & 1 & 1 & & 6 \\ & 2 & & 2 & & & 1 & 1 & 1 \\ & & 1 & 1 & 1 & 1 & & & 1 & & & 1 \\ & 2 & & & & 2 & & 1 & & & 1 \\ & 1 & 1 & & 2 & & 1 & 1 & 1 & & & 1 \end{smallmatrix}$$

SORTING. Dividing the fleece according to the grade of wool. The grades are designated by numbers or special terms:

> *Britches*—wool on hind legs (very coarse)
> *Prime*—immediately above the Britches (short and weak)
> *Diamond* (No. 56)—still higher than Prime and in the hollow of the back (rather coarse and long)
> *Extra Diamond* (No. 58)—on shoulders and flanks (best wool, medium long, soft and strong)
> *Shafty* (No. 50)—around the Diamond, or in poorer fleece it can take the place of Diamond (long, strong and coarse)
> *Kemp*—stiff, discoloured wool of inferior quality.

SPANISH LACE WEAVE. A free lace weave in which the openings in a tabby ground are made by performing a double hair-pin turn with the weft, and then by pulling the weft more or less tight around the corresponding warp ends.

SPECK WEAVE. The same as Spot Weave (R).

SPETSVAV (Sc.). The same as Honeycomb (Colonial).

SPIDER NET. A Net-Weave (v) which differs from Whip Net (v) insofar as there are additional pairs of Gauze between pairs of Whip Net.

SPINDLE (fr. AS *spindel*). 1. A fast rotating shaft of any spinning equipment on which the yarn is wound. 2. The stationary shaft in a shuttle. 3. 15,120 yards of woollen or cotton yarn, or 14,400 yards of linen yarn.

SPINNING (fr. AS *spinnan*). Action of twisting together the fibres which are to be made into yarn. Since the fibres are overlapping each other, a thread of any length can be made from comparatively short fibres. The simplest spinning can be made without any implements by twisting the fibres between fingers. The simplest spinning implement is a spindle or a long rod with a weight (whorl) at its end. The whorl gives a uniformity to the rotation of the spindle and the long rod serves to accumulate the spun yarn. The upper end of the spindle has a notch by which it hangs on the fibres being spun.

SPINNING WHEEL. The main part of a spinning wheel is the spindle. The rest serves only to rotate the spindle and to guide the fibres. It is composed of a tripod, a large wheel, and a pedal which turns the wheel. Sometimes it has a Distaff to hold the unspun fibres. The spindle itself is a metal rod hollow on one end, so that the yarn passes axially into the spindle, and then out through a small hole in the side. The spindle has a pair of Fliers attached on both sides, and a pulley wheel fixed on the other end. It revolves in two leather bearings. The bobbin turns freely on the spindle, and has a groove cut around one of its ends. The large wheel turns the spindle and the bobbin at the same time, but the bobbin has a tendency to turn faster, the circumference of the groove being smaller than that of the pulley wheel on the spindle. The yarn comes through the hollow end of the spindle, then through the hole and around one of the hooks in the flier to the bobbin on which it is wound. The spinner regulates the twist by letting the yarn slip through the fingers slower or faster.

The spindle rotates between two vertical supports called Maidens, which are set in a horizontal piece (Mother-of-all). The tension of the cord which drives the spindle is regulated either by turning or sliding the Mother-of-all. The large wheel is connected with the pedal by a flat stick called the Footman.

SPLIT. 1. (fr. splitting the reed) The same as Dent in a Reed (v). 2. 90 inches of linen yarn.

SPLITFUL. The same as Dentful.

SPLIT HARNESS. The same as Shaft Harness (v).

SPOOL RACK. The same as Bobbin Rack.

SPOT LACE (See Spot Weave). A Lace Weave which produces lace effect particularly with linen. The weave may have floats (vertical or horizontal)

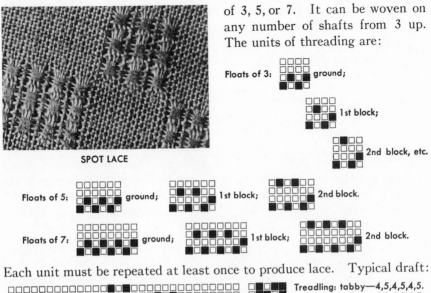

of 3, 5, or 7. It can be woven on any number of shafts from 3 up. The units of threading are:

Floats of 3: ground;

1st block;

2nd block, etc.

Floats of 5: ground; 1st block; 2nd block.

Floats of 7: ground; 1st block; 2nd block.

SPOT LACE

Each unit must be repeated at least once to produce lace. Typical draft:

5x 4x 6x 4x 5x 5 4 3 2 1

Treadling: tabby—4,5,4,5,4,5.
1st block—4,3,4,3,4,5.
2nd block—4,2,4,2,4,5.
both blocks—4,1,4,1,4,5.

The units of treadling must be repeated also at least once Blocks of pattern with a larger number of shafts can be combined at will. One block may be woven with horizontal floats when another block will have at the same time vertical floats (See Turned Spot Weave). Synonym: Bronson Lace.

SPOT WEAVE

SPOT WEAVE. Originally in England this term meant pattern weaves with patterns in colour on a tabby ground. The weave had no floats, because all floats were cut off. Because of its similarity to the Swivel Weave used in industrial weaving, we call it now Swivel (v). In U.S.A.

144

Bronson (see Bibliography) described a similar weave, which was known later on as Spot Weave. The terminology was further complicated by the literal translation of Scandinavian "Spetsvav" also as a Spot Weave. To avoid misunderstanding we call now: Old English "Spot Weave"— Swivel; "Spetsvav"—Colonial Honeycomb; and Bronson Weaves are synonymous with Spot Weave.

A typical draft for plain spot weave is:

Treadling: 4, 3, 4, 3, 4, 3 (tabby),
2, 3, 2, 3, 2, 3, 1, 3, 1, 3, 1, 3,
2, 3, 2, 3, 2, 3, 4, 3, 4, 3, 4, 3.

4 3 2 1

In England the first shaft was called "fore leaf," the second "ground leaf," and the remaining shafts "spotting leaves."

See also: Turned Spot Weave, All-Over-Spots, Spot Lace, Bronson.

SPOTTING LEAF (En.).   One of the pattern shafts in Spot Weave (v).

SPREADER. The same as Raddle (v).

SPREADING. Passing the warp through a Raddle (v) before Beaming (v). The warp should be wider on the warp beam than in the reed to compensate for the take-up and to reduce friction in the reed. If the fabric loses one inch in width (when compared with the width of warp in reed), about two inches should be added in spreading. This rule is seldom observed in hand-weaving, and is important only when working with very fine or very brittle warp yarn. Spreading does not need to be precise, and is always done in full number of portees (crosses). Thus one dent of the raddle will contain 1, 2, 3, etc., full portees. To get the right average number of ends per inch, the next dent may have smaller or larger number of portees.

SPUN YARN. Any yarn which went through the process of spinning. Short fibres (wool, linen, cotton) must be spun, but very long fibres or filaments (silk, synthetic fibres) may be loosely twisted, or even not twisted at all. Thus Spun silk or rayon mean yarn spun from waste. In case of many synthetic fibres Spun yarns means that the filaments were first cut into Staple (v) and then spun to imitate natural yarns. Spun metallic yarns are made by twisting a flat, narrow strip of metal around a cotton core.

SPYNDLE. Obsolete spelling of Spindle.

SQUARING A PATTERN. Weaving a pattern in such a way that the finished piece will look the same from all directions. This applies to the pattern, but not to the texture or weave. The pattern to be squared must be first divided into blocks, and then each block is squared separately, starting with one end of the draft and moving block by block to the other end. In weaves where the blocks do not overlap they are made quite

145

square (see example), in other weaves they must be corrected for overlapping, so that they all lie on one diagonal. The treadling which gives a squared pattern with two diagonals is a basic treadling, and it serves to find out other variations of squaring (v Pattern Variations). Pattern squared with diagonals is sometimes called "woven as drawn in," when the patterns squared without diagonals are "rose-fashion woven."

STANDARD. The front heddle-frame with plain heddles used in Cross-Weaves.

STANDARD WEAVE. A vague term, which may mean either a Basic Weave (v), or any simple weave in which repeats in threading and treadling are the same.

STAPLE. Natural short fibres. Also short fibres made by cutting filaments of silk and of synthetic yarns.

STAR. A component of a larger pattern. E.g.:

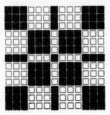 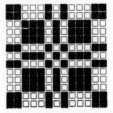

146

STAR OF BETHLEHEM. Colonial pattern (v) of the Blooming Leaf group. Short draft:

```
 4  10      4   4     10
    4   10  5 10     4
    4   10    4 4  10   4
    4  10    4  4   10  4
```

STAR OF THE SEA. Colonial pattern (v) of the Diamond-and-Table group. Short draft:

```
16 12 12 12 12 12 16      5 5     5 5     5 5
                    15       11      11      15
 4  4  4  4  4  4   16 6  4 6 6  4 6 6  4 6 16
                  16     6   6   6   6   6    16
```

STAVE (fr. AS *stoeff* = stick). The same as Shaft (R).

STITCHED DOUBLE WEAVES. Any double weave in which the two layers of cloth are stitched together from time to time. The purpose of stitching may be: to make a heavy fabric with fine texture, or to reinforce a loose fabric with a strong ground (similar to lining), or finally to produce a faint pattern.

In the first case we use plain double weave stitched closely (see Double Weave). In the second we may have, for instance, a very open basket stitched to a ground of tabby. In the third we have Quilt Weave (v).

STITCHING. 1. Weaving two layers of cloth stitched together. 2. Cutting down the length of floats in pattern weaves.

STOCK DYEING. Dyeing of fibres before spinning.

STOCKINET. Called so because of a certain resemblance to stockinet knitting. Twill weave similar to the Wave, but with shorter repeat in treadling.

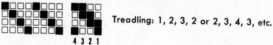

Treadling: 1, 2, 3, 2 or 2, 3, 4, 3, etc.

4 3 2 1

STRAND COTTON. 1. Loosely spun cotton. 2. 6- or 4-ply mercerized cotton.

STRETCHER. The same as Templet (v).

STRING HEDDLE. The same as Cord Heddle (v Heddle).

SUEDE (fr. Fr. = Sweden). Woollen or cotton fabric with short nap made by rubbing the surface of the fabric with emery. It imitates the Suede leather.

SUMAK (or Soumak or Summak—fr. Greek). A flat tapestry weave (v) in which the weft passes under two and then over four warp ends in the opposite direction.

SUMMER-AND-WINTER. The origin of the term is unknown. The weave is of Scandinavian origin. If Bronson Weave is now the same as Spot Weave, then Summer-and-Winter (called afterwards "S-and-W") should be called Double Spot Weave, since it requires two "fore leaves," or two shafts which carry half of the warp instead of one.   S-and-W played an important part in Colonial Weaving (v), although it required often more than 4 shafts.   Elements of pattern peculiar to S-and-W are: Snowball, Slate, and Tree, plus all the elements used in 4-shaft weaving.

SUMMER-
AND-WINTER

The weave has several advantages: short floats, well defined blocks of pattern, and solid blocks of colour when woven as a Bound Weave. It has units of pattern in threading:

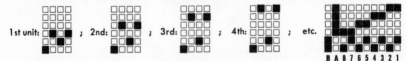

1st unit: ; 2nd: ; 3rd: ; 4th: ; etc.

B A 8 7 6 5 4 3 2 1

In treadling it requires *two* treadles for each block of pattern, not counting the tabby.   Thus the treadling for the 1st block (1st unit) is: 8B7A; for the second, 6B5A; 3rd, 4B3A; 4th, 2B1A, etc.   The units of threading and treadling can be repeated indefinitely.   The blocks of pattern can be combined without restrictions provided that we have enough treadles. Compound tie-up (v) is often used.

A typical draft of a 4-shaft S-and-W is:

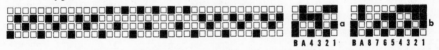

B A 4 3 2 1   B A 8 7 6 5 4 3 2 1

Tie-up "a" is the traditional one.   However, to get the full advantage of the weave tie-up "b" must be used.   The latter gives: ground only, 8B7A;

148

1st block, 6B5A; 2nd block, 4B3A; both blocks, 2B1A.

SUMMER-AND-WINTER (traditional)

The only limitation of S-and-W is the number of treadles required. Therefore it is often woven as Crackle (v) with only one treadle for each block of pattern, as in tie-up "c." The texture now is changed, but there is no need to use a compound tie-up. The treadling for the ground is: 4A4B; for the 1st block, 3A3B; for the 2nd, 2A2B; and for both blocks together, 1B1A.

Any S-and-W draft can be also Woven-as-drawn-in, and it gives a very satisfactory texture, but here again it requires a large number of treadles.

All floats in weft in S-and-W are of 3 or less, exactly as in Crackle Weave. From the point of view of drafting S-and-W is Crackle on opposites. Both weaves are identical in texture.

SUN, MOON AND STARS. Colonial pattern of the Star-and-Wheel group. Short draft:

$$\begin{matrix} & 5 & & 5\,5 & & & & & & & 5\,5 & \\ & & 6\,5\,6 & & & & & & & 6\,5\,6 & \\ 4 & & & 10\,3\,3\,3\,3\,10 & & & & 4 \\ 4 & & & 9\,9\,9\,9\,9 & & & & 4 \end{matrix}$$

SUNFLOWER. Colonial pattern (v). Short draft:

$$\begin{matrix} 4 & 4 & & & & & & 4 & 4\,3\,3\,4 & 3 & 4\,3\,3\,3 \\ & 4 & 3\,3\,3\,3 & & & 3\,3\,3\,3 & 4 & 3\,3\,3\,3 & & 3\,3\,3\,3 \\ 4 & 4\,3\,3\,3\,4 & 3 & 4\,3\,3\,3\,4 & & 4 & & \\ 4 & 4 & 3 & 3 & & 4 & 4 & & 3 & 3 \\ & & |8x| & & & & & & |8x| \end{matrix}$$

SUNRISE. Colonial pattern or a component of a pattern. Short draft:

$$\begin{matrix} 9 & 8\,8 & & 4 & & 5\,11\,5 & & 4 & & 8\,8 \\ & 9 & & 6 & & 4 & & 4 & & 6 & 9 \\ & & & & 4\,4\,4\,4 & & & \\ 8 & 8 & & 4 & & 4\,4\,4\,4 & & & 4 & 8 & 8 \end{matrix}$$

SWEDISH EMBROIDERY WEAVE. The same as Dukagang (v), or only pattern woven in Dukagang on plain background.

SWEDISH LACE. A Lace Weave (v) nearly identical in texture with Bronson Lace, but written in nearly the same way as Huckaback Lace. Compared with Bronson it has the same number of blocks but a better (more balanced) tie-up. When two or more blocks are combined there is a mark between the blocks (absent in case of Bronson). On the other hand, when Turned Lace is woven its blocks are better adjusted than in Bronson. Typical draft:

tabby   1st block   2nd block   tabby   B A 4 3 2 1

Treadling: Tabby, BA; 1st block, A2A2AB; 2nd block, B1B1BA; both blocks, B1212A; turned lace: 1st block, A4A4AB; 2nd block, B3B3BA.

149

There are incidentals both in threading and in treadling when two blocks join each other.

SWEDISH LOOM. The term has no definite meaning. Sometimes designates Double-Tie-Up Loom (see Independent Action Loom).

SWEDISH WEAVE. A tapestry weave of uncertain origin. It is the simplest weave of the flat knotted type (compare Sumak). The "knot" consists of only one turn of the weft around each warp end. The effect on one side is similar to plain flat tapestry; on the other side the fabric is corded.

SWEDISH WEAVING TERMS (simplified spelling). *Atlas* = satin; *avig-sida* = reverse; *avskara* = to cut; *barntacke* = baby blanket; *bereda* = prepare; *beredning* = set up; *bindning* = tie-up; *blekning* = bleaching; *bobinmaskin* = bobbin winder; *bobbin stalning* = bobbin rack; *bomull* = cotton; *bonad* = tapestry; *botten* = ground; *bredd* = width; *brostbom* = breast piece; *bundvav* = tabby; *bard* = edge; *borja* = begin; *damast* = damask; *dividera* = divide; *draga* = pull; *draperi* = drapery; *drakt* = dress; *drall* = cloth; *dubbel* = double; *enkel* = single; *figur* = pattern; *filt* = felt; *fin* = fine; *flor* = gauze; *flossa* = pile; *flossakniv* = trevette; *flossalinjal* = velvet rod; *frans* = fringe; *fall* = hem; *fardig* = finished; *farg* = colour; *fargning* = dyeing; *gagnefkrus* = honeycomb (colonial); *garn* = yarn; *garnbom* = warp beam; *garnharva* = skein; *garn-nummer* = count of yarn; *garnwinda* = swift; *gas* = gauze; *grov* = coarse; *halveblekt* = half-bleached; *hampa* = hemp; *harnes* = harness; *halkrus* = honeycomb (colonial); *halsom* = hemstitch; *harva* = skein; *harvel* = skein winder; *inlagd* = inlay; *inplock* = pick-up; *inslag* = weft; *kam* = reed; *kam-garn* = worsted; *kant* = selvedge; *kardull* = carded wool; *kavel* = roller; *kedja* = chain; *klinga* = blade; *klister* = size; *klot* = satin; *knut* = knot; *knyta* = tie· *knytning* = tying; *konst* = art, artificial; *korg* = basket; *krok* = hook; *krympa* = shrink; *kypert* = twill; *latta* = lever; *lin* = flax; *linne* = linen; *lod* = weight; *lang* = long; *los* = loose; *matta* = mat; *munkabalte* = monk's belt; *mang skaft* = multi-shaft; *mobeltyg* = upholstery; *monster* = pattern; *nickepinne* = rocking shaft; *nymodig* = modern; *nystvinda* = swift; *obalanserad* = un-balanced; *oblekt* = unbleached, natural; *par* = pair; *pinne* = peg; *plat* = flat; *plocka* = pick-up; *prov* = sample; *ram* = frame; *rand* = edge; *red* = reed; *redkam* = reed; *rips* = rep; *rullar* = roller; *ror* = dent; *sammet* = velvet; *sida* = page; *siden* = silk; *silke* = silk; *skaft* = shaft; *sked* = reed; *skedrok* = sleying hook; *skedtathet* = sett of reed; *skyttel* = shuttle; *skal* = shed; *skalpjalor, skalsticka* = lease rods; *slagbom* = batten; *slut* = end; *slat* = smooth; *solve* = heddle; *solvning* = threading; *solvnota* = threading draft; *solvskaft* = shaft; *solvtrissa* = jack; *spets* = lace; *spinnrock* = spinning wheel; *spole* = bobbin; *spolmaskin* = bobbin winder; *spannare* = template; *stad* = selvedge; *taft* = tabby; *tagghjul* = ratchet; *trampa* = treadle; *trasmata* = rag rug; *trad* = thread; *tuskaft* = tabby; *tyg* = cloth; *tygbom* = cloth-beam; *ull* = wool; *ulls-*

garn = woollen yarn; *uppknytting* = tie-up; *utreda* = unweave; *vadmal* = homespun; *varp* = warp; *varpa* = warping mill; *varpbom* = warp beam; *varpning* = warping; *vaffelvav* = waffle; *vaft* = weft; *vav* = weave; *vavknut* = weaver's knot; *vavning* = weaving; *vavnot* = draft; *vavsol* = loom; *ylle* = woollen cloth.

SWEET BRIAR BEAUTY. A Colonial pattern of the Star-and-Rose group. Short draft:

SWIFT (fr. AS *swifan* = to turn). A reel which serves either to wind the yarn into skeins, or to unwind it from skeins. The circumference of the

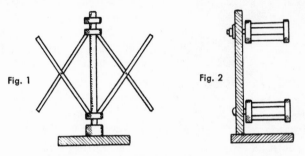

Fig. 1   Fig. 2

swift can be regulated according to the size of skeins, either by inserting wooden pegs into holes in the arms, or by other means, e.g.: folding swift (Fig. 1), or squirrel-cage swift (Fig. 2). Synonym: Windle, Reel.

SWINGLE (fr. AS *swingele*). A wooden appliance for breaking the flax.

SWISS. Light, stiff, transparent cotton fabric woven in tabby, with a simple pattern embroidered or woven.

SWIVEL WEAVE (*swivel* = a small shuttle). Weaving technique which gives an inlay effect. Usually small patterns are woven on a tabby background. The pattern weft makes long floats at the back of the fabric and the floats are cut off later on. Draft for a two-block pattern:

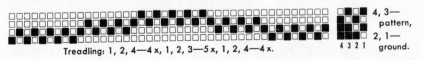

5 4 3 2 1

Treadle 1—1st block, treadle 2—2nd block, treadle 3—1st and 2nd blocks, treadle 4 and 5—tabby. Treadling: e.g., 1, 4, 5—5 x, 2, 4, 5—4 x, 1, 4, 5—5 x. The weft used in sheds 1, 2, 3 must be of different colour than the ground or binder.

For counterbalanced looms a more convenient draft is:

4, 3— pattern, 2, 1— ground.

4 3 2 1

Treadling: 1, 2, 4—4 x, 1, 2, 3—5 x, 1, 2, 4—4 x.

151

A better texture and pattern will be produced with the following tie-up and treadling:

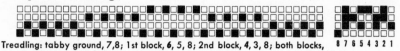

Treadling: tabby ground, 7,8; 1st block, *6, 5*, 8; 2nd block, *4, 3*, 8; both blocks, **8 7 6 5 4 3 2 1**
2, 1, 8.   Pattern weft (colour) on treadles 6, 4 and 2; ground weft on 1, 3, *5, 7*, 8.

All-over patterns in Swivel may have 3 blocks, but without tabby ground.   Then the treadling is: 1st block, *1, 2*, 8; 2nd block, *6, 5*, 8; 3rd block, *4, 3*, 8; 1st and 2nd blocks, *3, 4*, 8; 2nd and 3rd blocks, *2, 1*, 8.

SWIVEL WEAVE

Colour on numbers in italics.

Swivel can be woven on any number of shafts, provided that we have a sufficient number of treadles. The blocks of pattern can be of any size, but not smaller than 8 warp ends.   For smaller blocks use Turned Swivel (v).

The floats can be cut off close to the fabric after washing and ironing if the fabric is to be used on both sides.   They can be left intact for upholstery, bags, cushion covers, etc.   Or if too long, they can be trimmed about ½ inch from the fabric.

Swivel effect can be obtained with traditional weaves such as Diamond Twill, Overshot, Crackle, and Summer-and-Winter.   E.g.:

Treadling: 1, 3, 2, 4—all the way, but the colour follows the threading, when the   **4 3 2 1**
ground is thrown on the treadle which makes tabby with the first treadle.   Thus: *1,* 3, *2,* 4, *1,* 3, *2,* 4, *1,*
3, *2,* 4, *1,* 3, *2,* 4, 1, *3, 2,* 4, 1, *3, 2,* 4, etc.

All hand-woven Swivel Weaves have the pattern in Tabby on one side of the fabric, and long floats on the other.   Swivel can be also woven in Twill, on twill ground, or in Twill on tabby ground, but then it is not very practical, because the cut floats of the pattern have a tendency to pull out.   Synonyms: Spot Weave (En.), All-Over Spots (En.).

SYNTHETIC FIBRES.   Fibres made by chemical synthesis from raw materials which are completely different in all respect from the final product.   For instance, terylene fibre made from petroleum, salt, and coal. When the fibre has the same chemical composition as the raw material from which it was obtained it is not synthetic, but only artificial (e.g., Rayon, Glass, Metallic fibres).   More common synthetic fibres are: Nylon, Orlon, Perlon, Vinyon, Terylene, Polythene, etc.

SYNTHETIC YARNS.   Yarns made or spun from Synthetic Fibres.

152

TABBY WEAVE (fr. *Attabiya* near Bagdad). The simplest weave possible. It has a repeat of two threads in both directions. It may be executed on two shafts, although in most cases four are used to reduce the friction:

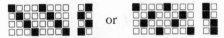 or

TABBY

Tabby is used widely not only in making cloth, linens and other fabrics, but also for ground in pattern weaving, and as binder in many weaves. When the count of threads is the same in warp and weft, the tabby is called "fifty-fifty" or Taffeta. When the warp is very open it may be completely covered with weft as in Tapestry weaving. On the other hand, by using very closely set warp we may cover the weft with warp (compare Corded Fabrics, Rep Weave, Warp patterns).

Two-block patterns can be woven in tabby, by alternating two contrasting colours both in warp and weft. One block has then horizontal stripes, and the other vertical ones. E.g.:

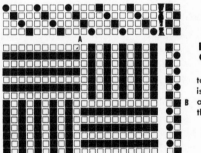

■—white
●—black

To change from one block to another, one of the colours is repeated both in threading and in treadling: A and B in the example.

Tabby produces very strong fabrics resisting both friction and tension, but the fabrics are comparatively stiff. When we try to get softer fabrics by making them more open, there is the danger of slippage. Also the insulating quality of the cloth is very low, because of the small amount of air between tightly packed fibres. From this point of view an improvement on tabby is Basket Weave (v), a derivate of tabby. Synonym: Plain Weave.

153

TABLE. A component of a larger pattern. It is a square made of rows of smaller blocks. E.g.:

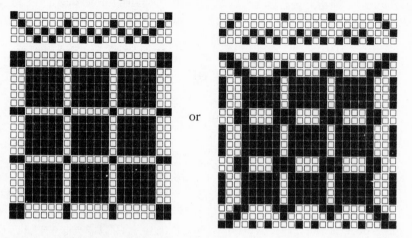

or

The first table is made on opposite sheds (1, 2 and 3, 4), the second has overlapping blocks (shed 1, 2 and 4, 1).

Since a table can have any size, it becomes very useful when a small pattern is enlarged several times. Then each block of the original pattern is replaced with a table of appropriate size (v Modern Overshot).

TABLE LOOM. Small loom operated by hands only. It has levers, usually on its right hand side. When a lever is depressed, the corresponding shaft rises. There are no lamms and consequently no tie-up. Since most treadling drafts are written for sinking shed (v) they should be corrected for table looms, or the cloth will be woven upside-down. The advantage of table looms is that they belong to the class of Independent Action Looms (v), the disadvantage that the weaving is very slow compared with foot-power looms.

TABLET WEAVING. The same as Card Weaving (v).

TACK (fr. Ir. *tacca* = fastening). A short cord connected with one of the cords in the simple (v Draw-Loom). A bunch of tacks tied together (Lash) opens one shed.

TAFFETA (fr. Persian *taftan* = to weave). 1. The same as 50:50 tabby. 2. Any fine, closely woven, light fabric of wool, wool on cotton, rayon or silk.

TAIL CORDS (or just Tail). The horizontal cords of a draw-loom harness.

TAIL STICK. The stick to which all Tail Cords are tied, and which in turn is fixed to the wall.

TAKE-UP. Reduction in width or length of the fabric during weaving. A fabric is always shorter than the warp on which it was woven, and it is narrower than the width in reed. The take-up of the warp may be anything from zero (weft-face corded fabrics) to 30 per cent (warp-face corded fabrics). Most often it is from 5 to 15 per cent. The take-up in weft should never exceed 10 per cent, and must be kept as low as possible by the properly set warp. Take-up during weaving depends on the following factors:

1. The weave. The longer the floats of a weave, the less take-up. Tabby shrinks more than any other weave. Satin shows very little take-up.

2. Sett of warp, and beating. Open warp shrinks less than a close one. Hard beating increases take-up both in warp and weft, but more in weft when the warp is open, and more in warp when it is a close one.

3. Tension of warp. When the warp is comparatively loose, there is less take-up in width; when it is tight, less take-up in length.

4. Tension in weft. The effect is just opposite to the tension in warp.

TAKE-UP MOTION. A part of a loom, which automatically moves forward the cloth after every beat of the batten. It is always found in power looms, very often in fly-shuttle looms, but seldom in ordinary hand looms. It consists of a combination of gears and weights, and of an additional roller which pulls the cloth uniformly. The advantage of a good take-up motion is not only the saving of time, but an even spacing of weft shots, quite independent of the weaver.

A simplified Take-Up Motion can be made by hanging a very heavy weight on the cloth-beam, and by adjusting the friction brake on the warp-beam so that it releases the warp at every beat.

TAPED ENDS. Warp ends threaded in pairs.

TAPESTRY (fr. Lat. *tapete* = hangings). A piece of elaborate weaving made for decorative purposes. In most cases tapestries are woven in free weaves peculiar to this kind of work. Heavy tapestries are called rugs or carpets.

TAPESTRY LOOM. The same as Vertical Loom.

TAPESTRY

TAPESTRY WEAVES. All Tapestry weaves belong to the Free weaves (v). They can be classified according to the way in which the

155

weft is attached to the warp into: Flat, Knotted, and Pile Tapestry Weaves.

The flat type can be woven in any of the simple weaves, provided that the warp is covered by the weft. In most cases it is tabby, sometimes broken twill, or just two staggered sheds of 1:3 twill, or even one shed of such a twill (with tabby binder). The problem here is to connect two adjacent blocks of different colours without leaving a hole or a ridge between them. In certain Oriental tapestries a slit is left whenever two blocks meet on a vertical line. In others the vertical lines are avoided or replaced by a very fine zigzag line (Navajo, Kilims). In still other cases the wefts are interlocking either between two warp ends or on one of them (compare Interlocking). When besides the pattern weft, a much thinner binding weft is used, this problem does not arise. Compare Brocading.

Knotted tapestry has weft which encircles each warp end, or makes knots on single ends, or on groups of them. It can be woven with or without binder.

Any flat or knotted tapestry can be executed in Low-Warp or High-Warp technique (v), but no binder may be used in High-Warp.

Pile tapestry is made so that the weft forms loops between each two knots on the warp. These loops may be later cut, or remain uncut. The binder is necessary here, and only Low-Warp technique is possible. Compare Rug Weaving.

TARLATAN (fr. It. *tarlantanna*). Light, sheer and stiff cotton fabric, woven in tabby.

TARTAN

TARTAN (fr. Sp. *tiritana* = fine silk). A sequence of coloured stripes, the same in warp and weft, peculiar to each Scottish clan.

156

TEASEL (fr. AS *toesel* = to tease). An implement used for raising the nap on a fabric.

TEASING. A primitive way of preparing the fibres for spinning by pulling them apart with fingers.

TEETHING. Wrong adjustment of the pattern in Double-Spot Weave.

TEG (fr. Scand. *tacka* = ewe). First coat of fleece.

TEMPLET (or Temple, fr. Lat. *templum* = lath). A weaving accessory which keeps the woven cloth from "drawing-in" or shrinking during weaving. It consists of two flat pieces of wood either hinged or sliding on each other. Their ends have two or more rows of sharp points on their lower surfaces. These points penetrate the cloth at the selvedges. The total length of a templet should be easily changed in comparatively large limits. The use of a templet should be avoided as much as possible, since it spoils the edges. Synonyms: Stretcher, Tenter Hook.

TENNESSEE TROUBLE. Colonial pattern (v) of the Star-and-Table group. Short draft: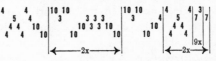

TENSION BOX. A braking device used in connection with Sectional Warp Beam (v). The warp coming from the bobbin rack passes through several short rollers, which constitute the tension box, and then through the raddle on the warp beam. The tension box when properly adjusted gives not only the same tension to all warp ends in one section, but to all sections as well.

TENTER or **TENTER HOOK** (fr. Lat. *tendere* = to stretch). The same as Templet.

TENTERING. Drying of finished fabrics, after washing, by stretching them on a frame, to avoid shrinkage.

TERRY or **TERRY VELVET** (fr. Fr. *tirer*). Velvet or any pile weave with loops left uncut.

TERYLENE. Synthetic yarn made of petroleum, salt and coal. As strong as nylon. Resistant to sunlight, and more resistant to heat.

TEXAS CHECK. Colonial pattern (v) of the Four-Block-Patch group. Short draft: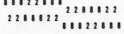

TEXTILE (fr. Lat. *textilis*). Anything woven, used in weaving, or relating to weaving, as Textile fibres, Textile industry, etc.

157

TEXTURE (fr. Lat. *texere* = to weave). Physical properties of a fabric. The arrangement of threads (without regard to their colour), their thickness, composition, twist, and count of cloth, all influence the texture. Sometimes by texture we mean only the appearance of a fabric, i.e., its roughness or smoothness, presence or lack of a nap, and so on.

For centuries the utmost effort of weavers went in the direction of fine texture, smooth or even glossy fabrics. It is only recently that weavers' interest turned towards rough yarns, or to simultaneous use of yarns of very different thickness and composition. The general tendency is to create fabrics which would present an irregular texture in appearance, but not in fact. That is, that the physical properties of the fabric do not change from inch to inch, although the apparent texture does. To achieve this aim we have three ways: 1st, Texture Weaves; 2nd, Texture Yarns; 3rd, combination of both.

TEXTURE WEAVES. There are many traditional weaves which produce uneven surface of the fabric: Waffle, Lace, Cross Weaves, Honeycomb, Crepe. Also many Pattern Weaves such as Overshot, Crackle, All-Over-Spots. But the changes in texture are too regular for modern effects. To achieve the "regular irregularity" they must be adapted to the modern requirements. The units of a weave may have different length both in threading and treadling. E.g.:

5 4 3 2 1

Treadling: 1, 4, 1, 4, 2, 4, 3, 4, 3, 4, 3, 4, 3, 4, 2, 4, 2, 4, 1, 4, 1, 4, 1, 4, 1, 4, 2, 4, 3, 4, 1, 4, 3, 4, 1, 4, 1, 4, 1, 4, 1, 4, 1, 4, 3, 4, 2, 4.

Or several weaves may be mixed in one draft:

Treadling:
1, 5, 2, 6, 4, 5, 3, 6;
or:
6 5 4 3 2 1   1, 5, 2, 5, 4, 6, 3, 6.

Finally, a completely accidental threading and treadling drafts are made in the following fashion: a deck of cards is made with numbers from 1 to 4 (for instance, 25 ones, 25 twos, 25 threes and 25 fours). Then the cards are drawn at random until the desired length of a repeat in threading is reached. The same is done for treadling except that the numbers are from 1 to 6, and that the repeat is much shorter. A standard tie-up of any kind is used. Before weaving a complete draw-down must be made on graph-paper to check for too long floats in warp or weft. E.g.:

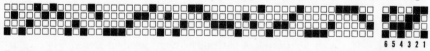

6 5 4 3 2 1

Treadling: 1, 5, 6, 2, 3, 4, 1, 3, 6, 5, 4, 2, 1, 3, 5, 6, 4, 2, 3; or 2, 6, 2, 5, 1, 6, 1, 5, 2, 3, 2, 4, 1, 3, 1, 4. etc.

158

All Texture weaves enumerated here are based on the probability calculus, and must produce an irregular yet uniform texture. However, in accordance with the same mathematical principle in each case, they must be

TEXTURE WEAVE

examined for too long and therefore impractical floats. Such floats if found are eliminated by crossing out the offending heddle (floats in weft), or the treadle (floats in warp).

TEXTURE YARNS. See Three-Dimensional Yarns.

THICKSETT (fr. closely set warp). The same as Corduroy.

THREAD. In handweaving the same as yarn. There is a tendency among handweavers to avoid the use of this word, except when speaking about sewing thread. The distinction does not seem to be justified.

THREAD CARRIER. The same as Slabstock (R).

THREAD COUNT. Number of threads per square inch in a fabric. It is expressed either by two numbers, first for warp, second for weft (e.g., 24x 32), or by their sum (56). Count of a finished cloth is always higher than the count on the loom, because of shrinkage.

THREADING. An operation which consists on passing the warp-ends through the heddle-eyes, or mails in a harness. As a rule this is done with a threading hook, but may be performed with fingers as well. The heddles should be pushed aside, to the left as well as to the right of the heddle to be threaded, then the hook is put through the eye, the warp-end placed in the notch of the hook, and pulled forwards. It is a good practice to tie together the ends of every repeat, after checking it up. The threading can be done either from the left hand side of the harness or from the opposite one. The latter is more common in America.

159

When threading and sleying is done in one operation, a longer hook must be used. It is first inserted into the proper dent of the reed, then into the heddle-eye, as before.

In cases when several warps are to be entered, it is advisable to thread them separately, leaving free heddles for the ends to come. This applies particularly to warp-pile weaves, quilt, and tissue weaves. Synonym: Entering.

Continuous threading. Such pattern threading which gives tabby as well. This applies particularly to such weaves as Overshot, Crackle and pattern Twills (Dornick Twill (v) does not give tabby sheds). *Broken* threading does not produce tabby regardless of the tie-up used. E.g.:

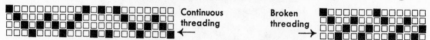

Continuous threading   Broken threading

Plain threading is one for the simplest twill. E.g.:

or   and so on.

THREADING HOOK. A flat steel blade with a notch at the end, mounted in a wooden handle. It should be narrow to fit into a heddle-eye, and thin, to pass between the blades of a fine reed. The shape and length

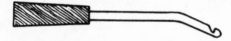

depends on the number of shafts in a harness, and on the manner of threading. It may be anything from 6 to 15 inches. The blade is often bent backwards.

THREAD MOUNTURE. The harness of a draw-loom. If there are two harnesses, the one with the comber board, or the back harness.

THREE-DIMENSIONAL. Anything which has three dimensions, i.e., anything at all. Three-dimensional or 3D weaves—the same as Texture Weaves.

THREE-DIMENSIONAL YARNS. The same as Novelty Yarns in industrial weaving. A yarn which has not only a length and width, but variations in thickness. See Bouclé, Nubby, Chenille, etc.

THROUGH-PUTS. Doups and Standards in old-fashioned gauze weaving, when clasped heddles (v) were used (R).

THROWING THE SHUTTLE. Throwing and catching the shuttle are the two most important operations in weaving, and the two most difficult to learn. Together with beating they have a decisive influence on the quality of a fabric. The shuttle should be held between the thumb (from above) and the middle finger (from below), the index slightly touching the point. The ring finger and the small finger hold the weft when a new bobbin in the shuttle is started, or when making fringes. In the moment of throwing the shuttle the index is the last to leave it and it gives the shuttle the proper direction.

When catching, only the thumb and the middle finger are working. The index must find its proper position before the next shot. The shuttle should not be stopped when it emerges from the shed, but carried away from it with a decreasing speed.

THROWN SILK. The same as Organzine (v).

THRUM (fr. Icelandic *thrömr* = edge). The end of a fabric taken off the loom, and cut off later on. These ends are sometimes used in rag-rug weaving.

TICKING. Any cotton fabric suitable for mattress covers, bed ticks, etc. It should be woven closely enough to be feather-proof.

TIE. 1. A cord or cords connecting one treadle with one lamm in a tie-up. 2. In weaves with long floats the point where the float in weft is caught under a warp end, or *vice versa*.

TIE-DYEING. A process in which the dye is unevenly distributed on a fabric, warp or yarn in skeins by tying it at regular intervals before dyeing. The places which are to remain undyed are tied first, then the yarn or fabric is dyed in the lightest colour, and the process of tying repeated for each consecutive colour, much in the same way as in Batik technique.

TIE-UP. An arrangement of ties connecting the lamms and treadles, or the treadles and shafts. In simple looms the tie-up consists of permanent single cords tying one shaft to each treadle, and is called *Direct Tie-Up*.

The purpose of the tie-up is to enable the weaver to open all sheds required for a certain weave with only one treadle for each shed. This is not always possible since the number of sheds which can be used on a loom is in most cases much larger than the number of treadles. Thus for more complicated weaves the tie-up should be so contrived that any shed could be opened with no more than two treadles depressed simultaneously.

E.g.:

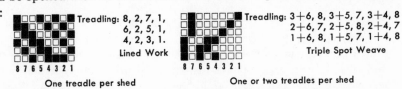

Treadling: 8, 2, 7, 1,
6, 2, 5, 1,
4, 2, 3, 1.
Lined Work

8 7 6 5 4 3 2 1
One treadle per shed

Treadling: 3+6, 8, 3+5, 7, 3+4, 8
2+6, 7, 2+5, 8, 2+4, 7
1+6, 8, 1+5, 7, 1+4, 8
Triple Spot Weave

8 7 6 5 4 3 2 1
One or two treadles per shed

The order in which the ties are placed depends on the treadling. The treadles which require more pressure to open the shed should be placed towards the ends of the lamms; those which are most often used should be in the centre. On the other hand, when there are some treadles for the pattern and some for the ground alone, it is advisable to separate them so that one foot operates the ground, and the other the pattern. These conditions are sometimes contradictory, and a perfect solution is impossible. In so-called Standard tie-up for overshot, crackle and twills, several variations are used:

The first is the best when there is about as much tabby as pattern in the weave. The second when there is little tabby, the third when most of the weaving is tabby.

Single tie-up (each shaft is connected with only one lamm) is used in all counterbalanced looms, and in the independent-action looms with weighted shafts. The double tie-up means that each shaft is tied to one lamm (short) which pulls it down, and to another (long) which pulls it up. In single tie-up drafts a mark (usually a circle) means that the corresponding lamm is tied to the treadle. In double tie-ups two kinds of marks are used: one to denote a tie with a short lamm, and another for a tie with a long lamm. In double-harness method some of the ground shafts are not connected at all, then a free space is left in the draft. E.g.:

The tie itself should be strong and adjustable. The classical way of tying consists on having two loops fixed: one to the treadle, another to the lamm and connected together with a snitch-knot (v). Two single cords tied with a square knot are nearly as good if heavy cord is used, although more difficult to undo. Modern ties are made with a single loop fixed to the lamm, and with a snap lock at its lower end. Its length is adjusted by a screw in the lock or, less satisfactory, by a square knot with which the ends of the cord are tied to make the loop. The lock snaps on an eye-screw in the treadle. Ties which cannot be adjusted are worthless. Synonym: Cording.

TISSUE WEAVES (fr. Fr. *tissu*). Any pattern weave which has a binder not only in weft but in warp as well. The binding warp and weft make a solid ground on which the pattern may be formed by floats of pattern weft, and of pattern warp. The latter may be made of light and soft yarn which otherwise would not stand the tension during weaving. As a rule this weave requires a separate harness for the ground, and always a separate warp beam for pattern warp. The tissue weaves are used mostly

162

for complicated patterns woven on a draw-loom. The only weave of this class, which can be made on an ordinary loom, is the turned quilt weave, on the condition that the warp for one layer will be made of fine and strong yarn, and that the tension of this warp during weaving will be much greater than that of the other (pattern) warp. Compare: Turned Quilt Weave.

TOBINE or **TABINE** (fr. *Tabby*). Warp overshot used for decorating edges of fabrics. Coarse silk fabric woven in twill.

TONGUE. An extension of a treadle which can be used at the same time as the treadle, or omitted, depending on the position of the weaver's foot.

TOP. Combed wool ready for spinning.

TOP-CASTLE. The horizontal beam on the top of a loom. The top-castle supports the rollers, pulleys, horses, or coupers. Synonym: Heddle-Bearer.

TOP MOUNTING. The same as Upper Tie-Up.

TORTOISE. Overshot pattern. Short draft: $\begin{smallmatrix} & & 9 & & \\ 4 & 9 & & 4 \\ & 3 & 3 & 6 \end{smallmatrix}$

TOW (fr. AS *tow*). Short flax or hemp fibres rejected in heckling.

TOW. About one pound of flax fibres.

TRAFALGAR. A cross-weave (v) essentially the same as Purles (v) but with the blocks of gauze forming diamond patterns.

TRAM (fr. Lat. *trama* = weft). Lightly twisted silk weft.

TRAMP. To tread, treadling.

TRANSCRIBING. Changing a draft written for one weave into another draft, both having the same pattern, but not the same weave.

TREADING. The same as Treadling.

TREADLE. In a foot-power loom, a pedal which operates a lamm, or which releases the brake on the warp-beam. The brake treadle is hinged at the back, the other treadles either at the back (in older looms) or at the front. The arrangement of treadles in a loom is a problem which is very difficult to solve satisfactorily, since the number of treadles which can be easily operated is about a dozen, and the number of sheds in some weaves much higher. Thus in industrial hand-weaving special machinery was introduced to open the required sheds with two treadles only. Compare: Shed, Shedding Machines, Tie-Up. Synonym: Pedal.

TREADLING. The order in which the treadles are depressed during weaving. Compare: Draft, Tie-Up. Synonym: Lifting, Looming Plan, Peg Plan.

163

TREVETTE (Fr.).   An adjustable knife for cutting the pile in pile fabrics, particularly Velvet.

TRIPLE HARNESS.   A harness built on the same principle as Double-Harness (see Two-Harness Method), but with three sections.   Each section handles a different colour.   By mixing the colours any shade and any pattern can be obtained, but the harness is rather complicated and suitable only for heavy fabrics.

TRIPLE SPOT WEAVE.   A Spot Weave (v) in which there are three "fore-leaves," i.e., in which half of the warp is equally distributed on three front shafts.   This changes the texture of the weave insofar that the pattern floats lie on a diagonal instead of being simply staggered as in the Double Spot Weave.   E.g.:

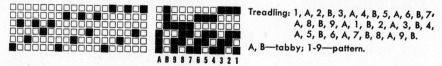

Treadling: 1, A, 2, B, 3, A, 4, B, 5, A, 6, B, 7,
A, 8, B, 9, A, 1, B, 2, A, 3, B, 4,
A, 5, B, 6, A, 7, B, 8, A, 9, B.
A, B—tabby; 1-9—pattern.

TRIVET.   Corruption of Trevette (v).

TROMP-AS-WRIT.   Colloquial colonial expression—the same as Woven-as-drawn-in.

TUBING.   Any fabric woven in circular weave, particularly a narrow fabric.

TUFTED WEAVE.   A free, weft-pile weave.   It may be executed on two shafts threaded for tabby, but a third shaft is very helpful in spacing the pile evenly.   The following draft may be used, although the distance between the ends threaded through the third shaft depends on the yarn used.   It should not be smaller than 4 ends.

Treadling: 1, 2, 1,
or: 1, 2, 1, 2, 1.

The last shed is the pile shed.   By depressing the treadle No. 1 we raise shafts 1 and 2.   Since there is always a slight difference in the height to which the shafts of the same shed rise, the places where the pile should be pulled out will be clearly visible.   A single round rod serves to make the pile.   The weft after being pulled up from the shed is wound once around the rod, and then the operation is repeated in the next place, and so on until a whole row is made.   Then come two or four shots of the binder. The larger the diameter of the rod, the longer the loops of pile.   Since the weave is free, any kind of pattern may be woven.

TUMBLER (fr. AS *tumbian* = to dance).   The same as Couper (v).

164

TUNING FORK. Colonial Summer-and-Winter pattern. Short draft:

TURKEY FOOT. Small colonial pattern, or a component of a larger one. Short draft: ₇ ⁶
⁷
⁶

TURKEY GAUZE. A cross-weave (v) in which one warp thread crosses two other threads between two shots of weft. As this first warp thread must be longer than the other two, two warp beams are used.

TURNED HUCKABACK. A huckaback weave in which two rows of floats alternate in direction. E.g.:

Treadling:
4,3,4,3,4,2,
4,1,4,1,4,1.

TURNED OVERSHOT WEAVE. (Compare: Turned Weave.) An overshot weave which has floats both in warp and weft. It is used for making

TURNED OVERSHOT

overshot borders on all four sides of a piece of weaving. Two-block overshot can be made in this way on 6 shafts, and 4-block one on 8 shafts. E.g.:

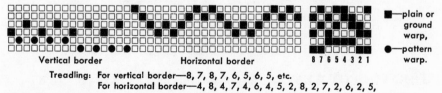

Vertical border   Horizontal border   ■—plain or ground warp,
●—pattern warp.

Treadling: For vertical border—8, 7, 8, 7, 6, 5, 6, 5, etc.
For horizontal border—4, 8, 4, 7, 4, 6, 4, 5, 2, 8, 2, 7, 2, 6, 2, 5,

On the same type of draft, and on the same tie-up, a horizontal border of 4 blocks, and a vertical one of 2 blocks can be woven, by substituting a 4-block draft to the right hand side of the above draft, and treadling accordingly.

165

TURNED LACE WEAVE. See Turned Spot Weave.

TURNED M'S-AND-O'S. A variation of Huckaback which looks like Waffle in appearance, but has no depth. E.g.:

Treadling: 4, 1, 4, 1, 4, 2, 3, 2, 3, 2, 3, 2.

TURNED QUILT WEAVE. It is really a double weave (v) in which the two layers have different count of cloth. Both layers are stitched together, but no wadding is used. E.g.:

Treadling:
1st block: 10, 6, 8, 9, 6, 7,
2nd block: 5, 1, 3, 4, 1, 2.

Turned quilt weave may have exactly the same texture as a Tissue weave, if proper yarn is used, but the pattern will remain much simpler than in most tissue weaves since four shafts are required for every block of pattern.

TURNED SATIN. The same as Damask.

TURNED SPOT
WEAVE (lace)

TURNED SPOT WEAVE. A spot weave which has floats in two directions on the same side of the fabric. It differs from the ordinary weave by the tie-up only:

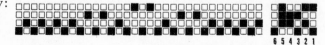

Treadling:

6,5,6,4,6,4,6,5,1,5,1,5,6,4,6,4,6,5 (fig. 1),

or: 6,5,1,5,1,5,6,4,6,4,6,5,1,5,1,5,6,5 (fig. 2),

or: 6,5,3,2,3,2,6,5,1,4,1,4,6,5,3,2,3,2 (fig. 3).

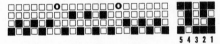

Fig. 1　Fig. 2　Fig. 3

In the same way Lace Weave patterns can be woven (tr. 3) with an effect similar to Damask.

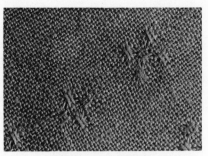

TURNED SPOT WEAVE

TURNED SWIVEL WEAVE. A Swivel weave with some blocks of pattern in the warp, or with all blocks of pattern in the warp. The latter case is of little interest for hand-weavers, but Swivel with blocks partly in weft and partly in warp is a great improvement on plain Swivel. E.g.:

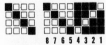

5 4 3 2 1

The warp on the first three shafts is the ground warp. Warp ends in shaft 4 are in slightly heavier yarn in a bright colour. They are added after the ground warp is threaded and sleyed (no space in sleying is left for the pattern ends). The pattern warp has usually very few ends and these can be hung on bobbins in the back of the loom, or wound on a separate warp beam.

In treadling, plain ground is woven on treadles 4 and 5. Treadles 3 and 4 give vertical lines; 2 and 4 one horizontal block of pattern; 1 and 4, another block of pattern. By combining vertical and horizontal lines a great variety of patterns can be woven.

TURNED TWILL. Any twill in which the ratio between warp and weft floats is reversed in the same piece of weaving. Treadles 1-4 in the draft will give 3:1 twill, and treadles 5-8, 1:3 twill. Thus alternating stripes can be woven. One of them will have horizontal floats, and the other vertical ones. When this principle is adapted to pattern weaving, the weave is Diaper (v).

8 7 6 5 4 3 2 1

TURNED WEAVE. Any weave in which the pattern is formed by blocks with floats going in two directions, or in which the back of one block is identical with the front of another block. In many weaves these two definitions amount to the same, since for instance the back of a 1:3 twill is 3:1 twill, or the back of a block of spot-weave with horizontal floats has vertical floats. But in case of turned overshot only the first condition is fulfilled, while in turned quilt weave it is only the second.

167

There are two different ways of "turning around" a weave: 1st, substituting the treadling draft for the threading draft, i.e., by turning the draft 90 degrees (both drafts must be full, not shortened in any way); 2nd, replacing all ties in the tie-up so that the fabric will be woven upside down. E.g.: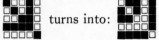

To obtain a pattern in any of turned weaves, we thread one block on one set of shafts, next block on another set, and so on. The tie-up is made so that when one block is woven in the original weave, the next block is in turned weave. E.g.:

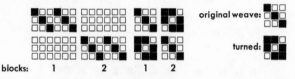

blocks: 1   2   1   2

TURN IN. To start or finish the weft at the selvedge, the end (half an inch or so) is usually tucked (turned in) into the next shed. When heavy pattern weft is used on a fine ground the turning-in should be avoided. It is better to cut off the end, if possible, after laundering.

TURNING ON. The same as Beaming.

TURNOVER REPEAT. Repeat of a pattern which is symmetrical to the first part but not joined with it, as in Point Repeat (v). E.g.: B is a turnover repeat of A.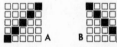

TWEED (uncertain origin, probably corruption of *Tweel*). Heavy woollen fabric, woven in coarse yarns in tabby or twill. Often checked.

TWEEL, TWEELING (Scot.). The same as Twill.

TWICE WOVEN FABRICS. The same as Chenille fabrics.

TWICE WOVEN RUGS. Heavy rugs woven in chenille (v). The rugs may have a uniform colour—then the weft in the first weaving is all of one colour. They may have a hit-and-miss pattern—then several colours of yarn alternate irregularly in the first weaving. If smooth commercial chenille weft is used, the second weaving may be done in Locked Wefts, and produce definite patterns, limited to only two colours in one row. More interesting patterns may be woven by carefully calculating the changes of colour in the first weaving, and cutting the chenille weft into strips of the same length as the width of the rug. These patterns

168

may have only vertical or horizontal lines, or even diagonals, but all running in the same direction in one section of the rug. Finally if we use Locked Wefts technique in the first weaving, the freedom of pattern is nearly unlimited: diagonals, curves, etc., can be made as well as straight lines in both directions. The only limitation is the size of the smallest elements of the pattern which should not be less than about four inches across, regardless of their shape, and this for purely practical reasons: theoretically any pattern can be made in Twice Woven Rugs, if the time factor is of no importance.

The texture of the rugs is very satisfactory. The pile if so desired may be much thicker than in the case of knotted rugs, and it may be of any length. They can be woven on very simple looms with only two shafts. In case of involved patterns it takes about 30 hours of work (including all operations) for one square yard of the finished rug.

TWILL (fr. G. *twillen* = to double). One of the basic weaves, probably a derivate of Basket. It may have floats of the same length as a Basket, but they are staggered instead of being parallel all the way. Twill is stronger than Basket but softer than Tabby. All twills have a tendency to produce diagonals in texture. If they do they are called Biased; if the

TWILL (broken)

diagonal is concealed, they are Broken. The different twills are designated by two numbers which indicate the length of floats on the two sides of the fabric. Thus 5:2 twill makes floats which are 5 threads long on one side and 2 threads long on the other. The sum of these two numbers gives the number of shafts necessary to execute the corresponding twill.

The simplest twill is 1:2 and can be made on 3 shafts:

Treadling: 1, 2, 3, or 3, 2, 1.

169

On 4 shafts two twills can be woven: 2:2 and 1:3 (3:1 being the back side of 1:3).

Three twills can be made on 6 shafts: 1:5 (and 5:1), 2:4 (and 4:2), and 3:3.

By changing the order of treadling we have: Reversed Twill (v), Wave (v), Stockinet (v), or Broken Twill. Broken twill of the type 1:N becomes a Satin when N is more than 3. Turned twill is a weave in which the ratio 1:N becomes N:1 on the same side of the fabric either in vertical or horizontal stripes. If these two twills (1:N and N:1) form a pattern, the weave is called Diaper Weave, and if they are broken we have Damask.

Higher Twills are those which form more than one diagonal. E.g.:

The simplest higher twill (2:1:1:1) can be woven on 5 shafts. None can be made on 4 shaft harness. All higher twills can be reversed or broken.

Herringbone twill is one with the diagonal changing direction in threading at regular intervals. Dornick twill is similar to the former, but the diagonals do not meet at the turning point. Diamond twill is a reversed (in treadling) herringbone twill.

TWIST. 1. The same as warp yarn. 2. The way in which the fibres in a yarn are twisted together. The twist is characterized by its direction (left hand twist, or right hand twist) and its degree: tight, light, loose, etc. As a rule the yarn for warp should have an opposite direction of twist than the yarn for weft, unless a crepe effect is intended. Usually warp yarn has a hard twist, which makes it strong and elastic (but hard and kinky at the same time), when the weft is loosely twisted, to make it softer.

TWIST WAY (in spinning). The same as right hand (Z) twist.

TWO-HARNESS METHOD. A method of weaving in which two harnesses (two sets of shafts) and two different types of heddle are used. Each warp end passes through a heddle in the Pattern harness, and then through another one in the Ground harness. The first harness (from the back) has ordinary heddle-eyes but long heddles, the second has heddles with long eyes. The back harness has two positions when working: upper and lower. The front harness has three positions: upper, lower and neutral. When any of the front heddles is in neutral position it does not affect the work of the back harness, since its eye is long enough to open a shed, but when it is lowered or raised it counteracts it. Thus the two harnesses can work independently of one another, or they can supplement each other. Thus one of them can weave the pattern only, when the other weaves the ground. Consequently the total number of shafts is much smaller than in ordinary, single-harness weaving. E.g., damask with a 6-block pattern requires 30 shafts (5 times 6), when with the two-harness method it takes only 11 (5 for the ground and 6 for the pattern).

Two-harness method is particularly well adapted for such weaves as diaper, damask, double weaves, and most of the turned weaves, but it may be used for any weave in which the ground and the pattern are clearly differentiated.

Another use to which this method may be put advantageously are compound weaves, particularly those which could not be performed simultaneously on an ordinary loom, e.g., 2:1 twill and tabby, overshot and spot weave, or two entirely different patterns in the same weave. The front harness is threaded for one weave, and the back harness for

TWO-HARNESS METHOD

another. When the front heddles are in neutral position the first weave is made on the back harness, and then the second weave on the front harness.

The number of shafts in the harnesses depends on the weave and on the pattern. The ground harness has as many shafts as the weave requires, i.e., 4 in most cases except for damasks, which have 5 or more. The pattern harness has as many shafts as blocks in the pattern except for double weaves, where the number of shafts is double the number of blocks.

A typical draft for a turned twill with a 3-block pattern is:

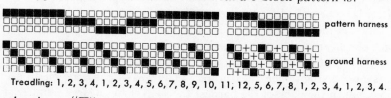

pattern harness

ground harness

Treadling: 1, 2, 3, 4, 1, 2, 3, 4, 5, 6, 7, 8, 9, 10, 11; 12, 5, 6, 7, 8, 1, 2, 3, 4, 1, 2, 3, 4.

In the tie-up "■" means sinking shed, and "+" means rising shed.

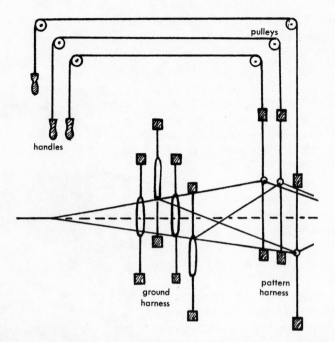

pulleys

handles

ground harness

pattern harness

When the number of treadles becomes too large, separate treadles are used for the ground and for the pattern. Two treadles must be depressed at the same time to open a shed. The former tie-up will become then: and the treadling: 1+7, 2+7, 3+7, 4+7, 1+7, 2+7, 3+7, 4+7, 1+6, 2+6, 3+6, 4+6, 1+5, 2+5, 3+5, 4+5, etc. When blocks of the pattern are rather large, so that in treadling one pattern shed remains open for a long time, it is better to use handles instead of treadles. The pattern shafts are hung on cords passing through pulleys at the front of the loom, where they can be pulled up and secured in this position for the duration of one block of the pattern.

With a very large number of blocks the pattern harness is replaced with a draw-loom harness. Then the front one is operated by treadles, when the back harness requires either a draw-boy, or a special arrangement of cords to be pulled by the weaver from the front.

Sometimes the front harness may be used as pattern harness, and the back one as ground harness, particularly in spot, lace, and dropped weaves.

The Two-Harness Method in a very crude form is often used in peasant weaving of central Europe. The weaving is done on an ordinary loom, but in the back of the harness the weaver ties a large number of half-heddles (doupes) to the warp. These doupes are grouped accordingly to the pattern woven and each group is attached to a stick, which can be lifted by hand, thus opening a pattern shed. The harness must have long-eye heddles, but the eyes are shorter than usual (about 1½ inches) so that the shed does not open completely and must be enlarged with a flat stick. The weaving is slower but gives good results. Synonyms: Double Harness, Presser Harness.

TWO-WARP CORDED FABRICS. Warp-face fabrics in which two warps are used. One warp remains very tight during weaving and is called Ground Warp. It is entirely invisible in the fabric and can be made of inferior but strong yarn. The second warp (Face Warp) is much longer (several times) than the ground warp, and set very closely. It is very slack (hardly any tension). The weft is usually much heavier than the warp, and is also invisible except at the edges. The face warp goes over  the ground warp, around one pick of weft, then below the ground warp, and around the second pick of weft. The draft is as follows:

The ground warp on shafts 3 and 4 (in the first draft); the face warp on shafts 1 and 2. Theoretically the two-warp corded fabrics can be woven on two shafts as in the second draft, but 4 shafts give better results and may produce a number of variations of this weave, particularly useful in texture effects.

The fabric is the heaviest and stiffest of all hand-woven fabrics.

TWO-WARP WEAVE. Any weave which requires two warp beams. E.g.: Turned Overshot, Turned Swivel, Tissue Weaves, Warp-Pile Weaves, many Net Weaves, many Crepe Weaves, etc.

TYING IN. Attaching the warp to the apron.

There are several ways of tying-in. The traditional (and the slowest) is to divide the warp into a number of even strands (bights), then pull each strand between the rod and the apron downwards, divide into two smaller strands and tie them together on top with a bow-knot. When correcting the tension the knots must be untied and tied again.

A better way is to tie each strand to the rod with a half-hitch; then to turn the cloth beam until the knots start slipping. Correct the tension by pushing down the strands which are too tight, and make the second half-hitch on each strand.

But probably the best method is to make a plain knot on each strand (approximately 2 inches from the end), and lace all strands to the rod with one long piece of cord. A space of about 1 inch should be left between the rod and the knot. The tension is adjusted with the lacing cord.

TYING ON. Attaching a new warp to the old one, thus saving several operations like threading, sleying, etc. This is usually done by placing the lease rods with the new warp on in front of the harness and of the batten, then cutting the new warp ends one by one and tying them to the old ones.

TYING THE WARP. Weaver's knot is used almost exclusively for tying broken ends. Sometimes, however, reef knot is preferable on stiff warps, as it is smaller than weaver's knot.

UNION DAMASK. Damask with linen or cotton warp and woollen weft in different colours. It is used as upholstery fabric.

UNION FABRICS. Fabrics with cotton warp, and woollen or linen weft.

UNIT OF WEAVE. The shortest repeat in threading and treadling which still contains all essential components of a given weave. Thus the units in threading are:

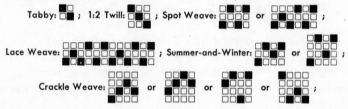

When transcribing short drafts into full threading draft each square of the short draft is replaced with one unit of the weave.

UNREADS. See Reads and Unreads.

UNWEAVING. Removing the weft from between the warp ends, usually to correct a mistake made in weaving. This operation is exactly the opposite of weaving: the proper shed is opened, the weft is loosened by pulling it towards the reed, and the shuttle thrown. Sometimes light beating is necessary to clear the shed. Unweaving is comparatively easy with cotton, more difficult with wool, and hardly possible with linen. When a large portion of the cloth must be unwoven, the weft is cut between the warp ends into short pieces, and pulled out with fingers.

UPHOLSTERY FABRIC. Any fabric suitable for upholstery, i.e., strong, closely woven, not too slippery, very resistant to friction, easy to clean. As some of the above requirements are contradictory, good upholstery fabrics are not easy to make.

The yarn should be tightly twisted, of two or more plies, smooth, and spun from long fibres to avoid formation of a nap. Colours fast and light-proof.

The weave must be rough to overcome the smoothness of the yarn, close, and without long floats. All simple weaves can be used except satin: tabby, basket (stitched or false), all twills, as long as they have short floats (biased, broken, herringbone, diamond, fancy). When the fabric has a pattern the following weaves are suitable: crackle, summer-and-winter, all-over-spot, swivel. For larger patterns diaper weaves are as good. To be avoided: lace, overshot, pile weaves (except very fine velvet with short pile). Tapestry weaves and tissue weaves can be used only on the condition that they are very firm and with short floats.

UPPER TIE-UP. The arrangement of rollers, pulleys, horses, jacks, or coupers together with connecting cords, on which the shafts of a harness are hung.

VEINING. Cross weave used as an ornament on tabby background, or leno on a background of gauze.

VELOUR (Fr.). The same as pile fabric. Particularly cotton fabric with short pile used for draperies.

VELVET (fr. It. *velutto*). A fine warp pile fabric. Pile rather short (⅛ inch or less). Silk on cotton ground or pure silk.

VELVET ROD. A flat piece of steel or brass slightly longer than the width of the fabric, and as thick as the pile is long. It has a groove on its upper edge. See Pile Weaves. Synonyms: Gauge, Flossa Rod.

VELVET ROSE. Colonial pattern of the Rose-and-Table group. Short draft:

```
6 5 5 5 5 5 5 6          8              8
          8          6  15 7 15  6              8
          6 3 3 3 3  13  5 5  13   3 3 3 3 6
5 5 5 5 5 5 5 5   3 3 3 6               6 3 3 3 3
```

VELVET WEAVE

VELVET WEAVE. The same as Warp Pile Weave (see Pile Weaves).

175

VELVETEEN. Weft-pile fabric similar to velvet.

VERTICAL LOOM. Any loom in which the warp is stretched vertically or nearly so. Most looms of this kind are obsolete and of historical interest only. At present the vertical loom is used only in making rugs, and certain types of tapestry. The loom has two treadles which operate the tabby sheds. The batten slides on the uprights of the loom, and it is controlled by a third treadle. Frame looms (v) are really vertical looms, too, since they are worked upon mostly in vertical position.

In tapestry weaving the vertical warp is called "high warp," and the horizontal one "low warp." Since entirely different methods of weaving were used in these two cases (v High Warp, Low Warp) these names became later synonymous with the method of weaving regardless of the position of the warp.

VERTICAL (tapestry) LOOM

VICTORIES. A cross-weave (v) in which pattern is formed by blocks of gauze on a background of tabby.

VINYON. Synthetic yarn made of resin. Weaker than nylon; less resistant to solvents. Softens at 165°F. It also shrinks in hot water (much below boiling point) more than any other fibre (12 per cent).

VIRGINIA BEAUTY. Colonial Summer-and-Winter pattern. Short draft:

$$\begin{matrix} & 2 & 2 & 2 & & 2 & 8 & & 1 & & 8 \\ & 2 & & 2 & 2 & 2 & & 2 & & 1 & 1 \\ 2 & & 2 & & 2 & & 2 & & 1 & & 1 \\ 2 & & 2 & & & 2 & & 2 & 1 & & 1 \end{matrix}$$

VISCOSE. Rayon made of wood pulp.

VOIDED PILE. Fabrics with pattern in pile on plain background.

VOILE (Fr. =*veil*). Sheer light fabric woven in tabby.

176

WADDING (fr. Swedish *vadd*). In Quilt weave a shot of heavy weft which comes between two layers of fabric.

WAFFLE WEAVE. A weave which produces a definite three-dimensional effect. It is woven partly in tabby areas surrounded by ridges of long floats. The floats rise high above the level of tabby. It can be woven on any number of shafts from 4 up. E.g.:

WAFFLE WEAVE

Treadling: 5, 4, 3, 2, 1, 2, 3, 4, 5, 4.

This produces a waffle on one side of the fabric with long floats poorly stitched to the ground. A much better waffle can be made also on 4 shafts, but with firmer floats, and with the same effect on both sides of the fabric:

Treadling: 5, 4, 3, 2, 1, 2,
1, 2, 3, 4, 5, 4.

Fabrics woven in waffle are very spongey, soft and warm. Synonym: Honeycomb.

WALLS OF JERICHO. Colonial pattern of the Sunrise group. Short draft:

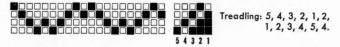

WARP (fr. AS *wearp*). A set of parallel yarns stretched on the loom before weaving begins. In most cases the warp is parallel to the longer side of the fabric. The warp is slightly wider than the finished fabric and slightly longer, too. On very simple looms its length is equal to the length of the loom itself (frame looms), or twice that much (cradle loom). In other looms it is much longer, up to several hundred yards. It is then wound on a special roller called Warp Beam.

The process of preparing the warp is called warping; winding it on the warp beam: beaming or turning-on; pulling it through the proper heddles: threading or entering; and getting it through the reed: sleying or reeding. Sometimes the last two operations are called entering. The mechanism which opens the warp to accept the weft forms different sheds (v) and is called shedding motion.

177

A warp is characterized by its length, total number of threads (called ends), sett or number of threads per inch, number of yarn (or grist), composition of yarn, and facultatively number of Portees (v).

The length may be anything from a fraction of a yard to several hundred yards. Number of threads from a few dozen (in an Inkle loom) to tens of thousands in fine silk weaving. The sett (v) is seldom less than 8 (except in net weaves), or more than 100 (except in silk). The grist of yarn depends on the weave and the sett of warp. The portees play a secondary role since they do not show after the warp is beamed. They have usually 4 or more ends—in a warping mill (v) several dozen. The yarn used for warp should be strong and resistant to friction. To increase this resistance it is often sized or dressed.

A complete warp ready for beaming must have some way of preserving the order in which the ends were wound. This is done by crossing single ends, or whole portees. The cross (or lease) is made at least at one end of the warp, sometimes on both.

Sectional warp is one beamed directly from tubes, cones, skeins or bobbins on the warp beam (Compare: Sectional Warp Beam).

Prefabricated warp is a sectional warp wound on flat spools, or reels, which can be inserted in the desired quantity on a square steel rod which then replaces the warp beam.

WARP BEAM. The roller or beam on which the warp is wound. Usually the warp is not attached directly to the beam but to an apron (v) which in turn is nailed to the beam. In some old warp beams there is a groove in which the warp is inserted, together with a Cane Stick or a flat stick of the same length as the beam, and fitting snugly in the groove so that it requires a certain pressure to be put there with the warp on. Every warp beam has either a brake (v) or a ratchet wheel which prevents the warp from unwinding during work. Compare: Sectional Warp Beam. Synonyms: Back Beam, Yarn Beam, Cane Roller.

WARP FACE FABRICS. Any fabric in which the weft is completely covered by warp (or nearly so) on both sides, or on one side only. In the first case this effect can be achieved with any weave on the condition that the warp is set very closely, and is kept at a low tension during weaving. In the second, special weaves are used such as Satins, or twills with long floats (1:7 or more), but here the warp must be set comparatively close, although not as close as in the first case. Compare: Weft Face Fabrics.

WARP PATTERNS. 1. Any pattern formed by floats in the warp. Every weft pattern may be transformed into warp pattern by "turning" it (v Turned Weaves), i.e., by threading it on a number of shafts equal to the number of treadles in the weft pattern, and taking the order of treadling as threading draft.   E.g.:

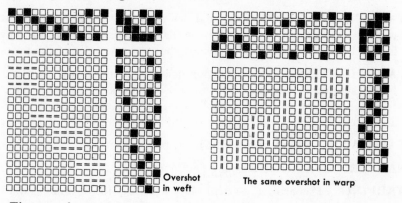

Overshot
in weft

The same overshot in warp

The yarn for warp in warp overshot must be the same as the yarn for weft in weft overshot.   This technique is particularly important in fly-shuttle weaving.   The different colours are set in warp, and only one kind of yarn (and consequently only one shuttle) used for weft.

2. The same applies to any weave which produces weft-face effect on both sides of the fabric.   It can be turned, and thus transformed into a weave with the same pattern in warp.   E.g., Diamond Twill or Summer-and-Winter woven on opposite sheds (v) give weft face fabrics. After turning, as the overshot in the example above, they will give warp face fabrics with the same pattern.   The order of colours in warp in the turned weave must be the same as the order of colours in weft of the original weave.

3. Patterns in any weave in which the weft is completely covered by warp.   For instance, in tabby warped in two alternating colours, any two-block pattern can be executed by using two wefts of different grist: one very thin, the other very heavy (Compare: Rep Weave).   E.g.:

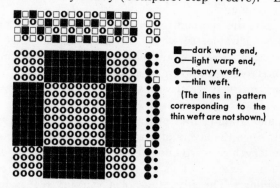

■—dark warp end,
O—light warp end,
●—heavy weft,
•—thin weft.

(The lines in pattern corresponding to the thin weft are not shown.)

All warp-face patterns are rather difficult to weave because of the close sett of warp.   The yarn must be very carefully selected so that the sheds will open without too much trouble.

WARP-PILE FABRICS. Fabrics with pile made from an additional warp. Compare: Pile Weaves.

WARP-PRINTED FABRICS. Fabrics in which the design is printed on warp before weaving. They can be distinguished from ordinary printed fabrics by subdued colours and somewhat hazy outlines of the pattern.

WARP PRINTING. This operation does not differ in any essentials from block printing of fabrics. The warp beamed and threaded is pulled out from the loom on to a long table in front of the loom. It is printed there, and after it is dry is wound back on the warp beam.

WARP WAY. About yarn: right hand twist.

WARPER. Operator of Warping equipment.

WARPING. Preparing the warp. A warp ready for beaming should have all ends of the same length and tension and, as far as possible, the order in which the ends come should be preserved all along the entire length of the warp.

The simplest way of making a warp is still used in Asia: a row of sticks is driven in the ground, the length of the row being equal to the desired length of warp. Then the weaver walks along the row unwinding the yarn and passing it alternately to the left and to the right of the sticks. When coming back, he crosses it with the former between each pair of sticks. All crosses are secured with string before the warp is taken off the sticks, and they are released gradually during the beaming. Although very

primitive, and not very practical, it is the only perfect way of warping. All threads are of exactly the same length and tension since they are not piled one on top of another, and continuous crossing prevents the ends from being tangled.

As this method requires too much space, it has been replaced with a warping frame (v) where the warp instead of going always in the same direction, goes there and back between two rows of pegs. However, there is no crossing between pegs except at the ends. Its drawback is that only comparatively short warps can be made in this way.

For longer warps a Warping Reel (v) is used. Here the warp is wound around a rotating frame, or rather around two perpendicular frames. But since the layers of warp come at least partly one on top of the other, the length of warp ends is not uniform, and the ends are usually tangled to some extent. This must be corrected by stretching or combing during beaming. The advantage of a warping reel is its compactness and the speed of warping.

For still longer warps, and partly to overcome the shortcomings of a warping reel, the Warping Mill (v) was constructed. It differs from the reel by a mechanical guide which distributes the portees much more uniformly than the reel. On the other hand, a warping mill is much more expensive and takes more room than the reel. The warping is still faster than on the warping reel.

WARPING BOARD. The same as Warping Frame (v) in which the frame is replaced by a wide and strong board. It is longer but narrower than a warping frame.

WARPING FRAME

WARPING FRAME. A strong rectangular wooden frame with pegs inserted in its sides. The pegs in the two horizontal beams serve to make the lease or leases (one on each end of the warp). The warp makes half a turn around each peg in the uprights of the frame. Its total length is equal to the length of the frame multiplied by the number of pegs used. Neither very bulky nor very long warps can be made on a warping frame.

WARPING MILL (horizontal)   WARPING MILL (counter)

WARPING MILL. Vertical warping mills were always used in industrial hand-weaving, but they are too large and complicated for hobby or home-weaving. A smaller and simpler type has been developed recently. It is

181

essentially a horizontal Warping Reel (v). The warp yarns do not need to be guided by hand, because this is done by a Guide (or Heck-Block) which slides along the frame of the mill. The warp is not piled up but spread flat in sections. Warping may be done from as many as 16 tubes, or from as few as two or even one. Single cross at one end of the warp can be made with two small heddle-frames. The number of portees made is shown by a counter. Finally the warp is beamed directly from the mill on the loom. All operations can be done by one person. A medium warp of 15 yards and 400 ends can be made and beamed in less than one hour.

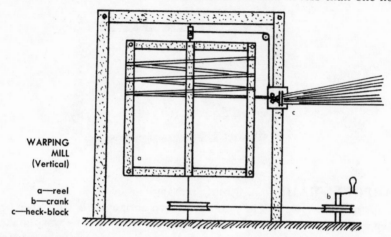

WARPING
MILL
(Vertical)

a—reel
b—crank
c—heck-block

WARPING REEL. Two rectangular frames made of wood are set at right angles and rotate on a common axis. They are mounted either vertically

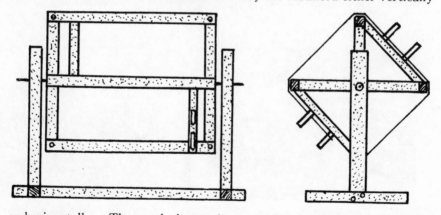

or horizontally. The vertical type is more often used but is inferior in all respects to the horizontal one.

The warp is wound on four sides of the frames. The lease is made between two pegs set in a small board which joins the two frames. This board is usually detachable and, after it is removed, the reel can be folded. The advantages of a warping reel are: the speed of warping when compared with a warping frame, the length of warp which may be several dozen yards, and the small space required for the reel when not in use. On the other hand, unless extraordinary precautions are taken, the quality of warp made in this way is the poorest. A horizontal warping reel is more satisfactory than the vertical one—it gives a still higher speed of warping, and there is no necessity of chaining the warp before beaming, as it can be beamed directly from the reel.

WASHINGTON BEAUTY. Colonial Summer-and-Winter pattern. Short draft:

```
         3 1 1 1 1 3      1 1      3 1 1 1 1 3
          1 3 1 3 1        2        1 3 1 3 1
   3   3   3                 1   1
   3 1 1 1 1 3              1 1   1 1
   3   1   1   3           2   2   2   2
```

WASHINGTON'S DIAMOND RING. Colonial pattern (v) of the Star-and-Wheel group. Short draft:

```
   3 10    9 10                     10 9    10
              3 3 3 3 3
      10   2   12 3 3 3 3 12   2   10
   9    10    10              10    10
```

WASTAGE. The part of warp which cannot be used. It includes the few inches necessary for tying-in, the heading or the part on which the threading is checked and the mistakes corrected, and finally the end of the warp which must be long enough to open the sheds. If the fabric is taken off the loom in several bolts before the whole warp is finished there is additional wastage for re-tying the warp. The smallest possible wastage is about 18 inches, but it is safer to count 36 inches.

WATERFALL. Colonial pattern (v) of the Three-Block-Patch group. Short draft:

```
   9 9  |9 |9  9 9            9 9 9  9 9
      5 |  5   11 11 11 11       5    11 11 11 11
   3 2 2|3| 2 2 3 2  3   3   3  2 3 3 2 2 3 2  3   3   3
        |7x|
```

WAVE WEAVE. Any biased twill woven so that the direction of the diagonal changes at regular intervals. It is similar to Herringbone Twill, except that the stripes go across the fabric.

WEAVE (fr. AS *wefan*). The order or system in which the threads of warp and weft intersect in a fabric.

WEAVE PLAN. The same as Draw-Down or Block-Out.

WEAVER. Anybody who operates a loom. At the present time there is hardly any classification of weavers based on their skill. Different schools and weaving organizations have different standards, as a rule very low ones. There is an attempt to standardize the requirements for weavers into four classes: basic, intermediary, senior and master. In old weavers' Guilds there were only three grades: apprentice, journeyman, and master.

183

 **WEAVER'S KNOT.** A knot used exclusively to tie the broken warp ends, or to tie a new warp on. It does not slip, but is slightly larger than the reef knot.

WEAVES (classified). All weaves are grouped into Basic (or Principal) and Derivate Weaves. There is a difference of opinion among authors as to which weaves are basic and which are not. There is still more confusion when the derivate weaves are discussed. *Encyclopedia Americana* divides all weaves into four groups: Simple, Compound, Crossed, and Pile. The Pennsylvania Museum knows only three: Simple, Compound, and Pile. The simple or basic are: cloth (tabby), cord, twill, and satin. Since satin is derivate of twill, and cord may be any weave at all, what remains is tabby and twill. Other authors consider as basic any weave which introduces a new principle into the construction of the web, or into the forming of patterns.

The simplest of all weaves is Tabby. Its derivatives are: Basket Weave, Rep Weave and other Cord Weaves.

Another simple weave is Twill. When it shows a diagonal it is Biased Twill. The twills of the type: 2:2, 3:3 and so on are Balanced Twills, when the twills 1:2, 1:3, 1:4, etc., show more weft on one side of the fabric, and more warp on the other. By changing the direction of the diagonal in threading we have: Herringbone Twill, Double-Point Twill, and Dornick Twill. Changing the order of treadling gives: Wave, Stockinet, and Broken Twill. When reversing both, we have Diamond Twill. Twills with more than one diagonal (e.g., 3:1:1:1) are called Higher Twills, and if they are of the Diamond type: Pattern Twills, or Lined Work, or Fancy Twills.

Overshot weave is a derivate of diamond twill with binder. Crackle is of the same derivation and an improvement on Overshot. Summer-and-Winter is Crackle on opposites (2 blocks instead of 4) with reservations.

Dropped Weaves are derivates of Tabby or Twill (accordingly to the ground used). Spot Weaves can be derived directly from Tabby, or from Dropped Tabby. Summer-and-Winter again can be derived from Spot Weaves and considered as Double Spot Weave (two front shafts instead of one). Huckaback, Waffle, M's-and-O's, etc., can be traced back to Spot Weaves.

Turned Twills, although obviously derivative of plain twill, form a separate division of weaving since they permit patterns of any size and of any number of blocks without changing the essential qualities of twill. Thus, starting with Dimity based on 1:2 twill, and Dornick (1:3), they go through all stages of Diaper Weaves (based on biased twills) and Damasks (based on broken twills of the satin type).

Double Weaves give two layers of fabric. Each layer can be woven

184

in any of the basic weaves, but most often tabby or plain twill are used. When the two layers are connected at the selvedges we have circular weave, when only on one side, Double-width cloth. When the layers are stitched together, it is Double Cloth Weave. If the layers are of different texture, and stitching forms a pattern, the weave is Quilt W. The two layers can penetrate each other, thus forming a pattern with clearly defined blocks. The weave is called now Double Weave, or in case of Quilt, Turned Quilt Weave. When the latter has two separate warps for its two layers, and the pattern is rather an intricate one, it becomes a Tissue Weave.

Turned Weaves are these which were transcribed from ordinary weaves into warp-pattern weaves, or which have both elements (i.e., original and turned) in the same piece of weaving.

The Pile Weaves are divided into Weft-pile and Warp-pile weaves. The pile may be cut (Velvet) or uncut (Terry). Pattern may be formed by blocks of uncut and cut pile (Ciselé), or by two piles of different length (Pile-on-pile), or by pile on plain background (Voided pile).

In Cross Weaves the warp ends are crossed between shots of weft, thus giving open and firm fabrics. When they are very open and have rather complicated texture, they are called Net Weaves. A particular case of Cross Weaving is Lappet technique. Here an additional warp with only few ends is used for embroidering the pattern on the fabric.

In all above weaves the shuttle travels the entire width of the fabric. When it traverses only a part of the shed, the weaving is called Free, and here belong all Tapestry Weaves, Brocades, Embroidery Weaves, and other Laid-In techniques.

WEAVING. 1. Art of producing cloth by interlacing two sets of threads running at right angles to each other. Thus knitted fabrics, lace and nets (not the same as Lace-Weave and Net-Weave), as well as braids and plaits are not considered as woven.

To have a general information about weaving see in the following order: History of Weaving, Warp, Warping, Loom, Beaming, Threading, Sleying, Tie-Up, Gating, Treadling, Shuttle, Throwing the Shuttle, Weaving 2, Draft, Weaves, Yarn.

2. Act of weaving. When the loom is set and adjusted, first the Heading (v) is woven. After correcting the mistakes (v) in threading and sleying, the weaving starts. The shuttle thrown by one hand is caught in the other, carried away from the shed, when at the same time the first hand comes on the cape of the batten. The movement of the batten forwards starts together with the closing of the shed, and should finish after the shed is changed. The return of the batten follows immediately, and the hand holding it comes to its side of the shed to catch the shuttle

thrown from the opposite side. When a few inches of the fabric are woven, the warp is moved forward, the tension of warp adjusted so as to make it exactly the same as before, and the whole operation repeated until the particular piece of weaving is finished.

WEB (fr. AS *webb*). 1. The interlaced threads of warp and weft, practically the same as Fabric. 2. The piece of cloth between the breast piece and the "fell."

WEB BEAM. The same as Cloth Beam.

WEFT (fr. AS *wefta*). The set of threads which goes across the fabric, at right angles to the warp. The weft is inserted between the ends of warp in the loom, usually with a shuttle. One or more wefts can be used in the same piece of weaving. Depending on what the weft is used for, it is called: ground weft (or binder), pattern weft, pile weft, and so on.

The qualities of yarn used for weft are very different from the warp yarn. It should be rather soft so as to get deeper between the warp threads. It should have as little elasticity as possible, or the fabric draws-in too much during weaving. The direction of twist should be opposite to the one of the warp, particularly with tabby, or a crepe effect will result. Synonyms: Woof, Filling, Shoot, Shute.

WEFT FACE FABRICS. 1. A fabric which has one side showing only weft, like Weft-face satins.

2. Any fabric in which the warp is completely covered with weft. This effect depends not so much on the weave, as on the sett of warp, and grist of yarn. When the warp is open and of comparatively thin yarn, it is easy to cover it with soft and heavy weft. If corded effect is wanted, the warp is heavy and open, the weft light and close. Patterns can be obtained by weaving on opposite sheds (v), or by turning the Rep Weave (v), i.e., making the warp of alternating heavy and light yarn, and weaving with two colours in the weft. Whatever the weave is, the difficulty of weaving weft-face fabrics lies in the fact that there is considerable shrinking of weft during weaving, and consequently the edges pull in, unless the weft is laid quite loosely in the shed.

WEFT PATTERNS. Patterns formed by floats in the weft.

WEFT-PILE FABRICS. Fabrics with pile made either by cutting floats in weft, or by leaving loops in weft. Compare: Pile-Weaves, 2 and 4, Tufted Weave, Corduroy.

WEFT-WAY. About yarn: the same as left hand twist.

WEIGHTING. A process by which the weight of a fabric is increased. The fabric is impregnated with a solution of mineral salts, kaolin, sugar, starch, wax, glue, or gum. Weighting may be soluble in water or not.

186

WHEAT EAR. A peculiar variety of Dornick Twill:

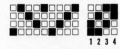 Treadling: 1, 4, 3, 2, 4, 1, 2, 3, 4.

1 2 3 4

WHEEL. A component of a Colonial pattern (v). Woven as drawn in. E.g.: (Read from the left).

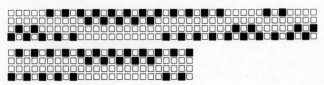

WHEEL OF FORTUNE. Colonial pattern (v) the same as Cup-and-Saucer (v).

WHEELING WOOL. Coarse worsted wool.

WHEELS OF TIME. Colonial pattern of the Wheel-Star-and-Rose group. Short draft:

$$\begin{array}{c} 3\ \ 3 \\ 3\ \ \ \ 3 \\ 4\ \ \ \ 4 \\ 4\ \ \ \ 4 \end{array} \begin{vmatrix} 7 & 2\ 2 & 7 \\ 11 & & 11 \\ & 13\ 2\ 13 \\ 8 & & 8 \end{vmatrix} \begin{array}{c} 3\ \ 3 \\ 3\ \ \ 3 \\ 4\ \ \ 4 \\ 4\ \ \ 4 \end{array} \begin{vmatrix} 13\ 2\ 13 \\ 8 & & 8 \\ 6 & 2\ 2 & 6 \\ 11 & & 11 \end{vmatrix}$$

← 2x → ← 2x →

WHIG ROSE (fr. G. *Wickenrose* = hedge-rose). Colonial pattern of the Wheel-and-Rose group. Short draft:

$$\begin{array}{c} 5\ \ \ \ 6\ 3\ 6 \\ 4\ \ \ \ \ \ 10\ 3\ 3\ 10 \\ 4\ \ \ \ \ \ \ 9\ 3\ 9 \\ 4\ \ 5\ 5 \end{array} \begin{array}{c} 6\ 3\ 6 \\ 4 \\ 4 \\ 5\ 5\ \ 4 \end{array}$$

WHIP. This part of the warp in Net-weaves, which passes through the bead lamms (v). It is made of tightly twisted, smooth and strong yarn, and is wound on a separate warp beam, called Whip Beam.

WHIP NET. A Net-weave in which each warp end crosses alternately two adjacent threads, and the weft passes through the crossings.

WHORL (fr. AS *hweorfan* = to turn). 1. A weight placed at the lower end of a spindle, and acting as a fly wheel. 2. A pulley in a Draw-Loom.

WILD SILK. Not cultivated silk.

WINDING. See Bobbin Winder.

WINDLE (fr. AS *windel*). A Reel, a Swift.

WINDOW SASH. Colonial pattern (v) of the Two-Block-Patch group.

8 8 8 8 8 8 2 2 2
2 2 2 2 2 6 6 6 6

WIRE HEDDLE. See Heddle.

WITCH. The same as Dobby (v).

WOOF (fr. AS *owef*). The same as Weft.

WOOL (fr. AS *wull*). Any fibres of animal origin used for making yarns; particularly those of sheep. All hair of sheep cut in one operation is called fleece. The fleece is sorted according to the quality of hair. Best wool comes from shoulders, sides and back (see Sorting). Wool is graded according to the number of hanks (of 560 yards) which can be spun from one pound. This number varies from 20 to 80. The wool must undergo the following operations to become yarn: scouring, carding, eventually combing, and spinning.

Fleece wool—sheared from living sheep. Dead wool—from skins of dead sheep.

Merino wool—medium long (2½ to 6 inches) and very fine. Cheviot wool—long and fine. Leicester wool—long and rough. Oxford wool—medium. Hampshire wool—short. Shropshire wool—very short.

WOOLLEN or **WOOLEN.** Made of wool.

WOOLLEN YARN. Any yarn spun of wool, but of inferior quality than worsted, i.e., shorter fibres, not combed.

WORLD'S WONDER. Colonial pattern of the Star-and-Wheel group.
Short draft:

WORSTED YARN. Originally woollen yarn manufactured in Worstead, Norfolk. Yarn of high quality, made of long fibres, combed and tightly twisted in spinning.

WOVEN-AS-DRAWN-IN. The order of treadling which gives a Squared Pattern (v) with a diagonal. This term is used most often in connection with Colonial weaving. Building a diagonal does not present any difficulties with most Colonial weaves, except with plain overshot. The blocks in overshot overlap each other by one warp end. Consequently, to get a straight diagonal, a compensation for this overlapping must be introduced. In practice this is done so, that to figure out the number of weft shots for each block, one unit is subtracted from the length of a float in the block. For instance, the block has floats which skip 8 warp ends: it will take seven shots of weft to "square" this particular block. Synonym: Tromp-as-writ.

WREATH ROSE. Colonial pattern (v) of the Wheel-and-Rose group.
Short draft:

```
3 2  7 7              7 7  2 3 2  7 7  2
    4     5 13 5 13 5      4      4      4
    4     12 5  5 5  5 12  4      4      4
3   8 3 8              8 3 8  3 3  8 3 8   3
```

X'S-AND-O'S. Small weaving pattern best adapted for a Spot Weave. E.g.:

YARDING or **YARDAGE** or **YARD GOODS.** Any fabric made and sold by the yard.

YARN

YARN (fr. AS *gearn*). Vegetable, animal or artificial fibres spun into a continuous thread. Yarn is characterized by its composition, its thickness (or grist, or count), number of strands (or plies), direction and degree of twist, and the colour.

According to their composition yarns are divided into:

Vegetable: Linen, Hemp, Jute, Sisal, Ramie, Cotton.

Animal: Wool, Silk.

Artificial and Synthetic: Gold, Silver, other metals, Glass, Rayons (Viscose, Cupprammonium, Acetate), Nylon, Saran, Terylene, Orlon, Polythene.

Mixed: Yarns made of two or more different fibres.

Grist or Count of yarn may range from 300 yds/lb (sisal mats, rug filler used in tapestry) to (theoretically) 3,000,000 yds/lb for a single filament of silk.

189

Yarn can be Single (one strand of fibres), or Plied (2, 3, 4 plies, etc.).

Single yarn may have right hand (or Z) twist, left hand (or S) twist, or no twist at all (in case of very long fibres or filaments). Plied yarn may have the same twist for both the fibres in singles, and for the plies, or an opposite twist.

In spinning, one ply of the plied yarn may have a different count, different twist, or different tension than the other. In this way are produced so-called Novelty Yarns, or Texture, or 3D Yarns. For instance: Ratine, Boucle, Nubby, etc. The yarn may be woven as Chenille yarn.

The yarn may be dyed before spinning or after. In the first case we have stock dyed yarns. When singles are dyed first and then spun again together, the yarn may have two or more colours.

Compare: Count of yarn, analysis of fabrics, spinning, twist, warp, weft, wool, flax, cotton, silk, rayon, etc.

YARN BEAM. The same as Warp Beam.

YELD. The same as Heddle (R).

YOUNG MAN'S FANCY. Colonial pattern (v). Short draft:

```
16 5 5 16
         16            5 5 5 5 5            16
            16 5 5 16 5 5 5 5 16 5 5 16
   5 5 5        5 5 5            5 5 5
```

YOUTH AND BEAUTY. Colonial pattern (v) of the Four-Block-Patch group. Short draft:

```
                    9 9 9 9 9 9 9     2     2
                                    8 8 9
                              9 9 9       9 9 9
                3 3 3 3 3 3 3 3 3   2 2   3 3
```

ZEPHYR (fr. Gr. *zephyros* = westerly wind). Any fine and light fabric.